LEARNING TEXT

LAW OF CONTRACT

LEARNING TEXT

LAW OF CONTRACT

Second Edition

Neil Lucas LLM, Dip. Ed.
Principal Lecturer in Law, Nottingham Law School,
Nottingham Trent University

 BLACKSTONE PRESS LIMITED

First published in Great Britain 1996 by Blackstone Press Limited, Aldine Place, London W12 8AA.   Telephone 0181–740 2277

© Nottingham Law School, Nottingham Trent University, 1996

ISBN: 1 85431 812 8

First edition, 1996
Reprinted with amendments, 1997
Second edition, 1998

British Library Cataloguing in Publication Data
A CIP catalogue record for this book is available from the British Library.

Typeset by Style Photosetting Limited, Mayfield, East Sussex
Printed by Livesey Limited, Shrewsbury, Shropshire

FOREWORD

The books in the LLB series have been written for students studying law at undergraduate level. There are two books for each subject. The first is the *Learning Text* which is designed to teach you about the particular subject in question. However, it does much more than that. By means of Activities, Self Assessment, and End of Chapter Questions, the *Learning Text* allows you to test your knowledge and understanding as you work. Each chapter starts with 'Objectives' which indicate what you should be able to do by the end of it. You should use these Objectives in your learning — check them frequently and ask yourself whether you have attained them.

The second book is a volume of *Cases and Materials*. This is cross-referenced from the *Learning Text*. It contains the primary sources of law such as statutes and cases plus subsidiary sources such as extracts from journals, law reform papers and textbooks. This is your portable library. Although each volume can stand alone, they are designed to be complementary.

The two-volume combination aims to support your learning by challenging you to demonstrate your mastery of the principles and application of the law. They are appropriate whatever your mode of study — full-time or part-time.

CONTENTS

Brief history of the law of contract — Definition of a contract — Essentials of a valid contract — Form of contract — Limitation of actions

1.1 Objectives — 1.2 Introduction — 1.3 The phenomena of agreement — 1.4 Offer — 1.5 Termination of offer — 1.6 Acceptance — 1.7 Inchoate agreements — 1.8 Intention to create legal relations — 1.9 Conclusion — 1.10 End of chapter assessment question

2.1 Objectives — 2.2 Introduction — 2.3 Executory, executed and past consideration — 2.4 Sufficiency of consideration — 2.5 Privity of contract — 2.6 Conclusion — 2.7 End of chapter assessment question

3.1 Objectives — 3.2 Introduction — 3.3 Express terms — 3.4 Terms and representations — 3.5 Implied terms — 3.6 Conditions and warranties and intermediate terms — 3.7 Conclusion — 3.8 End of chapter assessment question

4.1 Objectives — 4.2 Introduction — 4.3 The position at common law — 4.4 The Unfair Contract Terms Act 1977 — 4.5 The reasonableness test — 4.6 The Unfair Terms in Consumer Contracts Regulations 1994 — 4.7 Conclusion — 4.8 End of chapter assessment question

5.1 Objectives — 5.2 Introduction — 5.3 Performance — 5.4 Breach — 5.5 Agreement — 5.6 Frustration — 5.7 Conclusion — 5.8 End of chapter assessment question

6 Vitiating Factors   135

7 Remedies for Breach of Contract   178

PREFACE

My impetus for writing this Learning Text came from my experience in teaching contract law for nearly 20 years to first-year law students, the last five of those including distance learning students. I concluded that an alternative textbook, containing more information than any student is ever likely to need, was not what was required. I have tried to produce something appropriate to the needs of the law degree student, which is both clear and concise, and which places a premium upon explanation and understanding. In short I hope to have provided a stimulating learning experience.

There are not many statutory areas in the law of contract, but those which exist tend to be difficult and complex. I have attempted to ease the passage through the troubled waters of the Misrepresentation Act 1967, the Law Reform (Frustrated Contracts) Act 1943, the Unfair Contract Terms Act 1977 and the Unfair Terms in Consumer Contracts Regulations 1994 by a series of check-lists, flow-charts and diagrams.

In general the old adage in contract is: 'If you know your cases you know your contract'. This is only partially accurate. You must know and *understand* the *ratio decidendi* of your cases. If you do not appreciate *why* a particular case is decided as it is you do not understand it. Never stop until you can answer the question: 'Why?'. Most of the self-assessment questions and activities in this text are designed to help you to discover whether you can answer the question: 'Why?'. Frequently, the answer is to be discussed in the text shortly afterwards, but remember that cheating is self-defeating. You will learn far more by trying to work out the answers for yourself than by going straight to them. Learning may not be 'fun' in the conventional sense, but it can be an enjoyable voyage of discovery. Why spoil it? Have a stimulating journey.

I would like to thank my family for putting up with me in general, but in particular during the preparation of this Learning Text and my share of the *Cases and Materials* volume. I have endeavoured to state the law as at 31 March 1998.

Neil Lucas
Nottingham Law School
March 1998

TABLE OF CASES

TABLE OF STATUTES

INTRODUCTION

The law of contract is a collective body of legal rules relating to legally binding agreements made between persons in society. It is of relevance and importance to us all. Each day we all enter into a contract of some sort. Whenever we spend money, be it on food, travel, newspapers, books or even law courses, we make a legally binding contract.

Contract law is of vital importance to business organisations. Most of their business is performed by the making of contracts, be they with customers, suppliers or employees. Few organisations would want to enter into an agreement which could not be enforced, perhaps only at the last resort at least, by legal sanctions. (A note of caution though – check your football pools coupon!)

To the law student, the study of the law of contract is also of great importance. This subject forms the basis for the understanding of many other legal subjects. Obvious subjects to mention are employment law, commercial law, consumer law and the law of property, but there are many others.

Brief History of the Law of Contract

The modern law of contract developed from the old 'law merchant', i.e. the customs and rules established over the centuries and adhered to by early traders and business people. It thus dates back many centuries.

A particularly important period of development was during the nineteenth century. The expansion in trade caused by the extended dealings with Commonwealth countries and the Industrial Revolution resulted in a vast increase in the number of contracts made. In addition to this increase in numbers, there was a widening in the types of persons making contracts. Formerly contracts were made by landowners and merchants but, during this period, more and more people from all walks of life began to make contracts. The 'consumer society' was developing.

The accepted economic theory of the nineteenth century was 'laissez-faire'. This depends heavily on the freedom of the individual. Thus when persons freely enter into a contract by which they intend to be bound, then they are strictly bound. A court will not interfere in that agreement if it was made freely. This approach is known as the 'doctrine of freedom of contract' and it forms the basis of modern English contract law.

Are all contracts freely negotiated in reality? Can you write down below any examples of contracts which you think are not freely negotiated?

The courts will not therefore set aside a contract merely because one of the parties obtained an inadequate bargain, or because the parties' bargaining power was unequal. Thus a contract to sell a Rolls Royce for £5, or even less, is perfectly legally binding provided it is **freely** entered into.

The doctrine can work fairly when a contract is made between parties of equal bargaining power, particularly between two business persons each trying to negotiate the best deal. Severe problems arise, however, when the parties are of unequal bargaining power. It often seems unfair to enforce the contract against the weaker party, particularly if that party had little or no choice other than to enter into the contract. The classic example is an ordinary consumer dealing as an individual with a large organisation, the more so where the organisation insists on using a 'standard form contract', i.e. its own printed terms and conditions.

In everyday life an individual is frequently forced to accept the other party's contractual terms. If there is no 'on street' parking in a city (such as Nottingham) then a car park must be used. Most, if not all, car parks display terms and conditions which are not negotiable and which must be accepted. Try negotiating the conditions of a contract with the car park attendant in a multi-storey car park and then reversing back down the ramp, after the queue behind you has backed up to allow you to do so, when he says 'take it or leave it'! Leaving clothes to be dry cleaned creates a similar situation. Lastly, most large organisations, such as banks, insurance companies and finance companies insist on using their own standard forms of contract and refuse to negotiate or vary them.

In all these situations it is illusory to say that the contract is freely negotiated, but it is still a fact that, theoretically, the potential customer could refuse to enter the contract. Thus the doctrine of freedom of contract can operate very unfairly.

Under the common law, on which much of the law of contract is based, the courts were powerless against the doctrine of freedom of contract. Therefore, Parliament has had to intervene, particularly to protect the ordinary consumer. Various statutes have been passed which provide that protection, including the Consumer Credit Act 1974, the Rent Act 1977 and the Employment Protection (Consolidation) Act 1978. Two particular statutes which will be examined later in this course are the Sale of Goods Act 1979 and the Unfair Contract Terms Act 1977, both of which considerably reduce the hardship of the doctrine of freedom of contract, but which doctrine, it must be remembered, continues to form an important base of the law of contract. Statutory intervention has been increased by the Unfair Terms in Consumer Contracts Regulations 1994 (SI 1994 No. 3159).

It can be seen then that our study will be of the common law rules as developed over the centuries, influenced strongly by the doctrine of freedom of contract, to cover agreements made by individuals or organisations in society, and of the statutory intervention thereto whereby protection of the weaker party has been necessarily introduced, and whereby other anomalies have been put right.

Lastly, one note of caution concerning practicalities. While it is always good to know that legally one has a good case, it is not always a good thing to enforce that legal right. In practice most contractual disputes are resolved out of court. It is often more prudent, particularly for business organisations, to settle out of court rather than to jeopardise future dealings by going to litigation.

Definition of a Contract

A contract may be defined as an **agreement**, enforceable at law, between two or more persons to do or refrain from doing some act or acts; the parties must intend to **create legal relations** and must have given something or promised to give something of value as **consideration** in return for any benefit derived from the agreement.

While this definition is open to criticism in the sense that certain contracts (by deed) do not require consideration, or that a contract may be rendered unenforceable (perhaps due to lack of formalities), nevertheless it emphasises that the basic elements of contracts are agreement, intention to create legal relations and consideration.

Essentials of a Valid Contract

Offer ⎫
           ⎬ Phenomena of agreement
Acceptance ⎭

Intention to create legal relations

Written formalities in certain cases (exceptional)

Consideration (except for deeds)

Capacity

Genuine consent: Mistake ⎫
                                  Misrepresentation ⎬ Vitiating
                                  Duress ⎬ elements
                                  Undue influence ⎭

Contract must not be illegal or contrary to public policy

In the absence of one or more of these essentials, a contract may be **void**, **voidable** or **unenforceable**.

(a) **Void** A void contract has no legal effect at all and in reality the expression is a contradiction in terms. However, its usage is now well accepted in the law of contract. A contract is often described as void *ab initio* (void from the outset).

(b) **Voidable** A voidable contract is legally binding, but one of the parties has the option to set it aside (avoid it) if he so chooses.

(c) **Unenforceable** An unenforceable contract is valid in all respects except that it cannot be enforced in a court of law (usually due to lack of form). However, it can be set up by way of **defence**; thus, for example, money handed over under an unenforceable contract may turn out to be irrecoverable as the other party may argue the existence of the contract by way of defence.

Form of Contract

A contract made by **deed** is the only type of contract not requiring consideration. All other contracts, known as **simple or parol contracts**, require consideration. In most cases it does not matter which of the various forms of simple contract is used and a contract may be made in writing, orally or be implied from conduct, e.g., X goes into Y's shop and selects a loaf of bread which he hands to Y together with his purchase money (implied offer to purchase + money consideration); Y takes the money and hands the loaf to X (implied acceptance + loaf consideration). Thus most contracts are **not** made in writing, contrary to popular belief.

Similarly in:

Brogden v *Metropolitan Railway Co.* (1877) 2 App Cas 666
B had for several years supplied M with coal without any formal agreement. The parties decided to have a formal agreement drafted and M's agent sent a copy to B who inserted the name of an arbitrator and then returned the copy approved to M. M's agent put the agreement in a drawer, doing nothing to indicate his assent to the arbitrator selected by B. After the negotiations the parties carried on business with each other in accordance with the terms of the agreement (which was not itself a contract since it had never been accepted by M's agent). A dispute arose and B denied that there was a binding contract.

A contract existed, but the House of Lords could not say precisely when it was formed. The subsequent conduct of both parties could be explained only on the assumption that they had both approved the terms of the draft and that a contract came into existence either when M placed its first order for coal from B upon those terms, or at least when B supplied it.

However, in exceptional cases written formalities are required:

(a)   Contracts which must be made by deed, e.g., a lease for more than three years.

(b)   Contracts which must be in writing, e.g., cheques, bills of exchange and promissory notes, contracts of marine insurance, contracts for the sale of land.

(c)   Contracts which must be evidenced in writing, e.g., contracts of guarantee (s. 4 Statute of Frauds 1677).

Limitation of Actions

Lapse of time may render a contract unenforceable in a court of law.

The Limitation Act 1980 provides:

(a)   Actions on simple contracts are barred after six years from the date upon which the plaintiff could first have brought his action.

(b)   Actions on specialty contracts are barred after 12 years from the cause of action ('specialty' means 'by deed') A right of action accrues from the moment when a breach occurs, not from the date when the contract was made.

(c)   Where the plaintiff's claims include a claim for damages in respect of personal injuries, the limitation period is three years.

SAQ 2

Do all contracts need to be written? If not, what other forms may a contract take? List any examples which you can think of.

The need for writing is the exception rather than the rule, e.g., contracts for the sale of land must be in writing and contracts of guarantee must be evidenced in writing. Otherwise, contracts may be made orally or they may be implied from conduct, e.g., *Brogden* v *Metropolitan Railway Co.* (above), purchasing goods in a shop, travelling on a bus or train, going to the cinema or theatre etc.

CHAPTER ONE

THE PHENOMENA OF AGREEMENT

1.1 Objectives

By the end of this chapter you should be able to:

- understand the distinction between offer and invitation to treat and apply the objective test to problem situations;

- appraise critically the rules relating to offer and acceptance and apply them to problem situations;

- recognise the themes underlying the law relating to inchoate agreements and apply the law to problem situations;

- identify the presumptions underlying the law relating to intention to create legal relations and apply the law to problem situations.

1.2 Introduction

Whichever definition of the law of contract we look at, the word 'agreement' will be essential to it; in simple terms it is the law relating to and regulating agreements. A contract is a legally enforceable agreement creating rights and obligations for the parties to it. Agreement is often described as requiring *consensus ad idem* (a meeting of minds). This is misleading because the law does not adopt this subjective approach to agreement. Indeed, it adopts an objective approach, and is not so much concerned with what is in the minds of the parties, but with what can be inferred from what they have said, done or written.

However, not all agreements are legally binding contracts. Thus, social and domestic agreements are not generally enforceable, unless there is clear evidence of an intention to create legal relations. Similarly, although courts will try to give effect to apparent agreements, it may be difficult to do so in cases where the parties have expressed themselves in vague or incomplete terms. Much will depend upon how far a court is prepared to go in filling in any gaps left by the parties.

1.3 The Phenomena of Agreement

In the normal case, a contract results from an agreement between two or more parties, and indeed may be readily ascertainable, particularly where it has been reduced to writing. However, the description of a contract as an agreement is subject to qualification.

First, in the case of standard form contracts, where the powerful party can virtually impose his terms upon the weaker party, it can hardly be said to be a contract which rests upon 'agreement' in the true sense of the word.

Secondly, the law generally speaking applies an **objective** test of agreement. Consequently, if X by his conduct leads Y reasonably to believe that he, X, is assenting to contractual terms proposed by Y, then usually X will be deemed to have assented, and a contract to exist, even though X in his own mind had no such intention. In other words, the actual mental intention of the parties, a subjective test, is irrelevant and the existence of a contract or otherwise is to be determined by the application of an objective test, i.e. the court looks at what the parties said, did or wrote, and if a reasonable man would infer that agreement exists then such is the case, even if one of the parties in his own mind felt that there was no agreement. The logic behind this approach seems to rest substantially upon convenience, elimination of fraud on the part of persons who make promises and later claim never to have intended to carry them out, and a principle that a contracting party, especially in business circumstances, is entitled to have his reasonable expectations met.

ACTIVITY 1

Write down what standard you think might be adopted in the application of the reasonable man test, i.e. who is the reasonable man? Look at the extract from Treitel in *Cases and Materials* (1.1.1) for assistance.

The standard to be adopted is the view of the judge placing himself in the position of the reasonable man. However, judicial approach as to what standard this sets seems to vary. Sometimes the reasonable man seems to be the 'fly on the wall' third party observer, sometimes the reasonable offeree, i.e. a reasonable person in the position of the offeree in the case in question.

Whether agreement exists or not from an objective standpoint is usually analysed in terms of offer and acceptance, i.e. has one party made a firm offer which the other party has accepted? These concepts are helpful guidelines as long as they are not always rigidly adhered to. However, certain contracts do not always fit easily into this analysis.

Clarke v *Dunraven* [1897] AC 59
The owners of two yachts entered them for the Mudhook Yacht Club Regatta. In a letter to the club secretary each owner undertook to obey all the rules of the club. This included an obligation to pay 'all damages' caused by fouling.

The Santanita fouled and sank *The Valkyrie* and the owner of the latter yacht sued the owner of the former for damages. The liability of a colliding ship in such circumstances was limited by statute to £8 per ton on the registered tonnage of that ship.

The plaintiff argued that the general law was overridden by the defendant's contractual undertaking to pay 'all damages'. The vital question was whether or not there was a contract between the two owners, and the vital problem that the owners' immediate relationships were with the Yacht Club and not with one another.

A contract existed between the owners, such contract being created either when they actually entered their yachts for the race or, at the latest, when they actually sailed.

This approach, says F. R. Davies (Contract, Concise College Texts), calls to mind the good sense of the man who said: 'I can't define an elephant, but I know one when I see one'. It is also an approach which Lord Denning MR suggested should become the normal one to establishing the existence of a contract rather than a schematic and technical offer and acceptance approach (*Butler Machine Tool Co.* v *Ex-Cell-O Corporation* [1979] 1 All ER 965). However, this was firmly rejected by Lord Diplock in *Gibson* v *Manchester City Council* [1979] 1 All ER 972, where he emphasised that although offer and acceptance are not a requirement of the existence of a contract, they are nevertheless to remain the usual method of analysis, i.e. a *Clarke* v *Dunraven* approach is clearly exceptional.

Consequently, let us embark upon a detailed examination of the usual method of analysis, i.e. has one party (the offeror) made a firm offer which the other party (the offeree) has accepted?

1.4　Offer

What is an offer?

It is an intimation (viewed from an objective standpoint, i.e. the reasonable man test) by words or conduct, of a willingness to enter into a legally binding contract, specifying the terms of the binding agreement which will be formed should the offer be accepted by the party to whom it is addressed.

1.4.1　TO WHOM MAY AN OFFER BE MADE?

An offer may be made to a specific person, to a group of persons or to the world at large.

Carlill v *Carbolic Smoke Ball Co.* [1893] 1 QB 256
The company offered by advertisement to pay £100 to any person who succeeded in catching influenza after having used a smoke ball in the prescribed manner three times a day for two weeks. It was added that £1,000 was deposited with the Alliance Bank as an indication of sincerity in the matter.

Mrs C bought and used a ball in the prescribed manner, succeeded in catching influenza afterwards, and sued for her £100.

Several defences were put forward by the defendants, including no intention to create legal relations (i.e. the advertisement was merely an advertising puff), but particularly that there had been no offer to a specific person and that there had been no communication of acceptance to the company.

It was held that:

(a)　There was intention to create legal relations, the deposit of £1,000 at the Alliance Bank being evidence of a sincere offer.

(b) It is possible to make an offer to the world at large, which is capable of being accepted by a number of persons, and this offer had been accepted by Mrs C when she performed the stipulated conditions.

(c) In this type of contract (a unilateral contract) the offeror impliedly waives the need for communication of acceptance.

It is convenient here to distinguish between a **unilateral** contract and a **bilateral** contract:

(a) **Bilateral** X promises to do something for Y if Y will promise to do something for X in return. Normally the mere exchange of such promises renders them enforceable.

(b) **Unilateral** X promises to do something in return for an **act** by Y, e.g., to pay Y £500 if he walks from London to Brighton. Y is not bound to do anything at all; only if Y carries out the act will X's promise become enforceable.

An interesting example of a unilateral contract can be seen in *Bowerman & Another* v *ABTA, The Independent*, 23 November 1995. The plaintiffs were booked on a school skiing holiday with a tour operator who was an ABTA member. ABTA, a trade association of travel agents and tour operators, promoted its members by publishing how it protected the public from the risk of the agent's or operator's insolvency. An ABTA notice displayed in the operator's office described ABTA's scheme for protection against the financial failure of its members. The operator became insolvent, but the skiing holiday was transferred to another operator who received the ABTA refund. However, ABTA's refund did not include the holiday insurance premium paid by each party on the holiday. The plaintiff's claimed from ABTA the refund of a sum equivalent to the insurance.

The Court of Appeal held that the plaintiffs succeeded. ABTA, by displaying the details of its scheme for protection upon the operator's premises, was making a unilateral offer to protect the reader of the notice, the prospective customer. It was a unilateral offer to do something for the customer if the member should fail financially, which was accepted by booking a holiday with an ABTA member.

1.4.2 AN OFFER MUST BE DISTINGUISHED FROM AN INVITATION TO TREAT

The offeror must have completed his part in the formation of a contract by a final declaration of his readiness to undertake an obligation upon certain terms, leaving the offeree a choice between acceptance or refusal. If the alleged offeror is merely feeling his way towards an agreement, or has stated an intention only, i.e. he has initiated negotiations from which agreement might or might not arise, this will amount to an invitation to treat only, which cannot be accepted.

Obviously there are no set legal principles relating to the offer/invitation to treat distinction as everything depends upon an objective test of the parties' intentions. Hence the cases are not easy to reconcile, particularly as they often turn upon convenience considerations. These cases seem to fall into certain identifiable areas.

1.4.2.1 Shop and self-service situations

Fisher v *Bell* [1961] 1 QB 394
A shopkeeper who displayed a flick knife in his shop window was charged with the statutory offence of offering for sale the said flick knife.

The display of goods in a shop window is an invitation to treat only, and therefore no offence had been committed. It is the customer who enters the shop and offers to purchase.

Several factors seem to contribute to the rationale of this decision:

(a) A shop is a place for barter and negotiation over the terms of the contract of sale.

(b) A shopkeeper has a right to pick and choose his customers; if the display were an offer the shopkeeper might have to do business with rogues or vagabonds, and might be required to maintain an endless supply of the type of goods in question.

(c) Any erroneously marked goods in the window would have to be sold at that price if the display were an offer, e.g., a valuable coat marked at £40 instead of £400.

Pharmaceutical Society of Great Britain v *Boots Cash Chemists (Southern) Ltd* [1953] 1 QB 401
The defendants were operating a self-service system in one of their shops. Customers entered, selected articles from the shelves, put them in a wire basket and went to the cash desk to pay for them. The defendants had displayed on the shelves certain drugs which under statute were to be **sold** only under the supervision of a registered pharmacist. A registered pharmacist was present at the cash desk but not at the shelves and Boots were prosecuted for contravening the legislation. Clearly if the display of the drugs were an offer, and the customer's act of picking up the goods an acceptance, then the sale infringed the law. If the **sale** took place at the cash desk no offence was committed.

That the display of the drugs was merely an invitation to treat and not an offer, and no criminal offence was involved.

1.4.2.2 Advertisements and circulars

Advertisements and circulars are usually merely an invitation to treat.

Partridge v *Crittenden* [1968] 2 All ER 421
The appellant had inserted an advertisement in a bird fanciers' magazine (*Cage and Aviary Birds*): 'Bramblefinch cocks and hens, 25s. each'. He was charged with unlawfully **offering** for sale a wild live bird, to wit a brambling, contrary to the Protection of Birds Act 1954, was convicted and appealed.

The Divisional Court quashed his conviction as the advertisement was an invitation to treat and not an offer.

SAQ 3

Grainger & Son v *Gough* [1896] AC 325
The appellants, who were agents for a French wine merchant, canvassed for orders and distributed price lists on the merchant's behalf.

Was this distribution an offer or an invitation to treat?

Give a reason for your choice.

The appellants' canvassing was an invitation to treat and not an offer to sell goods on the merchant's behalf; otherwise the merchant might have been bound upon acceptance to supply an unlimited quantity of the wine described at the price named.

However, in exceptional cases, a person may well exhibit the intention to be legally bound via the medium of an advertisement, e.g., if X by advertisement offers £100 to anyone who returns his lost dog Spot, he is making a unilateral offer to the world at large; Y may accept such offer by the act of returning Spot. (Cf. *Carlill* v *Carbolic Smoke Ball Co.* at **1.4.1**).

Read the judgment of Lord Parker in *Partridge* v *Crittenden* in *Cases and Materials* (1.2.2.2) and write down in the space below when an advertisement might normally constitute an offer.

You should have identified the passage relating to advertisements placed by manufacturers.

1.4.2.3   Negotiations for the sale of land

Because there are so many detailed points to be settled between the parties to land transactions, the courts usually require very strong evidence indeed that the point of intention to be bound (offer) has been reached. A comparison of three cases is interesting:

Harvey v Facey [1893] AC 552
The plaintiff telegraphed to the defendant: 'Will you sell us Bumper Hall Pen? Telegraph lowest cash price'.

The defendants replied by telegraph: 'Lowest price for Bumper Hall Pen £900'.

The plaintiff telegraphed in response: 'We agree to buy Bumper Hall Pen for £900 asked by you. Please send us your title deed'.

Is there a contract here or not?

Give reasons for your choice.

The Judicial Committee of the Privy Council held that there was no contract. The second telegram was not an offer, but merely an indication of the minimum price the defendants would require if they eventually decided to sell.

Similarly in:

Gibson v *Manchester City Council* [1979] 1 All ER 972
A Council tenant who wished to buy his council house contacted the Council. The Council wrote him a letter telling him that it **might** be prepared to sell the house to him on stated terms and invited him to make a formal application on the attached form. The tenant did so, but the Council subsequently reversed its policy of selling to tenants.

The Council's letter contained the language of invitation to treat only and that no contract existed.

However, in:

Bigg v *Boyd Gibbins Ltd* [1971] 2 All ER 183
The correspondence between the parties negotiating for the sale of the plaintiff's property was as follows:

Plaintiff to defendant: 'As you are aware that I paid £25,000 for this property, your offer of £20,000 would appear to be at least a little optimistic. For a quick sale I would accept £26,000 . . .'

Defendant's reply: 'I accept your offer'. The defendant asked the plaintiff to contact the defendant's solicitors.

Plaintiff's final letter: 'I am putting the matter in the hands of my solicitors . . . My wife and I are both pleased that you are purchasing the property.'

A contract existed, Russell LJ saying: 'I cannot escape the view that the parties would regard themselves at the end of the correspondence, quite correctly, as having struck a bargain for the sale and purchase of the property'.

1.4.2.4   Tenders

Normally an announcement that provision of goods or services is open to tender is an invitation to treat and not an offer.

Spencer v *Harding* **(1870) LR 5 CP 561**
The defendants issued a circular offering for sale certain stock in trade for which tenders were invited, and the plaintiff's tender turned out to be the highest.

Do you think this circular was an offer or an invitation to treat?

Despite the usage of the word 'offer', the circular was an invitation to treat only and not a promise to sell to the highest tenderer.

However, it was said, *obiter*, in *Spencer v Harding* that a person seeking tenders will be held to have made an offer (and be bound to the highest tenderer) if it is clear that he intended automatically to be bound in such manner. This is well illustrated in a case which also deals with the question of 'referential' bidding, viz.:

Harvela Investments Ltd v *Royal Trust Co. of Canada Ltd* [1985] 2 All ER 966
The vendors of shares in a company sought a 'single offer' for the shares from each of two interested parties. Consequently, the vendors decided to dispose of the shares by sealed competitive tender and sent identical telexes to both parties:

> We confirm that if the offer made by you is the highest offer received by us we bind ourselves to accept such offer providing such offer complies with the terms of this telex.

The plaintiff bid $2,175,000. The other party bid $2,100,000 or $100,000 in excess of any other offer which you may receive . . . .'.

The House of Lords had to decide which of the two bids was the higher, thus constituting the acceptance necessary for the formation of the contract.

They held that:

(a) The telex was an offer of a unilateral contract to accept the highest bid, which would then be followed by a bilateral contract of sale with the highest bidder.

(b) The plaintiff's $2,175,000 bid was the higher and contractually bound the defendant to sell to the plaintiff.

(c) A term must be implied into the request for bids that referential bids would not be accepted; otherwise the defendant's definite intention to sell might well have been defeated if both parties had made referential bids.

Lastly, we should note that where tenders are invited from selected parties all known to the invitor, and the invitation prescribes a clear, orderly and familiar procedure, which is not open to negotiation, then the invitation contains an implied offer that any conforming tender submitted before the deadline will receive due consideration together with other conforming tenders: *Blackpool & Fylde Aero Club Ltd* v *Blackpool Borough Council* [1990] 3 All ER 25.

1.4.2.5 Tenders and standing offers

This really is a problem of acceptance in the context of tenders, but it is convenient to deal with it separately here. *Cheshire, Fifoot and Furmston's Law of Contract* poses the problem quite well (13th ed., p. 47):

> Suppose that a corporation invites tenders for the supply of certain specified goods to be delivered over a given period. A trader puts in a tender intimating that he is prepared to supply the goods at a certain price. The corporation, to use the language of the business world, 'accepts' the tender. What is the legal result of this 'acceptance'?

The tender is clearly an offer, but what is the effect in law of the 'acceptance'?

(a) If the invitation implies that the potential buyer **will** require **specified** goods over a **specified** period, acceptance of a tender sent in response to such an invitation results in a binding contract under which the buyer undertakes to buy all the goods specified in the tender from the person submitting it.

(b) If the invitation is vague and merely implies that the potential buyer **may** require goods of a specified description up to a maximum amount, the vagueness prevents a contract for the whole goods coming into existence.

Acceptance of a tender in response to such an invitation as in (b) above results in a **standing offer** by the supplier to supply the goods set out in the tender **as and when required** by the person accepting it.

Each time the buyer orders a quantity of goods a contract comes into existence for that quantity, but there is no breach of contract if the buyer does not order any goods at all.

Conversely, if the person submitting the tender wishes to revoke his standing offer, he may do so except in so far as the buyer has already ordered goods under the tender.

SAQ 6

Great Northern Railway Co. v *Witham* **(1873) LR 9 CP 16**
The plaintiffs invited tenders for the supply of goods, including iron, for a period of 12 months. The defendant submitted a tender to supply such goods over the period at a fixed price and in 'such quantities . . . as the company's storekeeper may order from time to time'. The plaintiffs accepted the tender and the defendant made several deliveries of iron, but before the end of the 12-month period refused to supply any more. The plaintiffs sued for breach of contract.

Explain the legal position of the parties by reference to the principles explained above.

The defendant had to honour the outstanding order already placed, but was entitled to withdraw his standing offer for the future.

1.4.2.6 Auction sales

The auctioneer's request for bids is an invitation to treat only. People bidding at an auction make an offer which the auctioneer is free to accept or reject. The offer can be withdrawn at any time before the auctioneer accepts (on fall of the hammer) *Payne* v *Cave* (1789) 3 Term Rep 148; Sale of Goods Act 1979, s. 57(2).

The advertising of an auction is a mere declaration of intention and not an offer to hold an auction. Thus potential buyers have no action against the auctioneers if they fail to hold the auction.

Harris v *Nickerson* (1873) LR 8 QB 286
The plaintiff broker, on the faith of an advertisement, travelled from London to Bury St Edmunds to purchase a particular lot of office furniture at an auction. When he arrived that particular lot had been withdrawn and he sued to recover for his wasted time and travelling expenses.

The plaintiff failed since the advertisement was a declaration of intention only.

What if the advertisement says that the sale will be **without reserve**? Does this constitute a definite offer to sell to the highest bidder? There is no decision on the point, but *obiter dicta* in *Warlow* v *Harrison* (1859) 29 LJ QB 14 suggest that it does.

If this is correct a complicated situation ensues, which you can see from the following SAQ:

The position might well be different depending upon whether the auction takes place or not.

Can you work out the possible legal positions in these alternative circumstances?

If the auctioneer refuses to hold any sale at all or withdraws the relevant lot before any bids are made, there is no breach of contract because of *Harris* v *Nickerson*. However, if the sale does take place and the relevant lot is included, the advertisement constitutes an offer to the public at large that the sale will not be subject to a reserve price. Thus if the auctioneer refuses to accept the highest bid and withdraws the lot, then even though there is no contract of sale he will be in breach of a unilateral contract to sell to the highest bidder: cf. *Harvela Investments Ltd* v *Royal Trust Co. of Canada Ltd* at **1.4.2.4**.

1.4.2.7   Offer of a place at university

Moran v *University College Salford (No. 2), The Times*, 23 November 1993
As a result of a clerical error, a prospective student received an unconditional offer of a place at university to study physiotherapy. He accepted the place by notifying PCAS (Polytechnic Central Admissions System) and the university in the prescribed manner. In so doing he ceased to be eligible to seek an alternative place through the clearing system. He also later gave notice terminating his employment and to leave his accommodation and did not attend a second interview for a job for which he had applied. It was contended by UCS that the offer of a place was merely an invitation to treat.

The unconditional offer of a place appeared to be an offer capable of acceptance, which Moran accepted at the latest when he notified UCS. An agreement was created under which UCS agreed to offer him a place if he sought to enrol on the due date. However, he would not have been bound to enrol or pay fees on the terms laid down by UCS.

1.5   Termination of Offer

An offer may be terminated in any one of the following ways:

1.5.1   REVOCATION

The offeror is at liberty to revoke his offer at any time before acceptance, but any such revocation is ineffective until communicated to the offeree.

Byrne & Co. v Van Tienhoven & Co. **(1880) 5 CPD 344**
A letter revoking an offer was sent from Cardiff to New York on 8 October. Acceptance of the original offer was telegraphed on 11 October from New York to Cardiff, followed on the 15 October by a letter confirming acceptance. The letter revoking the offer arrived in New York on 20 October.

What do you need to know about the purported acceptances in order to work out whether the offer has been validly withdrawn?

Due to the postal acceptance rule (a letter of acceptance is effective upon posting – see **1.6.3.2**) a contract came into existence before effective revocation had been made.

What if the offeror promises not to revoke his offer before a specified date? Any such promise is unenforceable unless supported by consideration (i.e. the other party must have promised or given something of value in return).

Routledge v Grant (1828) 4 Bing 653
The defendant offered to take a lease of the plaintiff's premises, and promised to keep the offer open for six weeks. After three weeks the defendant purported to revoke his offer, while at the end of six weeks the plaintiff purported to accept it.

There was no contract.

However, the result would have been different if, for example, the plaintiff had paid £5 (consideration) in return for the promise to keep the offer open – known as purchasing an option.

The English rule reflected in *Routledge v Grant* is out of step with most other legal systems and probably should be changed, at least in the case of 'firm offers' in a business context; such a 'firm offer' is a valuable tool in forward planning, especially where a firm wishes to rely on prices quoted by potential subcontractors when tendering for a major contract.

Apparently the communication of revocation need not necessarily be by the offeror, provided the offeree as a reasonable man ought to believe the source who informs him.

Dickinson v *Dodds* (1876) 2 ChD 463
On 10 June the defendant offered in writing to sell his house to the plaintiff for £800, 'to be left over until Friday 12 June, 9 am'.

On Thursday, 11 June the defendant sold his house to a third party, and that evening the plaintiff was informed of the sale by one Berry, the agent who had handled the transaction.

Before 9.00 am on 12 June the plaintiff handed a formal letter of acceptance to the defendant.

The Court of Appeal held that the manner of communication was irrelevant provided that the plaintiff knew without doubt that the defendant no longer intended to sell his property to him by the time the purported acceptance was made.

Read *Dickinson* v *Dodds*. **What difficulties are likely to be raised by this decision when trying to apply it to new situations?**

Answer in *Cases and Materials* (1.3.1).

You will see from the *Cases and Materials* that there are difficulties in identifying who is a reasonable source of revocation.

Revocation of unilateral offers presents certain difficulties, particularly as there is no English decision on this point. Let us consider an example:

X promises to pay £1,000 to the first person who succeeds in hopping the circumference of Ullswater on his left leg. Y undertakes the task and is 100 metres from completion when X cycles up to him and withdraws the offer.

If the general rule is applied, i.e. an offer can be withdrawn at any time before acceptance, then clearly acceptance is not complete until the act is fully performed and revocation seems possible, though this is most unfair to Y.

Read Lord Denning's judgment in *Errington* v *Errington & Woods* in *Cases and Materials* (1.3.2).

How might this judgment provide a satisfactory solution to the above situation?

A possible solution has been put forward in America (McGovney, 27 Harvard L Rev 644) – the so called 'two contract theory', viz. the offeror's statement consists of two separate offers:

(a)   an express offer to pay on performance of the act; and

(b)   an implied offer not to revoke until the offeree has had the opportunity to complete the act if the offeree begins the task within a reasonable time.

Thus once the act is commenced there comes into existence a separate contract, collateral to the main contract, not to revoke until the offeree has had the opportunity to complete the task. Any attempt to revoke before that time will be a breach of the collateral contract. This provides a satisfactory, albeit artificial solution.

The English cases on bilateral contracts suggest that whether such an offer not to revoke should be implied or not depends upon the intentions of the parties in the particular circumstances of each individual case: cf. *Luxor (Eastbourne) Ltd* v *Cooper* [1941] 1 All ER 33; *Errington* v *Errington & Woods* [1952] 1 All ER 149.

In *Daulia Ltd* v *Four Millbank Nominees Ltd* [1978] 2 All ER 557, the Court of Appeal stated, *obiter*, that it was too late for the offeror to withdraw his offer once the offeree had embarked upon performance.

1.5.2   REJECTION

Either express rejection or a counter-offer (see **1.6.1**) will destroy the original offer.

1.5.3   LAPSE OF TIME

Where it is expressly stated that the offer will remain open for a fixed period the offer cannot be accepted after the expiration of that period.

If there is no time stipulation the offer lapses after a reasonable time. What is reasonable is a question of fact in each case.

Ramsgate Victoria Hotel Co. Ltd v *Montefiore* (1866) LR 1 Exch 109
The defendant applied for shares in the plaintiff company in early June 1864. The shares
were allotted to him in late November 1864. The defendant refused to pay for the shares.

The defendant was not liable since the company's response to the defendant's offer had
not been made within a reasonable time.

1.5.4   DEATH

1.5.4.1   Death of the offeror

The death of the offeror will automatically terminate an offer to enter into a contract for
personal services, e.g. to sing at a concert.

Where the contract is not for personal services, the orthodox view is that the personal
representatives of the offeror should not have the burden of substituted performance
imposed upon them provided that notice of the offeror's death has been given to the
offeree. However, according to *obiter dicta* in *Bradbury* v *Morgan* (1862) 1 H & C 249, the
personal representatives may well be bound if the offeree has no notice of the offeror's
death at the time of acceptance.

1.5.4.2   Death of the offeree

This probably terminates the offer, since an offer is peculiar to the offeree and is not
intended to be made either to a dead person or to his personal representatives: *obiter dicta*
in *Reynolds* v *Atherton* (1921) 125 LT 690.

1.5.5   OFFER SUBJECT TO IMPLIED CONDITION PRECEDENT

In *Financings Ltd* v *Stimson* [1962] 3 All ER 386, the Court of Appeal **held** that an offer to
purchase a motor car had lapsed by the time of the purported acceptance because the
offer was subject to an implied condition precedent that the car would be in the same
condition at the time of acceptance as it was at the time when the offer was made (it had
been damaged in the meantime).

1.6   Acceptance

1.6.1   THE FACT OF ACCEPTANCE

What can constitute acceptance?

Acceptance may be express or inferred from conduct, i.e. an unequivocal act constituting
implied acceptance (unequivocal means an act the only logical explanation of which is
acceptance of the offer). Thus implied acceptance is clear in the case of unilateral
contracts, e.g., by returning the lost dog to accept the offer of a reward, or by using the
smoke ball appropriately in *Carlill's* case. Implied acceptance in the case of bilateral
contracts is well illustrated by *Brogden* v *Metropolitan Railway Co.* (see p. 4) or by the
dispatch of goods in response to an order.

The acceptor must have knowledge of the offer at the moment of acceptance.

Williams v *Carwardine* (1833) 5 C & P 566
The defendant offered a reward of £20 to anyone who gave information leading to the
conviction of the murderers of Walter Carwardine. The plaintiff knew of the offer but,

thinking that she did not have long to live, gave the information 'to ease her conscience and in hopes of forgiveness hereafter'.

The plaintiff was entitled to her reward and her motive was irrelevant provided that she was aware of the offer at the time of acceptance.

Acceptance must be unqualified. There are a number of branches of this requirement. First, acceptance must be absolute and unconditional. Hence, usage of the hallowed phrase 'subject to contract' will usually prevent a contract coming into existence, although, since each case depends upon the parties' intentions as discovered by the court, even that phrase may not negate acceptance in an exceptional case (see *Alpenstow Ltd* v *Regalian Properties plc* [1985] 2 All ER 545).

Other phrases which have failed to negate acceptance in the particular circumstances of the case in question are 'provisional agreement' (*Branca* v *Cobarro* [1947] 2 All ER 101) 'without prejudice' (*Tomlin* v *Standard Telephone & Cables Ltd* [1969] 3 All ER 201).

An offshoot of these difficulties is conditions precedent and subsequent. An agreement which appears to be a binding contract may never come into operation because it is subject to a condition precedent which is never fulfilled.

Pym v *Campbell* (1856) 6 E & B 370
An agreement to purchase a share in an invention was subject to the condition precedent that the invention was to be approved by a third party. The third party never gave approval and so no contract came into existence.

With regard to condition subsequent, the agreement will be binding unless and until the relevant condition occurs. If the condition does occur the contract will either automatically cease to bind, or one party will have the option to cancel it.

Head v *Tattersall* (1871) LR 7 Exch 7
A contract for the sale of a horse was subject to a condition subsequent that if the purchaser found within a stated time that the horse had not been hunted with the Bicester hounds the horse could be returned and the contract terminated. The purchaser discovered that the horse did not fit the description and was able to return the horse even though it had been injured in the meantime.

Secondly, the offeree's expression of assent must match exactly the terms of the offer – 'the mirror image rule'. Thus if the offeree, purporting to accept, introduces a new term not previously considered by the offeror, this will amount to a counter-offer, the effect of which is to destroy the original offer.

Hyde v *Wrench* (1840) 3 Beav 334
The defendant offered to sell his property to the plaintiff for £1,000. The plaintiff offered £950 which the defendant rejected. The plaintiff then purported to accept the original £1,000 offer.

The plaintiff's £950 counter-offer destroyed the original offer, which therefore was no longer in existence when the plaintiff purported to accept it at a later date.

However, a mere **request for information** not amounting to a counter-offer will not destroy the original offer.

Stevenson v *McLean* (1880) 5 QBD 346
The defendant offered to sell iron to the plaintiff at 40s. (£2) per ton, immediate delivery. The plaintiff asked the defendant by telegram if he would sell at the same price if delivery were staggered over two months. On receiving no reply, the plaintiff accepted the original offer. The defendant sold the iron elsewhere and claimed that the telegram was a counter-offer.

The telegram was a mere request for information and not a counter-offer. Therefore, the original offer remained open for acceptance and the defendant was in breach of contract.

The offer/counter-offer problem can be particularly acute in the business context in situations known as 'the battle of the forms'.

1.6.2 'THE BATTLE OF THE FORMS'

This problem arises where two parties deal with one another by reference to their own respective terms and these terms conflict. Whose terms comprise the terms of the contract?

One approach is illustrated in the following case:

BRS v *Arthur Crutchley Ltd* [1968] 1 All ER 811
The plaintiffs delivered a consignment of whisky to the defendants for storage. Their driver handed to the defendants a delivery note purporting to incorporate the plaintiff's 'conditions of carriage'. The note was stamped by the defendants: 'Received under [defendants'] conditions'.

This amounted to a counter-offer which the plaintiffs accepted by handing over the goods. Thus the contract was made on the defendants' terms.

This decision supports the 'last shot' doctrine, i.e. where conflicting terms are exchanged each is a counter-offer, so that if a contract results at all (perhaps from acceptance by conduct) it must be on the terms of the final document in the series.

The leading case is indecisive other than to indicate that the 'last shot' doctrine is not always the answer:

Butler Machine Tool Co. v *Ex-Cell-O Corpn* [1979] 1 All ER 965
The sellers offered to sell a machine tool to the buyers for a specified sum. The offer was made in a document containing certain terms, including a price variation clause, which were to 'prevail over any terms and conditions in the buyers' order'.

The buyers placed an order via a letter containing conflicting conditions, and in particular having no price variation clause. At the bottom of the order was a tear-off confirmation slip expressly subject to the buyers' terms.

The sellers completed and returned the tear-off slip together with a letter stating that the buyers' order had been entered into in accordance with the sellers' original offer.

When the tool was delivered the sellers claimed an additional sum under the price variation clause.

The sellers had contracted on the buyers' terms since return of the tear-off slip amounted to acceptance of the buyers' counter-offer. The accompanying letter was deemed not to qualify acceptance but to be mere confirmation of the price and description of the machine.

This decision turns entirely on the sellers' tactical error in returning the tear-off slip, and a different conclusion might well have been reached had the sellers refrained from returning such slip.

Read *Butler Machine Tool Co.* v *Ex-Cell-O Corpn* in *Cases and Materials* (1.4.2).

What alternative approaches are there to the 'last shot' doctrine?

What alternative views might have been adopted if the seller had not returned the tear-off slip?

1.6.3 COMMUNICATION OF ACCEPTANCE

1.6.3.1 General rule

There must be external manifestation of assent, and in particular acceptance has no effect until it is communicated to the offeror.

Acceptance is communicated when it is actually brought to the attention of the offeror. Thus, for example, if an oral acceptance is drowned by an aircraft flying overhead or is spoken into a telephone when the line has gone dead, there is no contract.

1.6.3.2 Exceptions

In the following circumstances acceptance may be effective even though it is not brought to the attention of the offeror:

Conduct of the offeror

The offeror may be estopped from denying that he received an acceptance if it is his own fault that he did not get it, e.g., if a listener on the telephone does not catch the words of acceptance, but does not ask for them to be repeated.

Terms of the offer

The offeror may expressly or by implication waive the need for communication of acceptance, e.g., in bilateral contracts a supplier may accept a retailer's order merely by dispatching the goods to him; in unilateral contracts acceptance is constituted by the precise performance of the act or acts specified in the offer.

The postal acceptance rule

In general a letter of acceptance takes effect upon posting rather than when it actually arrives. This is an arbitrary rule of commercial expediency, little better or worse than the alternatives, is subject to a number of qualifications, and is generally satisfactory unless the letter of acceptance is lost or delayed.

Adams v *Lindsell* (1818) 1 B & Ald 681
The defendants wrote to the plaintiffs to offer to sell some wool and asked for a reply 'in course of post'. The letter containing the offer was wrongly addressed and, because of this, the letter of acceptance was posted and received two days later than the defendants would reasonably have expected.

On the day previous to receipt of the letter of acceptance the defendants sold the wool to a third party, but the letter of acceptance had been posted before the day on which the wool was sold. The plaintiffs sued for breach of contract and succeeded because the contract was concluded when the letter of acceptance was posted.

Household Fire Insurance Co. v *Grant* (1879) 4 ExD 216
The defendant applied for shares in the plaintiff's company. The shares were allotted to the defendant and a notice of allotment posted to him which never arrived. The issue was whether the defendant had become a shareholder or not.

The Court of Appeal held that he had, because the contract was completed at the time of posting even though the letter of acceptance was never actually delivered.

In general the postal acceptance rule favours the offeree.

Read the extract in *Cases and Materials* (1.4.3.2) from Treitel, *Law of Contract*, 9th ed., p. 24.

Is the rule justifiable?

There are three qualifications for the operation of the postal acceptance rule:

(a) Reasonable means of acceptance.

(b) Properly addressed and properly posted.

(c) Letters and telegrams/telemessages.

Thus:

(a) Post must be a reasonable means of acceptance. Thus in *Henthorn* v *Fraser* [1892] 2 Ch 27, the Court of Appeal **held** that the fact that the parties lived some way from one another justified postal acceptance of an oral offer. Conversely, it would not usually be reasonable to reply by post to an offer made by swifter means, e.g., telephone/telex/fax. What if the offeror prescribes a means of acceptance? If he lays down an exclusive means of acceptance, e.g., carrier pigeon **only**, then only that method will suffice. However, the offeror must be careful to use exclusive language, because in *Yates Building Co. Ltd* v *Pulleyn & Sons Ltd* (1975) 119 Sol Jo 370 a stipulation to use registered post was held to be merely directory and not mandatory and acceptance by ordinary post was justified. Thus in the absence of a prescribed, exclusive means of acceptance any mode of acceptance which is as swift or swifter than that prescribed by the offeror, or which is equally or more advantageous to the offeror than his prescribed mode, will suffice: *Manchester Diocesan Council for Education* v *Commercial and General Investments Ltd* [1969] 3 All ER 1593.

Note that the postal acceptance rule can be excluded, either expressly or by implication, by the terms of the offer.

Holwell Securities Ltd v *Hughes* [1974] 1 All ER 161
An offer to sell a house was made in the form of an option expressed 'to be exercisable by notice in writing to the Intending Vendor . . .'. The notice was posted but failed to arrive.

There was no contract of sale as the terms of the offer, on true construction, required acceptance to be communicated.

(b) The letter of acceptance must be properly addressed and properly posted: *Re London and Northern Bank* [1900] 1 Ch 220. What if the letter of acceptance is wrongly addressed? There is no English decision on the point, but it has been suggested, *obiter*, that the postal acceptance rule should not apply: *Getreide-Import Gesellschaft* v *Contimar (Contimar's case)* [1953] 1 WLR 207.

(c) The postal acceptance rule applies to letters and telegrams/telemessages, but not to telephone acceptances or acceptances by telex which are regarded as equivalent to instantaneous communication. Which rule is likely to apply to an acceptance made by way of fax? Presumably an acceptance by fax is likely to be effective when communicated (although the point as yet has not been decided) as fax is virtually an instantaneous communication, and the postal acceptance rule is unlikely to apply. However, with regard to the difficulties of determining when a telex/fax is communicated, read the speeches of Lord Wilberforce and Lord Fraser in the *Brinkibon* case (below).

Entores v *Miles Far East Corporation* [1955] 2 QB 327
The plaintiffs had offices in London, the defendants in Amsterdam. The parties entered into an agreement by means of telex whereby each company had in its office a teleprinter connected by the Post Office to a teleprinter in the other office so that a message typed on one machine was automatically typed out by the other. The contract was broken and a question arose as to where the contract had been made.

The contract was made when and where the acceptance was received, i.e. in London.

Entores was confirmed by the House of Lords in *Brinkibon Ltd* v *Stalag Stahl und Stahlwarenhandels GmbH* (the *Brinkibon Case*) [1982] 1 All ER 293.

What is the position regarding revocation of a postal acceptance?

SAQ 9

What if the offeree purports to recall his postal acceptance, perhaps by telex/telephone, after the letter of acceptance has been posted but before it reaches the offeror (the telex/telephone revocation reaching the offeror before the letter of acceptance)?

A strict application of the postal acceptance rule would rule out any such revocation. However, there is no English decision on the point and what authorities there are are ambiguous.

In favour of the offeree being able to withdraw is the Scottish case of *Dunmore (Countess)* v *Alexander* (1830) 9 Sh (Ct of Sess) 190, though the scope of the decision is unclear.

Against are *Wenckheim* v *Arndt* 1 JR 73 from New Zealand and *A to Z Bazaars (Pty) Ltd* v *Minister of Agriculture* 1974 (4) SA 392 from South Africa.

ACTIVITY 7

For an alternative approach to the above read the extract in *Cases and Materials* (1.4.4) from Treitel, *Law of Contract*, 9th ed., pp. 27–8.

Silence

An offeror cannot impose silence as a means of acceptance upon an unwilling offeree by writing to him saying, 'If I hear nothing from you I'll assume you have accepted my offer'.

Felthouse v *Bindley* (1862) 11 CB NS 869
The plaintiff offered to buy his nephew's horse for £30.15s by a letter which said: 'If I hear no more about him, I consider the horse mine at that price'. The nephew did not

reply to the letter, but indicated to the defendant, an auctioneer, that the horse was to be kept out of a forthcoming auction sale. The defendant sold the horse by mistake and was sued by the plaintiff for the tort of conversion. The plaintiff could not succeed unless he could establish that he owned the horse, and that depended upon proving a contract between himself and his nephew.

The uncle failed, since he had no right to impose silence as a means of acceptance upon an unwilling offeree who would otherwise have to go to the time and expense of rejecting the offer.

However, there appears to be no reason why pre-agreed silence should not constitute acceptance (the offeree is willing) and it has frequently been held that silence plus external manifestation of assent by conduct amounts to acceptance both in unilateral contracts, e.g., *Carlill's* case (see **1.4.1**) and in bilateral contracts, e.g.:

Weatherby v *Banham* (1832) 5 C & P 228
Unrequested periodicals were sent to the defendant by the plaintiff who said that if they were not returned within a specified period the plaintiff would assume that the defendant had purchased them.

There was a contract because the defendant had accepted by implication by reading and keeping the periodicals.

The technique involved in *Weatherby* v *Banham* is known as inertia selling. The recipient is obviously bound if he uses the goods, but what if he does not want them and does not want to go to the time and expense of returning unsolicited goods? The problem is now regulated by the Unsolicited Goods and Services Acts 1971 and 1975, which provide:

(a)   If the sender of unsolicited goods does not retrieve them within six months he makes a gift of them to the recipient.

(b)   If the recipient serves written notice requiring the sender to retrieve the goods, the sender makes a gift of them to the recipient unless he retrieves the goods within 30 days.

(c)   It is a criminal offence to demand payment for unsolicited goods.

ACTIVITY 8

The fact that the nephew in *Felthouse* v *Bindley* told the auctioneer not to sell the horse is evidence that he was willing to sell to his uncle. So why was the case decided as it was?

Would silence have been acceptance if it were the uncle who had denied the existence of a contract?

After you have written down your suggestions read Miller (1972) 35 MLR 489 in *Cases and Materials* (1.4.5).

Identical cross-offers?

If X posts a letter to Y offering to sell his car for £2,000, and simultaneously Y posts a letter offering to buy X's car for £2,000, is there a contract between X and Y? There is no decision on the point but *obiter dicta* in *Tinn* v *Hoffman* (1873) 29 LT 271 suggest that there would not be due to a lack of identifiable offer and acceptance.

1.7   Inchoate Agreements

Even though there may be apparent offer and acceptance, still there may be no contract because the terms of the agreement are uncertain or the agreement is qualified by reference to the need for future agreement between the parties.

However, a particular problem here is that businessmen often enter into what they believe to be a contract as a matter of urgency in broad general terms, leaving the details to be sorted out later. If litigation arises the court has the unenviable task of deciding whether or not there was a contract in the first place, particularly if the agreement has to some extent been performed.

The court is faced by two conflicting elements:

    (a)   lack of certainty of essential terms; and

    (b)   the need to give effect to the reasonable expectations of the commercial world.

The approach of the judiciary seems to be that while it will not construct a contract for the parties, it will endeavour to construe the existence of a contract if at all possible.

What guidelines can be gleaned from the cases?

1.7.1   AGREEMENTS WHICH ARE IRRESOLVABLY VAGUE

Scammell Ltd v *Ouston* [1914] 1 All ER 14
The House of Lords **held** an agreement to buy goods 'on hire purchase terms over a period of two years' too vague to be enforced. Since there were many kinds of hire purchase agreements in widely different terms, it was impossible to say upon what terms the parties intended to contract.

British Steel Corporation v *Cleveland Bridge and Engineering Co. Ltd* [1984] 1 All ER 504
Work was begun on a major construction before all the elements of the contract had been agreed, though both parties confidently expected that reaching an agreement would not be a problem. However, final agreement was never reached, and eventually the plaintiffs ceased work and claimed for work done; the defendants counter-claimed for breach of contract.

There was no contract; there had been no final agreement on price, delivery or relevant terms and conditions. The plaintiffs recovered a reasonable sum for work done on what is known as a *quantum meruit* basis.

This represents an unusual decision in that normally the court finds a contract to exist where performance has begun.

1.7.2 VAGUENESS AND NO PERFORMANCE

May and Butcher v *R* [1934] 2 KB 17
An agreement was entered into whereby the plaintiff was to purchase from the defendant surplus war tentage, leaving the price to be determined by the parties. The parties failed to agree and the plaintiff sought enforcement of the agreement at a reasonable price.

The House of Lords **held** that there was no contract due to failure to agree upon price, date of payment or the delivery period.

1.7.3 VAGUENESS BUT PERFORMANCE BEGUN

SAQ 10

Hillas & Co. Ltd v *Arcos Ltd* (1932) 38 Com Cas 23
The plaintiffs agreed to purchase from the defendants '22,000 standards of softwood goods of fair specification over the season 1930'. The contract also contained an option for the purchase of timber during the 1931 season on very favourable terms, but the option clause did not describe the goods to be sold. The plaintiffs purported to exercise the option in 1931, but the defendants claimed there was no contract due to uncertainty.

Do you think a contract has been formed here?

Give reasons for your answer.

There was a contract as the terms could be ascertained by reference to the previous course of dealings between the parties in 1930.

Note: In similar circumstances one might be able to argue trade or business practice, e.g., 'within one month' is potentially vague, but not if it always means 31 days in a particular trade or profession.

Foley v *Classique Coaches Ltd* [1934] 2 KB 1
The plaintiff, a retail dealer in petrol, agreed to supply the defendants, who were the owners of motor coaches, with all petrol required for business purposes, 'at a price to be agreed by the parties in writing and from time to time'. No agreement in writing with regard to price was ever concluded and after three years the defendants purported to repudiate the agreement.

The contract was to be enforced on the basis of the defendants paying a reasonable price for the petrol supplied; what was reasonable in the circumstances was to be determined if necessary by arbitration as provided by another clause in the contract.

1.7.4 MEANINGLESS TERMS

Nicolene Ltd v *Simmonds* [1953] 1 All ER 822
The plaintiffs wrote to the defendant offering to buy a specified quantity of steel bars. The defendant wrote accepting the offer and stated 'usual conditions of acceptance to apply'. The plaintiffs acknowledged this acceptance in a further letter in which they made no reference to the 'usual conditions of acceptance'. The defendant failed to deliver the bars and when sued argued that the usual conditions had never been agreed and, therefore, there was no contract.

There were no usual conditions of acceptance to which the parties could refer; consequently, the clause could be ignored as meaningless and a contract enforced on the basis of the rest of the correspondence.

1.7.5 RETROSPECTIVE ACCEPTANCE

The parties may carry out certain acts assuming that a contract will eventually be made. Apparently in these circumstances acceptance can operate retrospectively to give legal effect to everything done towards the contract. Such intention may be express or inferred from conduct: *Trolloppe and Colls* v *Atomic Power Construction Ltd* [1962] 3 All ER 1035.

1.8 Intention to Create Legal Relations

Even where the parties have reached an agreement and have mutually furnished consideration, there will not necessarily be a contract. There is a further requirement of intention to create a legal relationship. For example, if X promises to cook dinner for Y, who must incur the expense of travelling to X's house to eat the meal, such arrangement is hardly likely to be intended to have legal consequences.

Whether intention to create legal relations exists or not is always a question of objective construction by the courts of what parties said, did or wrote. There is a strong presumption of intention to create legal relations in the case of agreements made in business/commercial circumstances, and a strong presumption against such intention in the case of agreements made in social/domestic circumstances. However, such presumptions are always rebuttable by evidence to the contrary.

1.8.1 EXPRESS EXCLUSION OF INTENTION TO CREATE LEGAL RELATIONS

The 'subject to contract' cases are all illustrations of express negation of legal intent.

With regard to business agreements, the courts will readily presume legal intention unless it is expressly negatived: *Jones* v *Vernon's Pools Ltd* [1938] 2 All ER 626; *Appleson* v *Littlewoods Ltd* [1939] 1 All ER 464. In both cases the plaintiff claimed to have sent in a successful football coupon and sued for the money. It was held in both cases that there was no contractual relationship due to an express clause in the coupon which said, 'binding in honour only; not subject to the jurisdiction of the courts'.

Rose & Frank Co. v *Crompton Bros Ltd* [1925] AC 445
The defendants, who were English manufacturers of paper tissues, entered into an agreement with an American firm, the plaintiffs, constituting them sole agents for the sale in the USA of tissues supplied by the English firm. A dispute arose between them.

There was no contractual relationship due to the following clause in the contract: 'This arrangement is not entered into . . . as a formal legal arrangement, and shall not be subject to a legal jurisdiction in the law courts.'

Sometimes legal intention can be excluded by legislation, e.g., s. 18 of the Trade Union and Labour Relations Act 1974 provides that collective agreements between employers and trade unions are not intended to be legally enforceable unless they are in writing and expressly affirm that they are intended to be binding.

1.8.2   NO EXPRESS EXCLUSION OF INTENTION TO CREATE LEGAL RELATIONS

1.8.2.1   Advertisements

Advertising 'puffs' are not normally treated as serious offers which can be accepted to bring a contract into existence, e.g., 'Heineken refreshes the parts which other beers cannot reach'. However, where there is evidence of intention an advertisement may constitute a unilateral offer which can be accepted. *Carlill* v *Carbolic Smoke Ball Co.* [1893] 1 QB 256.

1.8.2.2   Family arrangements

Husband and wife agreements
Whilst no precise conclusions can be drawn from the cases, it would seem that there is a presumption of no intention in certain situations. For example, where a husband and wife were living together at the time of the agreement, albeit extremely unhappily, on the basis that legal proceedings should not be used to resolve marital disputes: *Balfour* v *Balfour* [1919] 2 KB 571; *Spellman* v *Spellman* [1961] 2 All ER.

However, where the husband and wife were not living together at the time of the agreement the court may enforce it, particularly where the agreement was designed to deal with marriage break-up: *Merritt* v *Merritt* [1970] 2 All ER 760.

Where the words used by the parties were uncertain, the uncertainty may be evidence of lack of intention. See *Gould* v *Gould* [1969] 3 All ER 728, where a husband, upon leaving his wife, said he would pay her £15 per week 'so long as I can manage it.' It was held that there was no contract.

Other family arrangements
Although the agreement is made in social/domestic circumstances the court often infers legal intention if the agreement has a commercial flavour to it.

Simpkins v *Pays* [1955] 3 All ER 10
S was a lodger with P, an elderly woman, and her granddaughter. S was very keen on entering various competitions. S drew up the forms in P's name and the entry fees were shared. P promised to share any winnings obtained. One entry in a fashion competition won £750 which P refused to share.

There was a contract. S had been a competitor for many years, and had agreed to combine his efforts with the others only on the basis of their entries being a joint effort, each sharing expenses and each having the benefit of any prize money.

1.8.2.3   Other cases

Whether there is intention or not must be deduced from the circumstances of the case.

Peck v *Lateu* (1973) 117 SJ 185
Two ladies attended bingo sessions together and had an arrangement to pool their winnings. One of them won an additional 'Bonanza' prize of £1,107, and claimed it was not covered by the sharing arrangement.

In the circumstances the agreement was legally binding.

1.9 Conclusion

While we have studied offer and acceptance, intention to create legal relations and inchoate (incomplete) agreements apparently in isolation, we should not forget that they are interrelated issues, relevant to contract formation, and are frequently treated as such in problem questions. Although we can identify offer and acceptance, there will not necessarily be a contract where the agreement is made in social and domestic circumstances. Similarly, another way of expressing the view that something is too vague to constitute a contractual term is to say that it fails to express an intention to enter into a legally binding contract with sufficient certainty, i.e. it is not an offer.

1.10   End of Chapter Assessment Question

Bill is the proprietor of an antiques shop. On Thursday, he placed an advert in the *Antiques Gazette*, For Sale, Mahogany Table circa 1780, English £2,500.' Alan read the advert on Friday and telephoned Bill saying, 'I need such a table for a client, but I can only pay £2,000'. Bill replied that he could not accept less than £2,250, but stated that he would not sell that item to anyone else before Wednesday, while Alan considered the matter.

On Monday, Alan rang Bill, but, Bill had closed his shop to go to an auction. Alan therefore sent a fax message which was received on Bill's fax machine. In the message, Alan agreed to buy the table for £2,250. Later that day, Mary, Bill's cleaner, accidentally dropped the fax message into the waste bin, before Bill had read it.

While at the auction, Bill mentioned the table to another dealer, Tom, who immediately agreed to buy it for £2,500. The next day, Tom happened to meet Alan in the local pub and told Alan of his extraordinary luck in acquiring the table for £2,500. Alan went home and immediately posted a letter to Bill in which he agreed to buy the table for £2,250. That same afternoon, Bill had written to Alan stating that he was no longer willing to sell the table for £2,250.

Advise Alan.

There are a number of issues which require consideration in the question, but on one issue in particular it is necessary to read the judgments of Lords Wilberforce and Fraser in *Brinkibon Ltd* v *Stahag Stahl und Stahlwarenhandels GmbH* [1983] 2 AC 34; [1982] 1 All ER 293; [1982] 2 WLR 164.

See *Cases and Materials* (**1.8**) for the complete answer.

CHAPTER TWO

CONSIDERATION AND PRIVITY OF CONTRACT

2.1 Objectives

By the end of this chapter you should be able to:

■ explain in your own words what is meant by the concept of consideration;

■ distinguish between executory, executed and past consideration;

■ appraise critically the cases on sufficiency of consideration and be aware of why several of them are difficult to reconcile;

■ recognise how recent developments in the law relating to existing duties reflect a change in attitude by the judiciary (particularly *Williams* v *Roffey Bros and Nicholls (Contractors) Ltd*);

■ explain the common law problem which led to the development of the doctrine of promissory estoppel;

■ identify the essential ingredients of the doctrine of promissory estoppel;

■ evaluate critically the doctrine of promissory estoppel and identify the difficulties created by the uncertainty of its scope of operation;

■ apply the rules relating to consideration to problem situations;

■ understand the relationship between consideration and privity of contract.

2.2 Introduction

Despite an identifiable offer and acceptance, and a present intention to create legal relations, there may still be no contract in English law due to the absence of consideration (consideration is unnecessary if the agreement is made by deed, but this is very much an exceptional situation).

Both parties must furnish consideration in order to bring a contract into existence. Consideration is the price paid for the other party's obligation, e.g., in the sale of a car, the buyer's consideration is the payment of the price, and the seller's consideration is the handing over of the car; in a contract of employment the employer's consideration is the payment of wages and the employee's consideration is doing the work. Thus the payment of money, the handing over of goods, and the performance of a service will each constitute sufficient consideration.

Not only does the performance of an act, e.g., delivery or payment, constitute consideration, but also a promise to perform will suffice. Thus a promise given in return for a promise or an act will create a legally binding contract. However, a bare or gratuitous promise, one for which nothing is done in return, e.g., a promise to make a gift, is not enforceable as a 'contract'.

Thus it is probably true to say that the English law of contract is concerned with bargains, i.e. where something has been given in exchange for something else. However, the identification of the element of bargain sometimes produces no little difficulty. One reason is the approach of the judiciary, who, when faced with a situation where there is manifest offer and acceptance and intention of legal consequences, have sometimes leaned over backwards to discover the existence of some obscure element as satisfying the consideration requirement for one of the parties, particularly where the other party's promise has been relied upon.

2.2.1 DEFINITION OF CONSIDERATION

Consideration was defined by Lush J in *Currie* v *Misa* (1875) LR 10 Ex 153:

> A valuable consideration, in the sense of the law, may consist in some right, interest, profit, or benefit accruing to the one party, or some forbearance, detriment, loss, or responsibility given, suffered, or undertaken by the other.

The language of benefit and detriment is potentially confusing because usually they constitute the same thing looked at from different viewpoints, e.g., Ted agrees to purchase Charles's yacht for £10,000. Thus, Ted agrees to give Charles £10,000 (detriment to Ted) in return for the yacht (benefit to Ted). Charles agrees to provide Ted with the yacht (detriment to Charles) in exchange for the £10,000 (benefit to Charles). Consequently, a more useful definition is one given by Sir Frederick Pollock (*Principles of Contract*):

> . . . an act or forbearance of one party, or the promise thereof is the price for which the promise of the other is bought.

However, the benefit/detriment analysis cannot be ignored since many of the older cases approach the issue in this way.

2.2.2 CONSIDERATION AND CONDITION

Consideration must be distinguished from the fulfilment of a condition. If X says to Y, 'I will give you £500 if you break your leg', there is no contract, but merely a gratuitous promise subject to a condition. X is not **requesting** Y to break his leg, he is merely specifying an event which must occur before his **moral** obligation to pay £500 arises.

However, if X says to Y, 'You can have my old refrigerator if you disconnect it and take it away', the issue is less clear.

Can you explain from the example above how this might be interpreted as a contractual promise rather than a conditional gift?

It is a benefit to x and disconnection by Y may be consideration

An examination of all the circumstances might reveal an intention on X's part to **request** Y to take away the refrigerator, particularly if this is advantageous to X, and the disconnection and taking away might well be seen as the price to be paid for the promise. Thus, X might well be entering into a **legal** obligation with Y.

2.3 Executory, Executed and Past Consideration

2.3.1 EXECUTORY CONSIDERATION

An executory consideration consists of a promise to do, forbear or suffer, given in return for a similar promise. e.g., 'I promise to pay you £100 provided you promise to decorate my kitchen'.

The contract comes into existence at the moment the promises are exchanged, but its performance remains in the future.

2.3.2 EXECUTED CONSIDERATION

Executed consideration arises when one of the parties has, either in the act which constitutes the offer or in the act constituting acceptance, done everything he is required to do under the contract leaving outstanding liability on one side only, e.g., the act of acceptance in response to a unilateral offer to the world at large as in *Carlill* v *Carbolic Smoke Ball Co.* (**1.4.1**). See *Cases and Materials* (**2.1.1**).

2.3.3 PAST CONSIDERATION

Past consideration is no consideration.

In the case of executed consideration, both the promise and the act comprising the contract are essential and co-related components of the same bargain. In the case of past consideration, the promise is given subsequent to the act and independently of it, usually after the passage of some time. Thus if X rescues Y from a fire, and Y later promises X a reward, X cannot rely upon his rescue as consideration for Y's promise because it was past in point of time.

Roscorla v *Thomas* (1842) 3 QB 234

The plaintiff purchased a horse from the defendant. When negotiations had been completed and the contract formed, the defendant warranted the horse to be sound and free from vice. The horse turned out to be vicious.

The warranty was given after the sale had been completed; thus the previous sale was past consideration and so no consideration.

SAQ 12

Re McArdle [1951] Ch 669

The occupiers of a house carried out certain improvements and decorations at a cost of £488, and after the work had been completed, the remainder of the family, who were inheriting the property together with the occupiers, promised to repay the £488 in consideration of the work which had been carried out.

Had the occupiers furnished consideration in return for this promise? Explain your answer.

The Court of Appeal **held** that the consideration for the promise was past as the work had been done before the promise was made, and that the claim for the £488 failed.

There are certain exceptions to the past consideration rule

2.3.3.1   Bills of Exchange Act 1882, s. 27(1)

This Act provides that an antecedent debt or liability, though normally past consideration, is good consideration for a bill of exchange, e.g., a cheque. Thus a bank is deemed to have provided consideration in return for a customer's cheque paid in by way of reduction of overdraft on the basis that the customer's pre-existing debt to the bank is consideration for the transfer by him to the bank.

2.3.3.2   Limitation Act 1980, s. 27(5)

Where the debtor makes a written acknowledgement of a debt, the debt shall be deemed to have accrued on and not before the date of acknowledgement, even though the only consideration for the acknowledgement is the pre-existing debt. Thus if a debtor makes written acknowledgement of a debt some three years after first incurring it, the six year limitation period within which the creditor must bring proceedings to recover the debt will start to run all over again. However, once the debt has become statute barred by the expiration of the six-year period it cannot be revived by any subsequent acknowledgement.

2.3.3.3 The requested performance exception

It is not true to say that all acts which are not preceded by an express promise constitute past consideration. If an act is done by X at the request of Y in circumstances where X and Y must have understood that the act was to be remunerated (so that a prior promise of remuneration by Y can be implied), the act by X will be sufficient consideration.

Lampleigh v *Brathwait* (1615) Hob 105
B killed a man and asked L to obtain a royal pardon for him. L carried out B's request, and B then promised him £100.

A promise of payment by B would be implied at the time L commenced the act of obtaining a pardon, the actual promise later being treated as a mere clarification of the amount of the payment, i.e. what would otherwise have been past consideration became executed consideration.

In modern times the doctrine has been applied in *Re Casey's Patents* [1892] 1 Ch 104 and more recently by the Privy Council in *Pao On* v *Lau Yiu Long* [1980] AC 614, where the essentials were identified by Lord Scarman:

(a) The act must have been done at the request of the promisor.

(b) The parties must have understood that the act was to be remunerated.

(c) The payment, if it had been promised in advance, must have been legally recoverable.

2.4 Sufficiency of Consideration

The freedom of contract doctrine requires the parties to be free to make their own bargain. Therefore, the courts will not intervene even if the considerations furnished by each of the parties are disproportionate, unless there has been some fraud, misrepresentation, duress or undue influence.

This approach is embodied in the rule that the courts will not enquire into the **adequacy** of consideration, and are concerned only with the **sufficiency** of consideration, i.e. the consideration furnished by one party need not be of equivalent economic/commercial value to that provided by the other party, but will be sufficient if it is something of value in the eyes of the law. Thus if X agrees to exchange his Rolls Royce in return for Y's bicycle, then the bicycle will be sufficient consideration.

2.4.1 WHERE CONSIDERATION IS OF LITTLE ECONOMIC VALUE, BUT SUFFICIENT IN THE EYES OF THE LAW

2.4.1.1 General

Thomas v *Thomas* [1842] 2 QB 851
A deceased person had expressed a wish shortly before he died that his widow be allowed to occupy the house for the rest of her life. Upon his death the executors 'in consideration of such a desire' agreed with the widow to give her a life interest for £1 per year rent.

The deceased's wishes were not part of the consideration, but £1 per year was sufficient consideration.

Chappell & Co. Ltd v Nestlé Co. Ltd [1960] 2 All ER 701
The appellants were the owners of the copyright of a tune called 'Rockin Shoes'. The respondents offered records of the said tune to the public in return for 1s. 6d. (7.5p) and the wrappers from three of their chocolate bars. In connection with a dispute under the Copyright Act 1956, it became necessary to determine whether the chocolate bar wrappers (which were worthless in themselves) constituted part of the consideration or not.

What do you think? Set your reasons out on a separate sheet of paper.

They did. Since the object of selling the records was to increase the sales of chocolate, the stipulated evidence of such sales was part of the consideration.

2.4.1.2   Compromise of claims

Horton v Horton (No. 2) [1960] 3 All ER 649
A husband agreed to pay his wife £30 per month maintenance, and in return she agreed not to sue for maintenance. The husband should have deducted income tax before payment, but for nine months paid the sum without doing so. He later promised to pay such sum as would leave £30 after the deduction of tax, and made such payments for three years before stopping payments altogether.

In defence to his wife's action he claimed that the second agreement was unsupported by consideration. The only possible consideration was the settlement of the wife's claim for rectification of the original agreement, which might well have failed anyway (i.e. it was probably a worthless claim).

Nevertheless the Court of Appeal decided that consideration was present. Provided the wife had an honest belief that the action might succeed, it was irrelevant that it probably would not.

2.4.1.3   Forbearance to sue

Alliance Bank Ltd v Broom (1864) 2 Drew & Sm 289
B had an overdraft of £22,000. He was asked by the bank to provide security and promised to do so. Consequently, the bank did not sue immediately for its outstanding money. B failed to provide such security and was sued by the bank on his promise to do so.

The bank's forbearance to sue constituted sufficient consideration for the defendant's promise to provide security.

2.4.1.4 'Invented' consideration

These decisions support the view that where the court feels that it is in the interests of justice that a promise ought to be enforceable, it can always 'discover' something of value for which the promise was exchanged.

De La Bere v *Pearson* [1908] 1 KB 280
The financial section of a newspaper offered free financial advice. The plaintiff wrote asking for the name of a reliable stockbroker for advice on his investments. The newspaper negligently gave the plaintiff poor advice, causing him to lose money on his investments. The plaintiff sued the newspaper for breach of contract, but faced the difficulty of what consideration he had provided in return for the advice.

The plaintiff had furnished consideration in that the newspaper had the option of publishing the plaintiff's letter of inquiry in the newspaper if it wished to do so!

It should be noted that if the facts of *De La Bere* v *Pearson* were to recur in modern times the case would be decided under the law of torts under the principle of *Hedley Byrne & Co. Ltd* v *Heller & Partners* [1964] AC 465.

2.4.2 WHAT IS SUFFICIENT CONSIDERATION?

Note that in order to be sufficient, consideration must be real.

2.4.2.1 Moral obligation/love, affection etc.

Certain matters, e.g., moral obligation, natural love and affection or a promise not to nag, have been deemed to be too vague or too insubstantial to constitute consideration.

Eastwood v *Kenyon* (1840) 11 Ad & El 438
The plaintiff incurred expense in the maintenance and education of a child to whom he was guardian, and in the management and improvement of her property. The plaintiff borrowed money to enable him to make provision for the child, and when she became 21 she promised to repay the loan. The defendant, who became the girl's husband, made a similar promise.

The plaintiff could not recover as he had furnished no consideration to support the defendant's promise to pay and moral obligation was insufficient.

White v *Bluett* (1853) 23 LJ Ex 36
A son gave a promissory note to his father, and ultimately his father's executors sued him on the note. His defence was that his father had released him from the note in consideration of his promise to cease continually complaining that he was not treated as fairly as his brothers.

His promise did not constitute consideration since it amounted to no more than a promise not to bore his father.

2.4.2.2 The performance of existing legal duties

The question here is whether X's doing, or promising to do, something that he is already legally bound to do is sufficient consideration, in a contract with Y.

It is necessary to consider three types of duty:

(a) A duty imposed by the general law.

(b) A duty owed by X to Y under an existing contract.

(c)   A duty owed by X to Z (a third party) which he performs or promises to perform in return for Y's promise to him (X).

Duties imposed by the general law

Collins v Godefroy (1813) 1 B & Ald 950
An attorney had attended a trial for six days on the defendant's subpoena and alleged that the defendant had promised to pay him six guineas for doing so.

No consideration had been given by the attorney; having received a subpoena, he was already under a duty to attend, i.e. the defendant was receiving no more than he was already entitled to under the general law.

However, if a person exceeds his or her existing duty, that will be sufficient consideration.

SAQ 13

Glasbrook Bros v Glamorgan County Council **[1925] AC 270**
A police authority sued for the sum of £2,200 promised to them by a colliery company for whose mine the police had provided a stronger guard during a strike than was in their opinion necessary.

Explain in your own words what you think the outcome of this case was. Give reasons for your decision.

The plaintiff succeeded; the defendant had received more than it was entitled to under the general law. The public duty of the police was to be determined by the police.

An interesting decision follows:

Ward v Byham [1956] 1 WLR 496
The father of an illegitimate child wrote to the mother, from whom he was separated, promising to pay her £1 per week if she proved that the child was well looked after and happy, and that the child had been allowed to decide for herself whether she wanted to live with her mother or not.

The child chose to live with her mother and the father made the payments until the mother married another man, whereupon he stopped them. When sued, the father pleaded absence of consideration, arguing that the mother had merely performed an existing statutory duty because she was required by statute (s. 42 of the National Assistance Act 1948) to maintain an illegitimate child.

The Court of Appeal found for the mother, but for differing reasons:

(a) Morris and Parker LJJ found that the mother had promised more than her statutory duty by promising to keep the child well looked after and happy, and by allowing her to choose with whom she lived.

(b) Denning LJ found that the mother promised to do no more than she was bound to do, but this was good consideration because it was of benefit to the defendant.

Contractual duty

Stilk v *Myrick* (1809) 2 Camp 317
In the course of a voyage from London to the Baltic and back two sailors deserted. There were no substitutes available so the captain promised the rest of the crew the wages of the two deserters divided between them if they would work the vessel home.

Explain why you think the captain's promise was or was not legally binding.

The promise was not binding since the sailors had performed no more than their existing contractual duty.

However, in:

Hartley v *Ponsonby* (1857) 7 EL & B 872
A ship left England with a crew of 36. At Port Philip there was a multiple desertion leaving only 19 crewmen, of whom only five were able seamen. The captain promised the plaintiff (and others) an extra £40 to work the ship to Bombay. Ultimately the additional £40 payment was not made.

Explain why you think the captain's promise was or was not legally binding.

The plaintiff succeeded. As a result of the desertion the voyage had become dangerous and this went beyond the contemplation of the original contract. Thus, the plaintiff had either exceeded his existing contractual obligation, or had been released from his original contract and entered into a new contract for which his new promise to serve was good consideration.

The *Stilk* v *Myrick* principle seems to have been refined and limited to situations where the party promising the additional payment secures no benefit therefrom:

Williams v *Roffey Bros. and Nicholls (Contractors) Ltd* [1990] 1 All ER 512
The defendants were building contractors who were refurbishing 27 flats. They contracted with the plaintiff to carry out carpentry work, including work on the roof structure, for £20,000. The defendants' main contract contained a penalty clause and they became concerned when it appeared that the plaintiff, who was in financial difficulties, would not complete the carpentry work on time. Consequently, the defendants promised to pay the plaintiff a £10,300 bonus if he completed on time. The plaintiff made efforts to do so; the defendants did not pay the bonus.

The defendants were in breach of contract. *Stilk* v *Myrick*, though correctly decided on its facts, did not apply. Apparently the modern approach to the doctrine of consideration is that where benefits are derived by each party to a contract of variation, even though one party does not suffer a detriment, this will not be fatal to establishing sufficient consideration to support the contract, provided there has been no duress exerted to procure the promise of extra payment. The defendants here had received a benefit by avoiding the penalty for delay and in not having to engage alternative carpenters.

ACTIVITY 10

Why did the Court of Appeal go to such great lengths in this case to discover the existence of consideration? Read *Williams* v *Roffey Bros. and Nicholls (Contractors) Ltd* (in particular the judgment of Glidewell LJ) in *Cases and Materials* (2.1.2.2) in order to find out. List your responses below.

You should have identified that *Stilk* v *Myrick* was decided as it was because no doctrine of economic duress existed at that time. Now that the safeguard of economic duress exists it is legitimate to extend what is recognised as consideration in a commercial relationship where the parties clearly intended to enter into a contract.

Duties owed to third parties

If X promises Y that he will do something which he (X) is already contractually bound to Z to do, can X rely on that promise (or the performance of it) as consideration?

Jones v *Waite* (1839) 5 Bing NC 341 suggests not, but has since been discredited by three cases decided in the 1860s.

Shadwell v *Shadwell* (1860) 9 CBNS 159
The plaintiff's uncle wrote to him congratulating him on his engagement and promised to pay him £150 per annum until such time as his income from the bar reached £600 per annum. The plaintiff married Ellen Nicol (i.e. performed an existing contractual duty owed to a third party, contracts of engagement being legally binding at that time) and sued his uncle's executors upon the promise.

The plaintiff succeeded, Erle CJ and Keating J discovering that a detriment had been incurred by the plaintiff because by marrying he had materially altered his position and incurred the financial obligations of a married man in reliance upon his uncle's promise. Furthermore, the marriage was of benefit to the uncle as 'an object of interest with a near relative'. However, Byles J dissented, finding that the plaintiff had done no more than he was already contractually bound to do.

In *Shadwell* v *Shadwell* did the plaintiff really incur an additional detriment?

It is difficult to see that the plaintiff incurred an additional detriment *in reliance upon* his uncle's promise. Presumably he married Ellen Nicol because he was already contractually obliged to do so.

Chichester v *Cobb* (1866) 14 LT 433 requires no discussion since the facts and decision were virtually identical with those in *Shadwell* v *Shadwell*.

SAQ 17

Scotson v *Pegg* (1861) 6 H & N 295

The plaintiff had contracted with X to deliver a cargo of coal to X or 'to the order of X'. X sold the cargo to the defendant and, exercising his right under the contract, ordered the plaintiff to deliver it to the defendant. The defendant then promised the plaintiff that he would unload the coal at the stated rate, which he failed to do, and was sued by the plaintiff, who claimed that delivery of the coal to the defendant was consideration for the defendant's promise. The defendant argued that delivery of the coal was not consideration because the plaintiff was already contractually bound to X to deliver to the defendant.

Can you identify an additional detriment incurred by the plaintiff in this case? If so, critically consider the justification for your finding.

The plaintiff again succeeded, Martin B finding the delivery of the coal to be a benefit to the defendant, and Wilde B ingeniously discovering a detriment incurred by the plaintiff in that it might have suited him to break the contract with X and pay damages, and the delivery of the coal to the defendant extinguished this possibility.

Both *Shadwell* v *Shadwell* and *Scotson* v *Pegg* seem to stretch the boundaries of the imagination in terms of discovering a detriment incurred by the plaintiff, and it is submitted that the most logical interpretation of these two cases is that the performance of an existing obligation owed to a third party can be good consideration even though the plaintiff incurs no additional detriment.

This view seems to have been accepted in modern times by the Privy Council in two cases: *Pao On* v *Lau Yiu Long* (**2.3.3.3**) and *New Zealand Shipping Co. Ltd* v *Satterthwaite & Co. Ltd (The Eurymedon)* [1975] AC 154. In *The Eurymedon* the defendants, who were stevedores, unloaded goods from a ship, which they were already obliged to do under a contract with a third party. This act was held to be good consideration for a promise given by the plaintiff to relieve the defendants from liability for damaging the goods.

New Zealand Shipping Co. Ltd v *Satterthwaite and Co. Ltd* involves a three-party situation, whereas *Williams* v *Roffey Bros. and Nicholls (Contractors) Ltd* involves a two-party situation. However, in principle the two decisions are entirely consistent with one another.

Can you explain this consistency?

Williams v *Roffey Bros. and Nicholls (Contractors) Ltd* (where it applies) brings two-party situations in to line with three-party situations. In both cases the plaintiff need not incur an additional detriment (i.e. the law accepts that the plaintiff is performing merely what he is already **legally** obliged to perform). However, provided the he confers a **factual** benefit upon the other party to the contract, that is sufficient consideration.

A has received a factual benefit —

In two-party situations *Stilk* v *Myrick* will apply only where the defendant has received no **factual** benefit. However, whether it can realistically be claimed that the ship's master received no **factual** benefit in *Stilk* v *Myrick* must be a matter of some considerable doubt.

2.4.2.3 Discharge of existing financial obligations (repayment of debts)

The position at common law

If A owes B a debt of £200, and B agrees to accept £100 in full satisfaction of the debt, B is not bound by his promise and may subsequently sue for the full amount of the debt.

On the basis of the previous statement regarding the debt A owes to B, can you construct a rule in the form of a legal proposition which would cover this situation?

The rule which emerges is that payment by a debtor of a smaller sum in satisfaction of a larger debt is not good discharge of the debt because such payment is no more than the debtor is already bound to do, and the debtor has furnished no consideration in return for the creditor's promise to forgo the balance.

Pinnel's Case (1602) 5 Co Rep 117a
Pinnel brought an action in debt on a bond against Cole for payment of £8 10s. due on 11 November 1600. Cole pleaded that, at the instance of Pinnel, he had paid him £5 2s. 6d. in full satisfaction of the debt on 1 October.

The plaintiff succeeded because the defendant had drafted his plea incorrectly, but otherwise he would not have done as the payment had been made on a date earlier than the debt fell due, i.e. the debtor had provided consideration for the creditor's promise.

Thus the famous **rule in *Pinnel's* case** was stated to be:

> that payment of a lesser sum on the day (that it is due) cannot be any satisfaction for the whole because it appears to the judges that by no possibility a lesser sum can be satisfaction to the plaintiff for a greater sum . . .

However, the court went on to say:

> but the gift of a horse, hawk or robe, etc., in satisfaction is good for it shall be intended that a horse, hawk or robe, etc., might be more beneficial to the plaintiff than money, in respect of some circumstance, or otherwise the plaintiff would not have accepted it in satisfaction . . .

i.e. the creditor by way of consideration is receiving something more than he is already entitled to.

Consequently it would appear that the debtor may furnish consideration in such circumstances by:

(a) payment of a smaller sum before the due date at the creditor's request;

(b) payment of a smaller sum at a different place at the creditor's request, e.g., payment due in Nottingham but made in Sheffield;

(c) payment in kind, e.g., to use the language of *Pinnel's* case, a tom-tit or a canary, or a lesser sum and payment in kind at the creditor's request.

SAQ 19

A question arising from the rule in *Pinnel's* case is whether payment by cheque is payment in a form sufficiently different to cash to constitute consideration?

It was held in *Sibree* v *Tripp* (1846) 15 M & W 23 that payment by promissory note (a type of negotiable instrument, as is a cheque) constituted sufficient consideration, and this was extended to payment by cheque in 1882 in *Goddard* v *O'Brien* (1882) 9 QBD 37. However, this extension to payment by cheque was overruled, at least where the cheque is being used merely as a substitute for cash payment rather than as a negotiable instrument, by the Court of Appeal in *D & C Builders Ltd* v *Rees* [1966] 2 QB 617. (Very few cheques are negotiated to other people by endorsement (signing the back of the cheque) these days.)

In *D & C Builders Ltd* v *Rees*, the defendant owed £482 to the plaintiffs, a small firm of builders, for work done for him. He delayed the payment for several months and then offered the plaintiff £300, saying that if they failed to accept £300 they would get nothing. The plaintiffs, who were in a desperate financial position, accepted a cheque for £300 in full settlement of the debt. The plaintiffs later sued for the balance and succeeded. The main thrust of the decision was that the plaintiffs had been subjected to economic duress, but Lord Denning in particular emphasised that in modern times there is no sensible distinction between payment in cash and by cheque.

The rule in *Pinnel's* case received House of Lords approval in 1884 in *Foakes* v *Beer*:

Foakes v *Beer* **(1884) 9 App Cas 605**
Dr Foakes was indebted to Mrs Beer on a judgment for a sum of £2,090. A judgment debt bears interest as from the date of judgment. The parties agreed in writing that if Dr Foakes paid £500 in cash and the balance in instalments, Mrs Beer would not take any proceedings to enforce the judgment. The agreement did not refer to the question of interest. Dr Foakes paid the money as required, but Mrs Beer then claimed an additional £360 interest on the judgment debt.

Give reasons as to why you think Mrs Beer's claim might or might not have succeeded.

It was held (applying *Pinnel's* case) that Mrs Beer succeeded. Dr Foakes had furnished no consideration for Mrs Beer's promise; he had not done, or promised to do, anything that he was not already obliged to do.

There are one or two exceptional situations where the creditor cannot go back on his promise even though consideration is absent. The true explanation of these would seem to be fraud:

(a) **Composition with creditors** If X, who is unable to pay his debts in full, enters into an agreement with all of his creditors to pay each of them 75p in the pound no single creditor will be allowed to sue for the outstanding balance as this would be fraud on the other creditors.

(b) **Payments of debts by third parties**

Welby v *Drake* (1825) 1 C & P 557
The defendant owed the plaintiff £18 on a bill of exchange. The plaintiff accepted £9 from the defendant's father in full satisfaction. The plaintiff then sued the defendant.

He failed because by suing the son he was committing a fraud on the father.

In which of the following situations would the debtor (Donald) be deemed to have been released in law from his obligation to pay his original debt? Please write your answers in the spaces provided and then check them against the answers supplied.

(a) Donald owes Mickey £10. Mickey promises to accept £5 in full settlement of the debt.

> There is no valid release. *Pinnel's* case and *Foakes* v *Beer* apply. Donald has furnished no consideration.

(b) As in (a), but Mickey asks Donald to pay him £5 and a rubber duck in settlement of the debt.

> Donald is released from his obligation. Cash and something of value falls within the exceptions to *Pinnel's* case. Donald has furnished consideration. Presumably the rubber duck must be of value to Mickey, otherwise he would not have requested it.

(c) Donald owes Mickey £100 payable in cash in Nottingham on 10 December. Mickey asks Donald to pay £50 by cheque in Manchester on 8 December in settlement of the debt.

> Donald is released from his obligation. Payment by cheque does not constitute payment in a different form (*D & C Builders Ltd* v *Rees*), but Donald has paid on an earlier date than the due date, and in a different place.

(d) Donald owes £3 to Mickey, £4 to Pluto and £5 to Olive. Mickey, Pluto and Olive agree to release Donald from the remainder of his debt if he will pay them £2, £3 and £4 respectively.

> A valid composition with creditors. No single creditor can defraud his fellow creditors by going back on his promise.

(e) Donald cannot pay a debt of £50 to Mickey, but Olive pays Mickey £30 in exchange for a promise that he will not sue Donald for the £50.

A valid release by a payment made by a third party (Olive). If Mickey were allowed to recover the £50 from Donald this would be a fraud on Olive.

The position in equity

Foakes v *Beer* clearly illustrates the common law position, and despite being criticised for many reasons (contrary to normal commercial practice; the creditor may accept anything in satisfaction of his debt, even a peppercorn, except a lesser sum of money etc.) has never been overruled. Indeed, *Foakes* v *Beer* has been reinforced by a recent decision of the Court of Appeal which held that the fact that a creditor might take practical benefit from agreeing with the debtor to accept payments by instalments did not constitute consideration, i.e. the Court of Appeal confined *Williams* v *Roffey Bros. & Nicholls (Contractors) Ltd* (**2.4.2.2**) to an obligation to supply goods and services and refused to extend it to debtor–creditor obligations:

Re Selectmove Ltd [1995] 1 WLR 474
A company involved in negotiations with a collector of taxes had offered to pay its debts to the Inland Revenue by instalments. The inspector said that he would inform the company if the arrangement was not acceptable.

The fact that the company had begun paying the instalments and had not heard from the Revenue until October, when the Revenue threatened the company with winding-up proceedings if the arrears were not paid immediately, was insufficient to found a contract to pay an existing debt by instalments.

Consequently, it is perhaps not surprising that there have been attempts in equity to abrogate the consequences of *Foakes* v *Beer*. In particular we must consider a doctrine which started off in life as equitable estoppel but is now known as promissory estoppel.

Promissory estoppel

Central London Property Trust Ltd v *High Trees House Ltd* [1947] KB 130
In 1937 the plaintiffs leased a block of flats to the defendants for 99 years at a rent of £2,500 per annum. By 1940 the flats were virtually empty due to the war, and the plaintiffs agreed to reduce the rent to £1,250 per annum. By 1945 the flats were full again, and the plaintiffs brought an action against the defendants claiming the full original rent, both for the future and for the last two quarters of 1945.

Denning J (as he then was) held that the plaintiffs succeeded because it was implicit in the agreement between the parties that the rent reduction was to operate only while the flats could not be fully let, and ceased to operate early in 1945. However, he went on to consider (*obiter*) what the position would have been if the plaintiffs had sued to recover the full rent payable between 1940 and 1945. He concluded that the plaintiffs would have been estopped in equity by their promise (even though the defendants had given no consideration in return) from exercising their strict legal rights to payment in full.

In reaching this conclusion, Denning J relied upon the House of Lords decision in the following case:

Hughes v *Metropolitan Railway Co.* (1877) 2 App Cas 439
The appellant served upon the respondents a notice to repair within six months houses held on lease from him. Failure to comply with the notice within the stipulated period

would have entitled the appellant to forfeit the lease. The parties subsequently entered into negotiations for the purchase of the lease by the respondents, which negotiations continued for almost the entire period of the notice. Just before the notice was due to expire the appellant broke off negotiations, and upon expiry brought an action for possession claiming to have forfeited the lease.

The opening of negotiations amounted to a promise by the landlord that as long as such negotiations continued he would not enforce the notice, and, in reliance upon this promise, the respondents had acted to their detriment by not doing any repairs. Hence, the six-month period was to run only from the breakdown of negotiations, and the respondents were entitled in equity to relief against forfeiture.

Denning J (in *High Trees*) felt that the logical application of the *Hughes* principle led to the conclusion that 'a promise to accept a smaller sum in discharge of a larger sum, if acted upon, is binding notwithstanding the absence of consideration', i.e. it was the antidote to *Foakes v Beer*! However, in reaching this conclusion he faced a number of difficulties, some of which he seems to have failed to recognise, and others which he dealt with less than satisfactorily:

(a) In 1854, in *Jorden v Money* (1854) 5 HL Cas 185, the majority of the House of Lords ruled that only a representation of existing fact and not one relating to future conduct could give rise to an estoppel. Denning J distinguished *Jorden v Money* on the ground that the promisor in that case did not intend legal consequences, a fact not easily discovered from the report if at all, whereas the promisor in *High Trees* did!

SAQ 22

Why are *Hughes* v *Metropolitan Railway* and *Foakes* v *Beer* not really parallel situations? Is *Foakes* v *Beer* really an appropriate situation to which to apply the *Hughes* doctrine?

(b) *Hughes* and *Foakes v Beer* are probably not parallel situations. In *Hughes* the landlord sought to enforce a right to forfeit a lease which arose only because the tenant, in reliance upon the landlord, had failed to repair, i.e. a right to repair became a right to forfeit if the decision had gone against the tenant.

(c) *Hughes* was not considered by the House of Lords in *Foakes v Beer*, which was decided only seven years later, despite the fact that two judges were common to both cases!

(d) The decision in *Hughes* merely suspends rights, whereas Denning J concluded that rights can be extinguished (this is extremely controversial).

SAQ 23

Why is this view of Denning J controversial?

The view is controversial because it would enable a debtor to be released from his obligation having furnished no consideration in return.

There is no doubt in the light of subsequent decisions that a doctrine of promissory estoppel exists, though it has never been applied to a *Foakes* v *Beer* situation. The precise nature and scope of such doctrine is difficult to identify. 'But as is common with an expanding doctrine [the cases] do raise problems of coherent exposition which have never been systematically explored.' (Lord Hailsham LC in *Woodhouse AC Israel Cocoa Ltd SA* v *Nigerian Produce Marketing Co. Ltd* [1972] AC 741.)

Nevertheless, we must attempt to make some statement of what the doctrine is, to identify its essential characteristics and to examine some of its difficulties. It is perhaps useful here to bear in mind that there appears to be what might be termed an 'orthodox' view as against the 'Lord Denning' view!

(a) **Statement of doctrine (orthodox view)** If one party to an existing legal relationship, intending legal consequences, promises not to insist upon his strict legal rights arising from the relationship, and the other party to the relationship changes his position in reliance upon that promise, then the promisor will be estopped from going back upon his promise, even though he has received no consideration for his promise. However, as Lord Hodgson stated in *Ajayi* v *Briscoe (Nigeria) Ltd* [1964] 3 All ER 556, the promisor can withdraw from his promise on giving reasonable notice, which need not be formal, and the promise becomes final and irrevocable only if the promisee is unable to resume his original position.

(b) **Identification of the essentials and difficulties**

    (i)   The promise must be clear and unequivocal.

    (ii)   It must be inequitable for the promisor to go back on his promise and insist upon his strict legal rights. Thus promissory estoppel did not apply in *D & C Builders Ltd* v *Rees* (above) because the creditor's promise to accept £300 in full satisfaction had been extorted from him by economic duress.

    (iii)   The promisee must have changed his position in reliance upon the promise. What does this mean? Normally, in order to establish estoppel the promisee must show that he acted to his detriment in reliance upon the promise, i.e. if the promise were revoked he would be in a worse position than he would have been in had the promise never been made. This requirement was clearly satisfied in *Hughes* v *Metropolitan Railway Co.*

However, Lord Denning MR in *Alan & Co. Ltd* v *El Nasr Export Co.* [1972] 2 All ER 127, said that there is no requirement of detriment and all that is necessary is that the promisee must have been led to act otherwise than he would have done. The other two members of the Court of Appeal (Stephenson and Megaw LJJ) left the question open.

Lord Denning MR repeated the above view in *Brikom Investments Ltd* v *Carr* [1979] 2 All ER 753. The other two members of the Court of Appeal (Roskill and Cumming-Bruce LJJ) decided the case on different grounds.

Perhaps the best possible solution to the quandary is that put forward by Robert Goff J (as he then was) in *The Post Chaser* [1982] 1 All ER 19, when he suggested that detriment should not be necessary, and that the test should be whether or not it is equitable in the circumstances of the particular case that the party seeking to enforce his strict legal rights should be allowed to do so.

SAQ 24

Can you recognise any detriment or change of position identified by Denning J in the *High Trees* **case?**

No detriment or change of position was identified by Denning J in *High Trees*, though presumably he might have identified the tenants continuing to occupy the flats when otherwise they might have chosen to surrender the lease, if he had chosen to do so. This suggests that Denning J felt that reliance upon the promise alone was sufficient. Indeed, though obviously prevailed upon by fellow judges to accept eventually the need for change of position, his pronouncements in *Alan* and *Brikom* (above) seem to amount to nothing more than reliance.

(iv)   Normally promissory estoppel merely suspends rights and does not extinguish them, unless it is impossible for the promisee to resume his original position. The promisor may revive his suspended rights by giving reasonable notice thereof, which need not be formal.

Tool Metal Manufacturing Co. Ltd v *Tungsten Electrical Co. Ltd* [1955] 2 All ER 657
In 1938, the appellants granted the respondents a licence to import and manufacture hard metal alloys made in accordance with patent rights held by them. The respondents were to pay royalties on the material made, and to pay 'compensation' if the amount of material exceeded a named quota. Upon the outbreak of war in 1939, the appellants agreed to suspend the right to compensation, it being contemplated that a new agreement would be entered into when the war ended. In 1944, negotiations for such a new agreement were begun but broke down. In 1945, the respondents sued the appellants for breach of contract and the appellants counterclaimed for payment of

compensation as from 1 June 1945. The respondents' action was dismissed and the appellants' counterclaim failed because the Court of Appeal held that they had not given reasonable notice of an intention to resume strict legal rights. However, in 1950 the appellants brought a second action, claiming compensation from 1 January 1947.

The House of Lords found that this claim succeeded, the appellants' counterclaim in the first action in 1945 amounting to reasonable notice of an intention to resume strict legal rights.

Thus no one, other than Lord Denning, has suggested that promissory estoppel can extinguish rights (except where the promisee cannot be restored to his original position), a view which he repeated (*obiter*) in the context of part payment of a debt in *D & C Builders Ltd* v *Rees* (above).

It is submitted that this view is not reconcilable with *Foakes* v *Beer*, which would have to be overruled before such a view could be generally accepted. However, the meaning of rights being 'suspended' is not without controversy in the context of continuing obligations, e.g., the payment of rent, and will be investigated in the question at the end of the chapter.

> (v) Promissory estoppel operates only by way of defence and not as a cause of action. It is 'a shield and not a sword'. See Birkett and Asquith LJJ in the next case:

Combe v *Combe* [1951] 1 All ER 767
A husband, upon divorce from his wife, promised to pay her £100 per annum as a permanent allowance. In reliance upon her husband's promise, but not at his request, the wife did not apply to the courts for maintenance. The husband failed to pay the allowance, and his wife sued him upon his promise.

The wife failed as she had given no consideration for the promise, her forbearance to claim maintenance not being in return for the promise. Nor could she rely upon promissory estoppel as this would create a new cause of action where none existed before, i.e. promissory estoppel can be used only to vary an existing legal relationship and not to bring that legal relationship into existence in the first place.

2.5 Privity of Contract

2.5.1 THE DOCTRINE

The doctrine of privity of contract recognises that a contract is a private relationship between those persons who are party to it. Thus a person who is not party to the contract can neither acquire rights nor incur liabilities under the contract. This doctrine is very much akin to the separate rule that consideration must move from the promisee, though not necessarily to the promisor. The combination of the two rules means that anyone who wishes to enforce a contract must show that he is both party to the contract and has given consideration in return for the promise which he seeks to enforce (unless the contract be by deed).

Tweddle v *Atkinson* (1861) 1 B & S 393
H and W were married, and after the marriage their respective fathers, X and Y, contracted that each would pay a sum of money to H, and that H should have the power to sue for such sums. After the death of X and Y, H sued Y's executors for the money promised to him.

H's action failed. There was no consideration moving from H, nor was he a party to the contract between X and Y.

Consideration must move from the promisee, either to the promisor or to some third party. For illustrations of consideration moving to a third party see *Shadwell* v *Shadwell* and *New Zealand Shipping Co. Ltd* v *Satterthwaite & Co.* (at **2.4.2.2**).

Jack agrees to pay Rose, a florist, £25 to send some flowers to Gill.

   (a)   Rose sends the flowers to Gill but Jack refuses to pay. Can Rose successfully sue either Jack or Gill for breach of contract? Justify your conclusions.

   (b)   Jack pays £25 but Rose fails to send any flowers to Gill. Can either Jack or Gill successfully sue Rose for breach of contract? Justify your conclusions.

The plaintiff who is suing is always to be treated as the promisee. Your answers should have been:

   (a)   Rose can successfully sue Jack. Consideration (the flowers) has moved from her, not to the promisor (Jack) but to a third party, Gill. Rose cannot successfully sue Gill because Gill is not a party to the contract.

   (b)   Jack can successfully sue Rose because consideration (£25) has moved from him to the promisor, Rose. Gill cannot successfully sue Rose because no consideration has moved from her at all, and she is not a party to the contract.

Perhaps the leading case on privity of contract is the House of Lords decision in *Beswick* v *Beswick*:

Beswick v *Beswick* [1968] AC 58
Peter Beswick, the owner of a small coal merchants business, decided to retire. Consequently he transferred the business to his nephew in return for a promise from the nephew to employ him as a 'consultant' for the remainder of his life, and after his death to pay an annuity of £5 per week to his widow. After Peter Beswick's death his nephew failed to pay the annuity to the widow. The widow sued the nephew, both in her personal capacity as beneficiary under the contract and in her capacity as administratrix of her husband's estate (in law an administratrix stands in the shoes of the deceased).

The widow failed in her personal capacity as she was a stranger to the contract; but she succeeded as the administratrix of Peter Beswick (the promisee) and a decree of specific performance of the contract was granted requiring that the money be paid.

However, the doctrine of privity could lead to impracticalities in the commercial world, and as with the doctrine of consideration can lead to a situation where X and Y, intending legal consequences, enter into an agreement for the benefit of Z, but Z is unable to enforce that agreement. Therefore, it is not surprising that exceptions, both statutory and judicial, have been developed.

2.5.2 EXCEPTIONS TO THE DOCTRINE

2.5.2.1 Statutory exceptions

There are many statutory exceptions designed to enable the commercial world to function, but two of the more important ones are as follows:

(a) The Married Women's Property Act 1882, s. 11 permits a husband to insure his life for the benefit of his wife and children, and a wife to do the same for the benefit of her husband and children.

(b) The Road Traffic Act 1988, ss. 151 and 152 permit an injured third party to proceed directly against the insurance company upon obtaining judgment against the insured motorist.

2.5.2.2 Assignment of contractual rights

Contractual rights can be assigned to third parties, either under s. 136 of the Law of Property Act 1925 or under equitable rules.

2.5.2.3 The law of agency

Where one person (the principal) appoints an agent to contract on his behalf with a third party, the contract is enforceable both by and against the principal. Normally the agent drops out and ceases to be party to the contract.

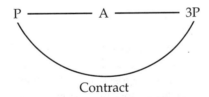

Contract

This is perhaps a genuine exception when the principal is undisclosed, i.e. the third party is unaware of the principal's existence at the time of contracting.

2.5.2.4 Negotiable instruments

If X is the holder for value of a bill of exchange (e.g. a cheque) which has been negotiated, usually by signed endorsement on the back, along a chain of parties, he may sue A, the original drawer of the cheque: Bills of Exchange Act 1882.

2.5.2.5 Third party joined in proceedings

Snelling v *J G Snelling Ltd* [1972] 1 All ER 79
Three brothers were co-directors of a small company. They agreed that if any one of them resigned he would not claim money due to him from the company. One of the brothers resigned and sued the company for the money due to him. The company was not party to the agreement between the brothers, but the other two brothers applied for a stay of proceedings.

Although the company could not rely directly upon the agreement, the co-defendant brothers were entitled to a stay of proceedings. Thus, because all the parties were before the court and in reality the plaintiff's claim had failed, the action was dismissed.

2.5.2.6   Trusts of contractual promises

One of the earliest cases in which a trust of a contractual promise was inferred was the following:

Gregory and Parker v Williams (1817) 3 Mer 582
P owed money to both G and W. He agreed with W to assign to him the whole of his property if W would pay his debt to G. P duly assigned his property, but W did not carry out his promise. G and P joined as co-plaintiffs and filed a bill in equity to compel performance.

They succeeded, P being trustee on behalf of G of W's promise.

Because P was trustee on behalf of G and W, either or both of them could have compelled P to sue W. If P had refused, G could have joined P and W as co-defendants and sued them.

Such a trust was still being readily inferred as recently as 1919: *Walford's Case* [1919] AC 801. However, since the decision in *Re Schebsman* [1943] 2 All ER 768, which denied the existence of a trust, the device is rarely implemented. The modern law of trusts requires an irrevocable expression of intention to create a trust, which is most unlikely to be exhibited unless that was the express intention of the parties in the first place. Otherwise, the overriding presumption is that a party to a contract reserves the right to vary the contract terms at a later date.

2.5.2.7   The restrictive covenants doctrine applied to contractual rights

Land law is much less concerned with the doctrine of privity of contract than is the law of contract, and it has been held that a restrictive covenant, voluntarily accepted by the purchaser of land as part of the contract of sale, can bind persons who later acquire the land.

Tulk v Moxhay (1848) 2 Ph 774
The plaintiff, who owned several plots of land in Leicester Square, sold the garden in the centre to one Elms, who agreed not to build upon it. After a series of transactions the garden was sold to Moxhay, who proposed to build even though he was aware of the restriction. The plaintiff sought an injunction and succeeded.

ACTIVITY 12

Can this doctrine be used to enforce against third parties restrictions upon the use of goods? For example, X is the owner of a caravan, and agrees to rent it to Y for one week from 21 August. Before 21 August X sells the caravan to Z, but informs Z of his agreement with Y. Can Y compel Z to make the caravan available if he refuses to do so?

Read the judgment of Brown-Wilkinson J in *Swiss Bank Corporation v Lloyds Bank Ltd* [1979] 2 All ER 853 in *Cases and Materials* (2.2).

Most of the cases in this area seem to involve charterparties of ships. The answer to the above question seems to have been given in the affirmative by the Judicial Committee of the Privy Council in *Lord Strathcona SS Co.* v *Dominion Coal Co.* [1926] AC 108 (a charterparty case). However, the Court of Appeal in *Clore* v *Theatrical Properties Ltd* [1936] 3 All ER 483 thought that the *Strathcona* decision must be confined 'to the very special case of a ship under a charterparty', and Diplock J in *Port Line Ltd* v *Ben Line Steamers Ltd* [1958] 1 All ER 787 felt that the *Strathcona* decision was not good law.

Perhaps, in conclusion, we should suggest that the better view is that the *Strathcona* decision applies only to charterparties of ships, if at all, and our caravan-hire example is better resolved by resort to the tort of knowing interference with contractual rights, a view put forward by Browne-Wilkinson J in *Swiss Bank Corporation* v *Lloyds Bank Ltd* [1979] 2 All ER 853.

2.5.2.8 Collateral contracts

Privity of contract may be avoided by construing the existence of a collateral contract.

Shanklin Pier Ltd v *Detel Products Ltd* [1951] 2 All ER 471
The plaintiffs, the owners of Shanklin Pier, contracted with X and Co. for the repair and repainting of the pier. The plaintiffs had consulted with the defendants, a firm of paint manufacturers, who had advised that their paint was suitable for painting the pier. Consequently, the plaintiffs specified in the contract with X & Co. that the defendants' paint must be used. The paint proved to be unsuitable and the plaintiffs sued the defendants for breach of warranty. The defendants argued that the contract for the paint was between X and Co. and the defendants, not between the plaintiffs and the defendants.

There was a collateral contract between the plaintiffs and the defendants by which, in return for the plaintiffs specifying that the defendants' paint must be used, the defendants warranted its suitability.

2.5.2.9 The law of torts

Sometimes the law of torts may provide a remedy where no contractual remedy is available.

Donoghue v *Stevenson* [1932] AC 562
The plaintiff consumed most of the contents of a bottle of ginger beer, which had been purchased by a friend. The ginger beer contained the decomposed remains of a snail and the plaintiff became ill. The plaintiff could not sue for breach of contract because the contract of sale was made between the friend and the cafe proprietor. However, the plaintiff succeeded in suing the manufacturer of the ginger beer for the tort of negligence.

2.6 Conclusion

In English law no contract, other than one made by deed, is enforceable in the absence of consideration. The cases on what constitutes consideration are not easy to reconcile because they often depend upon how hard the court was prepared to look to discover something which might be identified as consideration.

As we have seen, the doctrine of privity of contract is virtually synonymous with the doctrine of consideration. No promise is enforceable in the absence of consideration unless it falls within the exceptions to privity of contract or within the doctrine of promissory estoppel.

2.7   End of Chapter Assessment Question

Hartwell agrees to make all the costumes for Leonard's play, 'The Black Panther', which has its first night on 7 May. The price is £30,000 payable on 1 May, the delivery date under the contract. Early in April Leonard is alarmed to discover that Hartwell's seamstresses are substantially behind with their work, and in consequence his first night may be in jeopardy. Leonard therefore promises the seamstresses that he will pay them a bonus of £50 each if the work on his costumes is hastened. He also promises to pay Hartwell an extra £5,000 if he can ensure delivery of the costumes by 1 May. All other work is put to one side in favour of Leonard's costumes. On 30 April Leonard tells the seamstresses that his promise to pay the bonus is withdrawn.

On 1 May Leonard's costumes are delivered in accordance with the contract and Hartwell demands the sum of £35,000 from Leonard. Leonard explains that the costs of the play are far in excess of his expectations and that in consequence he is in financial difficulties. He offers to pay Hartwell £25,000 as this is all he can afford. Knowing that he will get less if Leonard goes bankrupt, Hartwell accepts this sum in full and final settlement.

On 1 June, learning that 'The Black Panther' is an outstanding success, Hartwell wishes to sue for the balance of £10,000 which he believes that Leonard owes him, and the seamstresses wish to sue Leonard for their promised bonuses.

Advise Hartwell and the seamstresses.

See *Cases and Materials* (2.4) for the complete answer.

CHAPTER THREE

TERMS OF A CONTRACT

3.1 Objectives

By the end of this chapter you should be able to:

- distinguish between terms and representations and understand the reason for doing so;

- distinguish between and identify the relationship between conditions, warranties and intermediate terms;

- identify the sources of implied terms and understand the necessity test in the context of both terms implied by law and terms implied in fact.

3.2 Introduction

We have looked so far at the essential requirements of a legally binding contract. Once we have established that a contract exists, it is then necessary to establish exactly what the obligations of the parties are under the agreement. We must therefore isolate the terms under which the parties have contracted.

Various types of terms may be present in a contract. The obvious type is an **express** term, i.e. a term which has been specifically negotiated by the parties in making their agreement. In addition, other terms may be **implied** into a contract from other sources, e.g., from custom and practice, by statute, or from the very nature of the contract by the common law.

3.3 Express Terms

Such terms are those specifically agreed between the parties to the contract. To find them the court examines exactly what the parties said to each other or wrote down. The aim is to discover the **intention of the parties**, i.e. did the parties intend a particular statement to be incorporated into the contract?

Where purely oral terms are involved, it is a question of proof, i.e. evidence as to what the parties actually said.

Where a written document has been created, the problem is one of construction of the written words, i.e. what do they actually mean?

A major difficulty arises where a contract is made partly orally and partly in writing. Such contracts are covered by a rule often known as the **parol evidence rule.**

3.3.1   THE PAROL EVIDENCE RULE

Basically, parol evidence (extrinsic evidence, oral or otherwise) cannot be admitted to vary, contradict or add to the written document.

The attitude of the courts is that if the parties have gone to the trouble of creating a written document containing the terms of the contract, then they must have intended that document to be the definitive contract. Anything intended by them to be a term would have been included in the document.

Hawkrish v *Bank of Montreal* [1969] 2 DLR (3d) 600
H signed a guarantee of a debt of a company. The form which the Bank gave him to sign referred to 'a continuing guarantee' up to $6,000 'of all present and future debts'.

H had intended that the guarantee should only cover a then existing debt of $6,000, and he therefore wanted to introduce evidence to this effect despite the wording of the guarantee, i.e. 'all present and future debts'.

Explain why this evidence will or will not be admissible?

H's evidence was inadmissible as it contradicted the document.

As a court's main aim here is to find the true intention of the parties, the parol evidence rule may be overruled. This will particularly be so where other evidence makes it clear that the parties did not intend the whole contract to be contained in the written document. In fact, in 1976 the Law Commission (Working Paper No. 76) recommended the abolition of the rule.

In practice, then, there are numerous examples of exceptions to the rule:

Smith v *Wilson* (1832) 3 B & Ad 728
The written contract referred to 1,000 rabbits. Oral evidence was admitted to show that under the local custom 1,000 rabbits meant 1,200 rabbits.

Oral evidence could be admitted to show that a term may be implied by custom.

Couchman v *Hill* [1947] 1 All ER 103
An auction catalogue described the defendant's heifer as 'unserved'. The catalogue also stated that the sale was subject to 'usual conditions'. These were exhibited at the auction

and one said, 'lots are sold with all faults, imperfections and errors of description'. The plaintiff asked both the defendant and the auctioneer, before bidding, whether the heifer was 'unserved' and both said it was unserved. He bid successfully for the cow but it later died as it was in calf (thus not 'unserved') but was too young.

The Court of Appeal allowed the plaintiff to recover damages. The oral assurance stood alongside the written documentation in forming the contract.

Birch v *Paramount Estates* (1956) 16 EG 396
The plaintiffs went to look at houses being built on a building site. The house on the plot which they wished to buy had not even been started. However, the sales person told them 'that it would be as good as the show home' and they then signed a written contract of purchase. That contract made no reference to the oral statement and the house, when built, was in fact inferior to the show house. The plaintiffs sued for breach of contract.

The oral statement was a part of the contract and therefore the plaintiffs were awarded compensation.

What does the plaintiff need to prove in order to displace the operation of the parol evidence rule?

Thus the parol evidence 'rule' is not really a rule at all but merely a presumption that the parties intended the whole contract to be contained in the written document. If this presumption can be rebutted by proving that the parties intended a partly written and partly oral contract, the 'rule' will not apply. A similar approach was adopted in the next case:

SS Ardennes (Cargo Owners) v *Ardennes (Owners)* [1950] 2 All ER 517
The plaintiff agreed with the defendant that his oranges would be carried from Spain to London by the defendant's ship. He was assured orally that the ship would sail direct to London. However, the bill of lading (the written contract) allowed the ship to proceed to London 'by any route and whether directly or indirectly'. The ship in fact travelled via Antwerp, and the delay caused the plaintiff to lose a favourable market and to sell at lower prices.

The plaintiff could recover damages as the oral promise constituted a term of the contract alongside the bill of lading.

This decision illustrates the almost total collapse of the parol evidence rule. Perhaps the final 'nail in its coffin' lies in the collateral contract device. Here, you would argue that the oral promise is enforceable because it is supported by consideration. The consideration would be entering into the written contract in reliance upon the oral promise.

City and Westminster Properties (1934) Ltd v *Mudd* [1958] 2 All ER 733
Mudd rented a small shop from the plaintiff who was aware that he often slept in a room
attached to the shop. When a new lease was being negotiated, Mudd was told that he
would still be allowed to sleep in the room after signing the new lease. A clause in the
document restricted the use of the premises to 'showrooms, workrooms and offices only'.
Alternative accommodation was available to him but, relying on the oral statement,
Mudd signed the lease. Subsequently, it was claimed that Mudd had forfeited the lease
by continuing to sleep on the premises contrary to the above clause.

Write down the terms of the collateral contract below.

Mudd was in breach of the contract but a collateral contract existed which afforded him
a defence. His entering into the new lease in reliance on the promise constituted
consideration, thus enabling him to enforce the promise, i.e. a collateral contract to that
effect had been granted.

Before moving on to look at implied terms, we need to notice that not everything said
by the parties during negotiations will form a part of the actual contract. Some statements
made will not be intended by the parties to be legally binding. These statements are
normally known as representations. It is therefore necessary to distinguish between
terms and **representations**. We can start by noticing that whereas a term can be breached,
a representation will be either true or false.

3.4   Terms and Representations

If a term of a contract is breached this can give rise to an action for **breach of contract**.
If, however, a representation is in fact false, this does not permit an action for breach of
contract. The only possible action is for **misrepresentation**.

Before the Misrepresentation Act 1967, the only action available to claim damages for
misrepresentation required the proof of fraud. In the absence of fraud, for example
where the false representation was made innocently or negligently, then damages could
not be recovered. Thus, in these circumstances, it was crucial to distinguish between a
term and a representation. If the statement was the former, damages could be recovered;
if the latter, they could not. You should bear this in mind when studying cases decided
before 1967. It could be argued that the absence of a remedy, were a statement not to be
decided to be a term, often influenced the court in making the distinction, particularly
in instances of negligent misrepresentation. This might explain the contradictions to be
found in a study of such cases.

The Misrepresentation Act 1967 introduced an award of damages for negligent misrepresentation and, in certain circumstances, for innocent misrepresentation, and thus the distinction between terms and representations became no longer as crucial.

3.4.1 HOW DOES THE COURT DISTINGUISH BETWEEN A TERM AND A REPRESENTATION?

The main factor is the **intention of the parties**. If it appears to the court, applying an objective test, that the parties thought the statement sufficiently important to be a part of the contract then it will be classed as a term.

In order to facilitate the application of this test, two factors are considered important:

(a)   the time at which the statement was made; and

(b)   whether one of the parties had specialist knowledge.

3.4.1.1   At what time was the statement made?

If the statement is made at the time that the contract is made, or near to it, then it is more likely to be intended to be a term. If a statement is made some time before the contract is made, and is not subsequently repeated, then it is less likely that it was intended to be important enough to be a term and it will merely be a representation.

 SAQ 28

Routledge v *McKay* [1954] 1 All ER 855
When selling his motor bike (a Douglas combination) the defendant, on 23 October, told the plaintiff that the bike was a 1942 model. On 30 October a written contract was concluded which made no reference to the date of the bike. Subsequently it was discovered that it was a 1930 model. The plaintiff claimed damages for breach of contract. (In the absence of proof of fraud he would not have obtained damages for misrepresentation.)

Explain, with reasons, why you think the statement was a term or a representation.

The statement was made some time before the contract and was therefore only a representation. The plaintiff failed in his action.

The facts of *Routledge* v *McKay* are relatively simple and the rule is easily applied. The facts of other cases are often more problematical.

Schawel v *Reade* [1913] 2 IR 81
This was an Irish case on appeal to the House of Lords. The plaintiff wanted to purchase a stallion to use for stud. When he began to examine the defendant's horse he was told, 'You need not look for anything, the horse is perfectly sound'. The plaintiff did not examine it any further. A price was agreed a few days later, and three weeks later the sale was concluded. The horse was not fit for stud and the plaintiff claimed damages for breach of contract. The defendant argued that the statement was made too long before the sale was concluded to constitute a term.

The contract was made over a prolonged period and therefore the statement was a term of the contract.

Bannerman v *White* (1861) 10 CB NS 844
A buyer who was negotiating the purchase of some hops asked the seller if they had been treated with sulphur, saying that if they had he would not even bother asking the price. The seller said that they had not and a contract for the purchase of 300 acres of hops was agreed. When the buyer discovered that five acres of the hops had been grown using sulphur he no longer wanted any of the hops. He was sued for breach.

Although not stated at the actual time of making the contract, the statement was a term because of the emphasis placed upon it.

SAQ 29

Can you identify a relevant connecting element between the last two cases which might explain why the court disregarded the time interval?

A connection between the last two cases can be found in the fact that the owners of the goods obviously had greater knowledge of those goods than did the prospective purchasers. Though not emphasised in the judgments, this could be a relevant factor. It has been said to be so in other cases.

3.4.1.2   Does one party have specialist knowledge?

Where the person making the statement has special knowledge over and above that of the other then the statement may be a term. The parties are more likely to give extra emphasis and attach particular importance to a statement made by the expert. Two cases nicely illustrate this:

Oscar Chess Ltd v *Williams* [1957] 1 All ER 325
W was selling his Morris car to the plaintiff, a car dealer, in part exchange for a new car. The registration book said it was a 1948 model. W, in good faith, gave the plaintiff that date in order to value the car. The plaintiff allowed him £290 as the part exchange price in the contract for the new car. Later it was discovered that the car was a 1939 model

and was worth only £175. The plaintiff sued for the balance of £115, claiming that the statement as to the year was a term.

Although made at the time of the contract, the statement was not a term. The car dealer had the specialist knowledge and was unlikely to have placed great emphasis on the statement.

Dick Bentley Productions Ltd v *Harold Smith Motors Ltd* [1965] 2 All ER 65
The defendant sold a Bentley car to the plaintiff, saying it had done only 20,000 miles since a replacement engine and gearbox had been fitted. The statement was made in the morning and the sale took place in the afternoon. The car in fact was in poor condition and the statement was untrue. The plaintiff sued for damages.

The statement was a term of the contract.

The decision seems reasonable but the problem here is that the facts of this case are almost identical to those of the previous case where the decision was the opposite. If both cases are correctly decided then they must be distinguishable on their facts.

SAQ 30

Can you identify the key distinguishing factor between these two cases?

The key distinction is the relative expertise of the makers of the statements. In the former case, the statement was made **to** the expert and was thus a representation; in the latter case it was made **by** the expert and was thus a term.

Lord Denning said negligence was the key distinction. In *Oscar Chess* the maker of the statement was not negligent, whereas in *Dick Bentley* he was. But you might care to consider whether negligence is relevant. If the *Oscar Chess* case had involved two private persons then the decision would surely have been different, and thus the same as *Dick Bentley*, even with the presence or absence of negligence. So the key distinction here must be the specialist knowledge.

Do you think that another solution to this problem could be the use of the collateral contract device? Entering into the contract of purchase is consideration to support the oral statement and thus the statement is binding. We saw this principle at work in *City and Westminster Properties (1934) Ltd* v *Mudd*, at **3.3.1**.

Lastly, a statement will not normally be a term if the person making it suggests that the other party should verify it. In *Ecay* v *Godfrey* (1974) 80 LL LR 286, the seller of a boat said that it was sound but suggested to the purchaser that a survey be done on it. It was held that the statement was not a term because the parties did not expect the buyer to rely on it.

3.5 Implied Terms

We have seen above that terms may be implied into a contract rather than being expressly agreed by the parties. The main examples of this are by custom and practice, by statute and by the common law.

3.5.1 CUSTOM AND PRACTICE

Even though not specifically negotiated between the parties, a term may be implied into a contract either from previous dealings between the parties or from standard practices in a particular trade, industry or profession.

British Crane Hire Corporation Ltd v *Ipswich Plant Hire Ltd* [1975] QB 303
A contract was agreed, by telephone, for the hire of a crane. A written document was sent and arrived subsequently. A clause in the written document stated that the hirer was responsible for the recovery of the crane. The crane sank in marshy ground with neither party to blame. The hirers claimed that the clause in the document was inapplicable as it was communicated after the contract had been made and was thus not incorporated.

Because it is the custom and practice in the plant hire industry for the hirer to be responsible, the hirer was responsible in this case.

It is worth noting that the decision is hardly surprising, as the hirers admitted that when they hired out plant they included the same clause in their contract!

Other examples of such implied terms are to be found in the discussion on the incorporation of exclusion clauses into contracts (see **Chapter Four**).

3.5.2 STATUTE

Various statutes imply terms into different specific types of contract. For example, the Equal Pay Act 1970 implies an 'equality clause' into every woman's contract of employment. If any term of her contract is less favourable than a similar term in a male employee's contract then that term is to be treated as modified so that it is not less favourable.

The Consumer Credit Act 1974 implies terms into hire purchase or other credit sale agreements.

By far the most important statute affecting our studies in this area is the Sale of Goods Act 1979 (originally enacted in 1893).

3.5.2.1 Sale of Goods Act 1979

The basic rule in the law of contract covering sales of goods is *caveat emptor* – let the buyer beware. This placed the obligation on the buyer to ensure that the goods were the seller's to sell and were not defective. In the absence of fraud, the buyer could not complain about any defect in the goods. This rule gave too much protection to the unscrupulous seller and, therefore, as early as 1893, the Sale of Goods Act was passed.

The main provisions of the Act concerning implied terms are ss. 12 to 15. You need to remember that this Act applies **only** to contracts for the sale of goods and **not**, for example, to exchanges of goods or to sales of land.

Section 12

There is an implied condition that the seller has the right to sell, i.e. that he has a good title to the goods at the time of the sale.

Rowland v *Divall* [1923] 2 KB 500
The defendant bought a car from X who had in fact stolen it from the true owner. The defendant then sold the car to the plaintiff, who in turn sold it to Y. The police then traced the car as having been stolen and seized it from Y to return to the true owner. Y recovered the price paid from the plaintiff who then sued the defendant.

The defendant was in breach of the term implied by s. 12. He had no title to the car and therefore no right to sell.

Section 13

Where there is a sale of goods by description there is an implied condition that the goods correspond with the description.

Varley v *Whipp* [1900] 1 QB 513
The plaintiff, when selling a reaping machine, said that it had been used for one season only and had cut only 50 to 60 acres. The defendant bought it without seeing it. He found that in fact it was an old machine that had been repaired at some time. He returned it and refused to pay the price. The plaintiff sued for the price.

Give reasons as to whether the buyer is entitled to repudiate the contract or not.

The plaintiff failed. The goods did not correspond with their description and this serious breach of condition entitled the defendant to treat the contract as repudiated and thus to refuse to pay the price.

Similarly, the packaging or the labelling of goods may constitute their description.

Beale v *Taylor* [1967] 1 WLR 1193
The defendant advertised his car as a 1961 Triumph Herald 1200 cc. The plaintiff inspected the car and saw a 1200 cc plate on the back. He bought the car but subsequently discovered that the car was in fact two cars which had been welded

together. The front half was a 1959 Triumph Herald 998 cc welded to the rear half of a 1961 1200 cc.

The advertisement and the plate on the back of the car constituted a description and therefore there was a breach of condition as the goods did not correspond with the description contrary to the term implied by s. 13.

The rule has, on occasion, been very strictly applied.

Re Moore & Co. and Landauer & Co. [1921] 2 KB 519
The plaintiff agreed to buy a specific quantity of fruit in cases of 30 tins each. Overall, the correct quantity was delivered but half of the consignment was in cases of 24. The defendant rejected the whole consignment and the plaintiff sued for damages for breach of contract.

The buyer was entitled to reject the goods as they did not correspond with the description. He could reject the whole consignment even though there was no evidence that it was essential for the fruit to be in cases of 30.

This case has not been overruled, though in *Reardon Smith Line Ltd* v *Hansen-Tangen* [1976] 3 All ER 570, Lord Wilberforce in the House of Lords said that such authorities were 'excessively technical and due for fresh examination'.

Section 14(3)

In a sale of goods in the course of a business there is an implied term that the goods are reasonably fit for the purpose expressly or impliedly made known by the buyer.

Baldry v *Marshall* [1925] 1 KB 260
The plaintiff owned a Talbot racing car in which his wife was scared to travel. She persuaded him to change it for a touring car. He therefore asked the defendant to supply a car which was 'comfortable and suitable for touring'. The defendant recommended a Bugatti. The plaintiff bought it not knowing anything about Bugattis. In fact it was a similar type of car to the Talbot.

The defendant was in breach of the implied term that the car be reasonably fit for the purpose made known.

The purpose will be impliedly made known when the goods have only one normal use.

Priest v *Last* [1903] 2 KB 148
The plaintiff bought a hot water bottle which his wife used for bodily application (relieving cramp). It burst and she was badly scalded.

The bottle was not reasonably fit for its purpose as required by the term implied by s. 14(3).

Section 14(2)

Where goods are sold in the course of a business there is an implied condition that they be of merchantable quality, i.e. they must be reasonably fit for the purpose or purposes for which they are commonly bought.

An important change in the law occurred on 5 January 1995. The term 'merchantable quality' has been replaced by the term 'satisfactory quality' (the goods must meet the standard that a reasonable person would regard as satisfactory, taking account of any description of the goods, the price (if relevant) and all the other relevant circumstances): Sale and Supply of Goods Act 1994.

Grant v *Australian Knitting Mills Ltd* [1936] AC 85

The plaintiff bought a pair of underpants which were packaged in a sealed, transparent bag. When he wore them for the first time he developed a severe rash and itching which was subsequently diagnosed as dermatitis. (Do not worry, the pants were long and the dermatitis was of the ankle, initially anyway!) The dermatitis was caused by sulphites which were present in the underpants as a result of a defect in the manufacturing process.

The plaintiff succeeded in an action for damages, one of the reasons being that the goods were not of merchantable quality, contrary to the term implied by s. 14(2). The goods were also not reasonably fit for their purpose impliedly made known, and the defendant was further liable in the tort of negligence.

The following is a fascinating case where it was decided that all the materials supplied under the contract are covered by s. 14.

Wilson v *Rickett, Cockerell & Co.* [1954] 1 QB 598

The plaintiff ordered some 'Coalite' fuel and used it on her fire. An explosion ensued caused by detonators mixed in with the coal. The defendant argued that the detonators were not sold under the contract but were given free and thus were not covered by the Act!

You will not be surprised to know that the Court found for the plaintiff. Section 14 covers **all** things supplied.

Section 15

In a sale of goods by sample there is an implied condition that the bulk of the goods corresponds with the sample in quality.

ACTIVITY 14

Read ss. 13 and 14 of the Sale of Goods Act 1979 in *Cases and Materials* (3.3.2). What restriction applies to the implication of terms under s. 14 which does not apply to s. 13?

Terms can be implied under s. 14 only where the seller sells **in the course of a business**. This restriction does not apply to terms implied under s. 13, i.e. s. 13 can apply to a seller conducting a private sale.

So much for ss. 12 to 15. Please bear in mind, however, that these terms being discussed are **implied** terms. Such terms cannot conflict with **express** terms, thus the terms implied by ss. 12 to 15 can be excluded by contrary intention, i.e. by express exclusion in the contract. The ability successfully to exclude them is restricted severely by the provisions of the Unfair Contract Terms Act 1977 (see **Chapter 4**).

How relevant is it whether the seller has been careless in selling goods which are of unsatisfactory quality or not reasonably fit for the purpose etc.?

It is not relevant at all. This is an example of what is known as strict liability. Lack of negligence is no defence. If the goods were supplied to the seller in an unsatisfactory condition he must seek to recoup his loss (if sued for breach of contract) from his supplier.

3.5.3 COMMON LAW

Various terms are automatically implied into contracts because it is deemed **necessary** for them to be so. This may be because the very nature of the contract requires a particular term to be implied, or because the application of an objective test makes it apparent that the parties must have intended a term to be implied, in order for the contract to make sense, particularly for business efficacy.

It must be emphasised that the test here is one of **necessity**. It has been suggested, particularly by Lord Denning, that a term may be implied because it is reasonable to do so. We shall see his comments on this in the Court of Appeal decision in *Liverpool City Council* v *Irwin* (discussed below) for clear evidence of this view.

You may consider the reasoning behind this to be logical. If we apply an objective test to ascertain the intention of the parties, then we are adopting the standards of a reasonable person. Surely a reasonable person would imply a term into a contract in order to produce a reasonable result, or at least to avoid an unreasonable result? The danger herein, though, is that we may be contradicting the doctrine of freedom of contract. It is for the parties to agree their bargain. It is not for the courts to interfere with a freely negotiated bargain. Many perfectly valid contracts involve one of the parties obtaining a bad deal, but that is the fault of that party as there was no compulsion to enter into the contract in the first place.

Thus the House of Lords has emphasised that terms will be implied where it is **necessary** to do so, **not** merely where it would be **reasonable** to do so. This is illustrated by the decision in the following case:

Liverpool City Council v *Irwin* [1977] AC 239
D was the tenant of a ninth floor flat in a block of flats owned by P. His contract contained no statement of the obligations of the landlord under the agreement.

Because of vandalism, the lifts rarely worked, the staircases were usually unlit and the shutes used for the disposal of refuse were frequently blocked. D withheld his rent, claiming he was entitled to do so because P was in breach of contract. P said that there was no express or implied term of which the council was in breach.

Because of the nature of the contract, it was implicit that the landlord was obliged to keep the common parts of the block of flats in a reasonable state of repair. However, because the standard required was one of reasonableness, the council had fulfilled its contractual duty by spending more on repairs than it took in rents.

The speeches emphasise the test of necessity and expressly reject the suggestion of Lord Denning, in the Court of Appeal, that the test be one of reasonableness. Indeed, Lord Denning himself seems to have accepted this in *Shell UK v Lostock Garage* [1977] 1 All ER 481.

It has been said that a term will be implied into a contract where it is 'necessary to give the transaction such business efficacy as the parties must have intended': *Luxor v Cooper* (below). A means of ascertaining such intention has been suggested by the 'officious bystander' test, to be found in *Shirlaw v Southern Foundries (1926) Ltd* [1939] 2 KB 206. McKinnon LJ said:

> Prima facie that which in any contract is left to be implied and need not be expressed is something so obvious that it goes without saying; so that, if while the parties were making their bargain, an officious bystander were to suggest some express provision for it in the agreement, they would testily suppress him with a common 'Oh, of course!'

As students of the law of contract, you may well greet this test with mirth, if not incredulity, but, ludicrous as it seems, it has been generally accepted by the judiciary over a number of years.

Luxor (Eastbourne) Ltd v Cooper [1941] AC 108
D employed P, an estate agent, to sell some property. The contract expressly provided for P to be paid commission 'on completion of sale'. P found a buyer but D had managed to sell the property himself. Therefore D did not pay P because a sale had not been completed by P. P argued that there was an implied term that D would not refuse to sell the property to persons introduced by P.

No such term would be implied because it was clear that both parties would not have agreed to the term at the time of the contract, i.e. D would not have accepted it.

Although the 'officious bystander' test was not specifically mentioned in this case, it is a classic example of its application. (As you may know, estate agents now expressly stipulate that they are entitled to payment 'on the introduction of a willing purchaser'.)

Certain types of contract automatically, by law, contain specific implied terms. A classic example is a contract for the lease of a furnished house, which automatically contains a term that the house be reasonably fit for habitation. Similarly, under a contract of employment, the employee owes various duties to the employer, one of these being a duty to provide faithful service and not to make a secret profit from that employment.

Boston Deep Sea Fishing Co. v Ansell (1888) 39 Ch D 339
A was the managing director of the company. He accepted a bribe in return for the awarding of a contract for the supply of new trawlers to the company and entered into contracts for the purchase of ice at a high price with a company of which he was a major shareholder.

He was in breach of the implied term requiring faithful service. He could therefore be summarily dismissed and was accountable for his secret profits to the company.

Read the judgment of Lord Denning in *Shell UK v Lostock Garage* in *Cases and Materials* (3.3.4) and, on a separate piece of paper or in the space below, distinguish between terms implied in law and terms implied in fact.

You might have said that terms implied in fact are implied in 'one-off' situations under the officious bystander test. Terms implied in law are implied as a necessary incident of a particular type of commonly recurring legal relationship, e.g., an employee's duty to provide faithful service and not to make a secret profit will be implied into all contracts of employment subject to any express provision to the contrary.

3.5.4 SUMMARY

The statement of the law in this area by the judiciary, particularly in *Liverpool CC v Irwin*, seems somewhat unsatisfactory. The very nature of the 'officious bystander' test and a close scrutiny of the application of the 'necessity' test to the facts of that case may well leave you with a strong suspicion that reasonableness is relevant. Using *Shell UK v Lostock Garage*, which was considered above, perhaps you would agree that a sensible compromise is to suggest that, although a court is most unlikely to imply an unreasonable term, nevertheless it is not free to imply a term merely because it seems reasonable to do so.

3.6 Conditions and Warranties and Intermediate Terms

The terms of a contract have traditionally been divided into two types, conditions and warranties, and, more recently, a third type has appeared, intermediate terms. It is important to distinguish between these different types as the consequences arising from their breach may be vastly different:

(a) A **condition** is an important term which goes to the root of the contract. A breach of condition entitles the injured party to repudiate the contract and/or claim damages.

(b) A **warranty** is a much less important term, the breach of which entitles the injured party to claim damages only.

The consequences of a breach of condition are therefore much more serious. As you can see, this makes it essential for a distinction to be made as to whether a particular term is a condition or a warranty. The following two cases illustrate this:

Poussard v *Spiers and Pond* [1876] 1 QB 410
An actress contracted to appear in a play commencing on a particular date. She fell ill and became available to appear only some days after the play's run had started. In her absence, a substitute had been engaged and the producers therefore refused her services when she returned.

What kind of term had been breached by the actress – a condition or a warranty?

The producers were entitled to refuse to employ the actress because her late arrival was a breach going to the root of the contract, i.e. a breach of condition. Thus they could repudiate the contract.

Bettini v *Gye* [1876] 1 QB 183
A singer was contracted to perform from 30 March to 13 July, and to attend six days before for rehearsals. Because of illness the singer did not arrive until 28 March and was told that his services were not required.

What kind of term had been breached by the singer – a condition or a warranty?

Missing a few days of rehearsals was not a breach which went to the root of the contract and thus there was no right to repudiate the contract. Damages for breach of warranty only could therefore be recovered.

When you compare the facts of these two cases, you should be able to see the logic of the respective decisions. In fact, the latter case was cited in the former. However, if the facts of *Bettini* v *Gye* are looked at in isolation, it is possible to assert that the breach was, perhaps, much more serious than was decided. Would an impresario who had invested a large sum of money in a production be satisfied if star players missed rehearsals?

This leads us to a discussion of **how** the courts distinguish between the different types of terms. Two tests seem to be important:

    (a) the intention of the parties; and

(b)   the consequences of the breach.

3.6.1   WHAT WAS THE INTENTION OF THE PARTIES?

Traditionally the courts attempted to ascertain the intention of the parties, i.e. were they treating the particular term as important or not? They would therefore examine the words used by, and the conduct of, the parties to construe their intentions.

Bannerman v White (1861) 10 CB NS 844
A buyer of hops asked whether sulphur had been used in their cultivation and said that if it had, he would not even bother to ask the price.

There was a clear intention that it be a condition of the contract that sulphur had not been used.

You might, perhaps, think that a more obvious situation is where the parties actually use the specific words 'condition' or 'warranty' in their negotiations, particularly in a written contract. However, a note of caution here. If the actual words are used then they must be used in their legal sense. A person often, for example, uses the word 'condition' as a synonym for 'term', e.g., 'The terms and conditions of the contract are . . . '. In such instances the language used by the parties will not be conclusive.

Schuler AG v Wickman Machine Tool Sales Ltd [1974] AC 235
A term of an agreement said that it was 'a condition' that a distributor should visit six named customers per week for each week of the duration of the contract, which was for four years.

What has been breached, a condition or a warranty? Give reasons for your decision.

Despite the use of the word 'condition', a breach of the term would not automatically give the right to repudiate. Taken literally, to miss just one visit would have been a breach of condition, which the parties could not have intended.

If the words used are not necessarily conclusive, then we need to look for other factors which may be important. As an example, the courts might look at the commercial importance of a term in relation to a particular trade, industry or profession.

Behn v Burness (1863) 3 B&S 751
In a contract for the charter of a ship, it was described as being 'in the port of Amsterdam'. The ship in fact arrived in Amsterdam four days after the date of the charter.

Because of the nature of the contract this was a breach of condition. Time is crucial in the chartering of ships, particularly as vast sums of money can be involved if there are delays.

You will, by now, be aware that our discussion so far has hardly produced a precise, accurate means of differentiating between the different types of terms. It is notoriously difficult to ascertain the 'intention of the parties'. However, the decisions in the last two cases lead us to a second method of making the distinction. In *Wickman* v *Schuler* the loss arising from the breach would have been minimal, and thus the term was a warranty. In *Behn* v *Burness* the loss from such a breach is considerable and thus such a term is a condition.

3.6.2   WHAT ARE THE CONSEQUENCES OF THE BREACH?

The suggestion here is that, in order to make the distinction, it is necessary to examine **the consequences of the breach**. The more serious the consequences, the more likely it is that the breach will entitle the innocent party to repudiate: the less serious the consequences, the less likely it is that the breach will entitle the innocent party to repudiate. This proposition originates from the following case.

Hong Kong Fir Shipping Co. Ltd v *Kawasaki Kisen Kaisha Ltd* [1962] 1 All ER 474
The plaintiffs owned a ship which they chartered to the defendants for a period of 24 months. A term in the contract required the ship to be 'in every way fitted for ordinary cargo service'. On a voyage to Osaka the ship was delayed for five weeks due to engine trouble, and at Osaka 15 more weeks were lost when the engines became even more dilapidated due to the incompetence of the engine-room staff provided by the plaintiffs. The ship was not made seaworthy until September. Meanwhile, the defendants had repudiated the charter in June. The plaintiffs claimed damages for wrongful repudiation.

It was held (perhaps surprisingly, bearing in mind that the ship had been unavailable for almost six months of a 24 month charter period) that the plaintiff's breach did not entitle the defendant to repudiate the contract and the plaintiff's claim succeeded.

However, the court refused to categorise the term as a condition or warranty, pointing out that the term in question could be breached in either a serious or a trivial manner, which was to be judged by the seriousness of the consequences of the breach, i.e. the term was an intermediate or innominate term. Presumably, the court felt that the consequences of the breach were not serious. Thus, while the defendant would have been entitled to damages for the equivalent of breach of warranty, he was not entitled to repudiate the contract for the equivalent of breach of condition.

This approach has been accepted in subsequent cases. The crucial issue is whether the innocent party has been substantially deprived of the whole benefit of the contract or not.

SAQ 36

Cehave NV v *Bremer Handelsgesellschaft mbH, The Hansa Nord* [1975] 3 All ER 739
Citrus pulp pellets to the value of £100,000 were sold. An express term in the contract stipulated 'shipment to be made in good condition'. Some of the pellets overheated during shipment and were thus not in good condition. The buyer therefore rejected the whole consignment.

The goods were then sold to a third party and were eventually acquired by the original buyer but at a price of £30,000, much lower than the contract price. He used the goods

for exactly the same purpose as originally intended, manufacturing animal feed, but in a slightly smaller quantity.

The seller sued for damages for the refusal to take delivery, but the buyer claimed this was justified by the breach of condition in relation to the express term.

Explain why you think the buyer was or was not justified in refusing to take delivery.

The seller obtained compensation as the rejection was not justified. The term was not a condition but was an intermediate term. The breach of such a term gives rise to a right to treat the contract as repudiated only if the consequences of the breach were particularly serious. Here, they were not.

A similar decision was reached in the next case:

Reardon Smith Line Ltd v *Hansen-Tangen* [1976] 3 All ER 570
A charter contract was made of a tanker which was still to be built. It was described in the contract as 'No. 354 at Osaka', Osaka being the shipbuilding yard. In fact the ship was not built at the Osaka yard but at Oshima as No. 004. The plans and specifications to which it was built were, however, identical.

The charterer refused to take delivery of the ship, claiming a breach of condition as the ship did not correspond to its contract description. The real reason for its refusal was the collapse of the oil tanker market.

Explain why you think the charterer was or was not justified in refusing to take delivery.

There was no breach of condition. The words 'No. 354 at Osaka' were merely a means of referring to the ship and did not constitute the contractual description. In their speeches their Lordships expressed a preference for the approach initiated in the *Hong Kong Fir* case.

Much of the argument in the last two cases arises from the provisions of the Sale of Goods Act 1893 (now 1979) and cases decided thereon. The terms implied into contracts for the sale of goods by ss. 12 to 15 of the Act are described specifically as conditions or warranties. The question then arises as to whether the breach of such a term described as a condition should entitle the injured party to treat the contract as repudiated even where the consequences of the breach were minimal.

The traditional cases affirmed this view but with somewhat extreme results.

Re Moore & Co. and Landauer & Co. [1921] 2 KB 519
A sale was agreed of a quantity of tinned fruit described as packed in cases of 30 tins. The correct overall quantity was delivered, but in cases of 24 tins. The whole consignment was rejected by the buyer, but without any reason being given other than the quantities packed.

The goods did not correspond with their description contrary to the term implied from s. 13 of the Act. As s. 13 stated that the term was a condition, there was a right to reject.

The evidence here showed that the fruit was perfectly merchantable as packed and thus the consequences of the breach were minimal.

Arcos Ltd v *Ronaasen* [1933] AC 470
Timber to be used for making barrels to store cement was described as being $\frac{1}{2}''$ thick. The timber actually delivered was $\frac{9}{16}''$ thick and was therefore rejected by the buyer. In fact the extra $\frac{1}{16}''$ made no difference to the use of the wood for making the barrels.

The buyer was entitled to reject the whole consignment because the goods did not correspond with their description contrary to the implied term from s. 13 of the Act.

You may think that these decisions in these cases seem extreme in allowing the contract to be repudiated merely on what might appear to be a technicality. They have been criticised in more recent years and the modern view is that they ought not to be followed. In the *Reardon Smith Line* case, Lord Wilberforce said:

> The general law of contract has developed, along much more rational lines (e.g. *Hong Kong Fir Shipping Co. Ltd* v *Kawasaki Kisen Kaisha Ltd*) in attending to the nature and gravity of a breach or departure rather than in accepting rigid categories which do or do not automatically give a right to rescind, and if the choice were between extending cases under the Sale of Goods Act 1893 into other fields, or allowing more modern doctrine to infect those cases, my preference would be clear.

However, we must remember that the speeches in this case, though critical of the older cases, do not specifically overrule them. We await further developments.

What difficulties can you think of in extending the intermediate term approach to sale of goods cases?

Your reply might be that most of the terms implied by the Sale of Goods Act 1979 are designated as conditions. How, therefore, can they be treated as intermediate terms if designated conditions by an Act of Parliament?

However, in some modern cases the courts have obviated this difficulty by restricting the scope of operation of s. 13. Apparently only descriptive words which are essential to the identity of the goods can fall within the condition implied by s. 13. Thus any inessential descriptive words can be treated as express, intermediate terms. Indeed, in the *Hansa Nord* (above) the Court of Appeal does not seem to have considered s. 13 at all.

However, such devious ingenuity is unnecessary in non-consumer transactions after 5 January 1995. The Sale and Supply of Goods Act 1994 provides that where the breach of the terms implied by ss. 13, 14 and 15 is so slight that it would be unreasonable for the buyer to reject the goods, then if the buyer does not deal as a consumer, the breach is not to be treated as a breach of condition but may be treated as a breach of warranty, i.e. a recognition of the intermediate term approach.

3.7   Conclusion

It now seems that we have three types of terms of varying degrees of importance: conditions, warranties, and intermediate terms. It may be argued that in fact there are now only two – conditions and intermediate terms. A breach of warranty which has serious consequences may now cause a contract to be treated as repudiated. However, attractive as this view may be, it cannot really be said to reflect the current position. Future developments are eagerly awaited.

However, a term which is clearly stipulated by the parties to be a condition will always allow the contract to be repudiated, no matter how trivial the consequences (apart from Sale and Supply of Goods Act 1994 situations previously noted). See *Bunge Corporation v Tradax Export SA* [1981] 2 All ER 513, where the House of Lords emphasised that in the interests of commercial necessity the parties should be able to stipulate the importance of particular terms and the consequences of their breach.

3.8 End of Chapter Assessment Question

'Common sense suggests and the law has long recognised that the obligations created by a contract are not all of equal importance. It is primarily for the parties to set their own value on the terms that they impose upon each other. But it is rare for them to express with any precision what, if anything, they have in their minds; and the resultant task of inferring and interpreting their intention is, as always, a matter of great difficulty.' (Cheshire, Fifoot & Furmston's *Law of Contract*, 13th edition p. 151).

Discuss.

See *Cases and Materials* (3.6) for the complete answer.

CHAPTER FOUR

EXCLUSION AND LIMITATION CLAUSES

4.1 Objectives

At the end of this chapter you should be able to:

■ appreciate the historical development of the law relating to exclusion clauses and the need for the Unfair Contract Terms Act 1977;

■ analyse critically the common law rules and identify why 'strained construction' is no longer necessary;

■ identify relevant bases of liability and types of exclusion clause so as to connect smoothly relevant sections of the Unfair Contract Terms Act 1977;

■ apply both the common law and statutory rules to problem situations in the appropriate order;

■ recognise and understand the principle of inequality of bargaining power which underlies this area of the law;

■ identify the overlap and relationship between the Unfair Contract Terms Act 1977 and the Unfair Terms in Consumer Contracts Regulations 1994.

4.2 Introduction

Exclusion clauses abound in our everyday lives. We have all seen notices saying 'The owners accept no liability . . .' etc., in so many public places – car parks, public houses, restaurants, dry cleaners, etc. The question for us is, what then is the legal validity of such clauses?

The doctrine of freedom of contract means that the parties are bound by all the terms of a contract freely entered into. Thus an exclusion clause is as valid as any other term of the contract. As a result, the judiciary cannot declare that such a clause is invalid merely because it seems unreasonable or unfair, or because one of the parties has obtained a bad bargain. To do so would be to renegotiate the contract for the parties, which the courts are not allowed to do.

This state of affairs is acceptable where the parties have entered into the contract from positions of equal bargaining power, such as where two large business organisations negotiate a contract. However, the position becomes much less acceptable where the parties do not contract on equal terms, e.g., where an ordinary consumer deals with a business, or where a small business deals with a much larger one. The use of a standard form contract by one of the parties accentuates the problem as the contract then is not negotiable but is presented in a 'take it or leave it' situation. (Have you ever tried negotiating an insurance or hire purchase contract, or arguing with a car park attendant about conditions of parking?)

To attempt to alleviate such problems, the judiciary has over the years developed certain rules which can be applied to restrict the application of exclusion clauses. **But** we must remember that a court cannot, at common law, declare a clause to be invalid merely because it is unreasonable.

In addition, because the judges' powers here are limited, Parliament has had to intervene to curb the excesses of the unreasonable use of exclusion clauses. The main statute which we will examine is the Unfair Contract Terms Act 1977. Thus, to assess the validity of an exclusion clause, we must examine the application of the common law rules and the provisions of the Unfair Contract Terms Act 1977. We also need to look at the Unfair Terms in Consumer Contracts Regulations 1994.

(Please note that throughout this chapter the expression 'exclusion clause' should be read as meaning 'exclusion or limitation clause' unless it is specifically stated that different rules apply to the separate types of clause.)

4.3   The Position at Common Law

There are two basic questions you must always consider:

(a)   Incorporation – is the clause part of the contract?

(b)   Construction – is the clause appropriately worded to cover what has occurred?

By answering these two questions and then applying the provisions of the 1977 Act and the 1994 Regulations, we can assess the validity or otherwise of any exclusion clause.

4.3.1   INCORPORATION

An exclusion clause is binding only if it is a term of the contract, i.e. it is incorporated into the contract. It may be incorporated in three ways:

(a)   by signature,

(b)   by notice, or

(c)   by a course of dealing.

4.3.1.1   Signature

If you sign a written contract then you are bound by its terms whether you have read and understood the terms or not. The lesson is that you should **not** sign documents without reading them and ensuring that you fully understand them. (How many times have we all done this!)

L'Estrange v *F. Graucob Ltd* [1934] 2 KB 394
A woman signed a written contract for the purchase of a cigarette vending machine without reading it. It contained an exclusion clause described by the judge as being 'in

regrettably small print'. The machine was defective but the sellers wished to rely on the clause.

The purchaser was bound by the clause as it was contained in the signed document.

This rule is qualified by the presence of fraud or misrepresentation.

Curtis v *Chemical Cleaning and Dyeing Co.* [1951] 1 All ER 631
The plaintiff took a wedding dress trimmed with beads and sequins to be cleaned. When given a document to sign she asked what it was. She was told that it exempted the company from liability for damage to the beads and sequins. She signed. The dress was stained during the cleaning process and the plaintiff claimed compensation. The defendant claimed the protection of an exclusion clause in the signed document which covered 'any damage, howsoever caused'.

To what extent do you think the exclusion clause was valid, if at all?

The exclusion clause was valid only in so far as it covered the beads and sequins. The misrepresentation, or half truth, by the assistant affected the validity of the clause.

4.3.1.2 Notice

An exclusion clause may be incorporated into the contract by notice of its existence being given to the other party. The rule is to be found in *Parker* v *South Eastern Railway Co.* (1877) 2 CPD 416.

Reasonable notice of the **existence** of the clause must be given by the party relying on it **before or at the time** the contract is made.

'Existence'   Only the existence of the clause needs to be notified, not necessarily the details of the clause itself.

Thompson v *LMS Railway Co.* [1930] 1 KB 41
A 2s. 7d (13p approximately) excursion train ticket said, on the front, 'See Back'. On the back it said that the ticket was issued subject to conditions, which were to be found in the railway company timetable. This could be purchased for 6d (approximately 20 per cent of the contract price). One of the conditions excluded the company from liability for personal injury to excursion ticket holders. The plaintiff, who was illiterate and had not read the timetable, was injured by the negligence of the company.

The existence of the clause had been reasonably communicated to her and therefore, as the clause was valid, she could not recover damages.

The judge in this case took the view that a reasonable person would be put on their guard by the mention of conditions being attached and would check them out before entering into the contract. He was very much adhering to a strict 'freedom of contract' approach. Although the decision has been criticised as to the reasonableness of the communication and would surely be decided differently today, it remains a good authority for the rule that only the **existence** of the clause needs to be communicated and not the clause itself.

SAQ 40

In *Thompson* v *LMS* a ticket was purchased a few days in advance of the excursion. **Might the decision have been different if the ticket had been purchased 30 minutes before the train was due to depart? If so, why?**

The rationale underlying *Thompson* v *LMS* assumes that Mrs Thompson would have had plenty of time to discover what the exclusions were, and could have changed her mind about the excursion and demanded her money back if she were not happy about them. How practical is this? Obviously the same logic does not apply if the ticket is purchased 30 minutes before departure.

'Reasonable notice'   Whether such notice has been given depends very much on the facts of each individual case.

Where an actual notice board is used, it must be sufficiently large and in a prominent position.

McCutcheon v *David MacBrayne Ltd* [1964] 1 All ER 430
The defendant ran a ferry service from the Scottish mainland to the islands. The plaintiff employed a Mr McSporran (what a lovely name for a Scotsman!) to arrange for his car to be carried on the ferry. He did so, but the ferry sank with the car, as a result of the defendant's negligence. When the plaintiff sued for compensation the defendant wished to rely on exclusion clauses. These were to be found on a risk note, which was usually signed by the customer but which had not been on this occasion, and on notices both inside and outside the defendant's offices at the pier. These contained 4,000 words in 27 paragraphs of small print.

The exclusion clauses had not been reasonably communicated to the customer and thus could not be relied upon.

> Where some form of document is used, then the clause will only be valid if a reasonable person would expect contractual terms to be present in or on the document. Generally, the more information there is to be found on the document, the more likely it is that the clause is correctly communicated.

Chapelton v *Barry UDC* [1940] 1 KB 532
The plaintiff hired a deck chair at a rate of 2d for three hours. The attendant gave him a ticket as proof of payment but he put this in his pocket without reading it. The deck chair collapsed as he sat on it and he was trapped and injured. When he claimed damages the Council wished to rely on an exclusion clause printed on the ticket.

Do you think that this ticket was a contractual document?

The clause was not valid as it was not reasonably communicated. A reasonable person would assume that the ticket was a mere receipt for payment and not a contractual document on which one would expect to find terms of a contract.

'Before or at the time' of the contract   The clause must be communicated before or at the time that the contract is made. It is not possible for a term to be unilaterally inserted into the contract after agreement has been reached.

Olley v *Marlborough Court Ltd* [1949] 1 KB 532
The Olleys entered an hotel and booked a room at the reception desk. They later went out having left Mrs Olley's fur coat and some valuables in their locked room. Mrs Olley left the room key at the reception desk. While the hotel porter was polishing a bust in the foyer, a thief stole the key and subsequently stole the fur coat. When Mrs Olley claimed compensation the hotel wished to rely on an exclusion clause to be found on a notice in the Olleys' room.

Had the exclusion clause been validly communicated?

The clause was not valid as it was communicated **after** the contract had been made, i.e. the contract was made at the reception desk before the Olleys could enter the room and see the notice.

An excellent case which illustrates the application of the rule on reasonable communication and which is essential reading is the following:

Thornton v *Shoe Lane Parking Ltd* [1971] 1 All ER 686
Mr Thornton was, as Lord Denning stated in the case, 'a freelance trumpeter of the highest quality'. He drove up to a car park entrance, thus causing the automatic machinery to proffer a ticket which he took, and entered when the barrier rose up. He left his car at the car park. On his return he suffered personal injury as a result of the negligence of a car park employee. When he claimed compensation the owners of the car park wished to rely on various exclusion clauses, variously displayed. At the entrance to the car park was a notice which said, 'All cars parked at owners' risk'. On the ticket it stated that it was 'issued subject to conditions displayed on the premises'. On a pillar inside the car park was a notice listing numerous conditions, one of which purported to exclude liability for injury 'howsoever caused'.

How relevant was the notice at the entrance to the car park?

Was the notice inside the car park effectively communicated to the plaintiff?

All three judges agreed that the notice at the entrance was inapplicable because it covered only damage to cars, and that overall, not enough had been done reasonably to communicate the existence of the other clause. The clause was an unusual and burdensome one and therefore a greater degree of communication than usual was necessary, perhaps requiring red arrows actually pointing to the clause.

Denning LJ was particularly concerned about notice being given by means of the wording on the ticket. He conducted a detailed examination of the exact time of the making of the contract with the machine and concluded that by the time Mr Thornton took the ticket, and so had chance to read it, the contract had already been made. Thus the existence of the clause was communicated too late and it was therefore invalid. He emphasised that split second timing is important when dealing with an automatic machine, as opposed to dealing with a person, because once the machine begins to operate it cannot be stopped and there is no going back: 'He may protest to the machine, even swear at it. But it will remain unmoved. He is committed beyond recall'.

However, Denning LJ's view was a minority one, and the other members of the Court of Appeal refused to express a view upon the precise moment of contract formation when using an automatic ticket machine. They emphasised the need for much more explicit steps to communicate the existence of a clause which was unusual and onerous. Indeed, Denning LJ expressed agreement with this view as an alternative to the approach adopted by him above: 'Assuming, however, that an automatic ticket machine is a booking clerk in disguise – so that the old-fashioned ticket cases still apply to it.'

You may be surprised at the variance between the decisions in *Thornton's* case and in *Thompson's* case (see above). After all, the court in each case is applying exactly the same test, as to reasonableness of communication, derived from *Parker v South East Railway Co.* to very similar facts and is arriving at a totally opposite conclusion.

Can you explain this disparity in view in *Thornton's* case and *Thompson's* case? A look at the dates of the respective decisions might prove helpful.

The answer probably lies in the nature of an objective or 'reasonable person' test. As society changes over the years then so do the standards of the reasonable person. In the 1970s there was greater emphasis placed on consumer protection by the law than back in the 1930s when the emphasis was more on freedom of contract. Thus more would need to be done **reasonably** to communicate the existence of the clause to a party to a contract in the 1970s than to a party in the 1930s, i.e. the 1930s decision assumes a contract made upon one party's standard terms and conditions to have been freely negotiated, and the parties to the contract to be of equal bargaining power; the 1970s decision recognises that such is not the case.

4.3.1.3 Course of dealing

Where it can be shown that there has been a consistent course of dealings, then even though no notice of the clause has been given on the occasion in question, the court may imply its presence in the contract, i.e. the parties will be deemed to have **constructive notice** of the clause from the previous dealings.

Spurling Ltd v *Bradshaw* [1956] 2 All ER 121
The defendant had stored goods at the plaintiff's warehouse over a number of years. On the occasion in question he left some barrels of orange juice to be stored, receiving the written documentation a few days later. This contained an exclusion clause. When the defendant collected the barrels they were empty. He refused to pay the storage charge and was sued. He counter-claimed for negligence and the exclusion clause was pleaded as a defence to the counter-claim. It was argued that the clause was not incorporated because it was communicated too late.

The clause was valid because it was deemed to be incorporated from the previous dealings between the parties. The defendant knew that the documentation would arrive subsequently and thus had constructive notice of the clause.

The course of dealings may be between the parties, as in the above case, or may be that accepted as customary in a particular trade or industry, as for example in *British Crane Hire Corporation Ltd* v *Ipswich Plant Hire Ltd* (discussed in **Chapter 3**). In either case the dealings must be consistent. In *McCutcheon* v *David MacBrayne Ltd* (**4.3.1.2**) the dealings were held not to be consistent because sometimes Mr McSporran was asked to sign the risk note and on other occasions he was not.

More difficult is the issue of whether there is a course of dealing or not. Consistency alone is not enough, and an element of frequency/regularity seems to come into operation. Thus, in *Hollier* v *Rambler Motors (AMC) Ltd* [1972] 1 All ER 399, involving the servicing and repair of a motor-car, three or four transactions over a period of five years was not deemed to be sufficient even though the same documentation had been issued on each of the previous occasions. It is significant, perhaps, that Mr Hollier was a consumer, and it should be easier to incorporate terms by reference to a course of dealing into a contract between two business people than into a contract between a business person and a consumer.

4.3.2 CONSTRUCTION

The judges scrutinise an exclusion clause very closely, and will declare it enforceable only if on its wording it covers the exact damage caused and the person who wishes to claim the protection of it. Thus, a clause which excludes liability for damage to red cars will be ineffective if the car damaged is a blue one.

A very strict approach is taken to ambiguous clauses. A valid clause must be clear and unequivocal. Any ambiguity will be interpreted against the person wishing to rely on the clause. This is known as the *contra proferentem* rule.

Houghton v *Trafalgar Insurance* [1954] 1 QB 247
A motor car insurance policy said the insurers would not be liable for damage caused 'whilst the car is carrying any load in excess of that for which it was constructed'. An accident occurred while six people were in a car designed to carry five. The insurers refused to pay, relying on the clause.

Can you identify the possible ambiguity? What is the decision likely to be as a consequence?

The word 'load' is ambiguous. It really refers to goods, not people. The clause therefore did not cover the carrying of excess **passengers**, and the insurance company had to pay.

Similarly, in *Thornton* v *Shoe Lane Parking* (see **4.3.1.2**), the notice at the entrance saying 'All cars parked at owners' risk' was interpreted as covering damage to cars and not damage to owners.

While the rule is enforced very strictly in relation to exclusion clauses, a more relaxed approach is adopted to limitation clauses. This is presumably because at least **some** liability is being accepted. See *Ailsa Craig Fishing Co.* v *Malvern Fishing Co.* [1983] 1 All ER 101, where a limitation clause covering 'failure in the provision of services' was held to apply even in a case of 'total' failure.

4.3.2.1   Exclusion of liability for negligence

Generally, unless, for example, a party contracts to take reasonable care of something, the liability imposed by a contract is known as **strict liability**. Thus a party is liable for breach even if that party had acted reasonably and could not help breaking the contract. However, a party may, in attempting to perform the contractual obligation, act negligently and thus be liable in the tort of negligence for damage caused by that negligence. Thus, in wrongly performing a contractual obligation a party may incur two types of liability: strict liability in contract and liability for the tort of negligence.

You should be able to see that a problem then arises. Where a clause excludes liability, which type of liability is being excluded – the strict liability or the negligence liability?

The logical conclusion is that the clause covers the strict liability in contract, i.e. because the clause is a term of the contract it must be referring to contract liability. Thus, if the clause makes no specific reference to negligence liability then that liability will not be excluded and the defendant will have to pay damages for negligence.

SAQ 46

White v *John Warwick Ltd* [1953] 2 All ER 1021
The plaintiff hired a bicycle from the defendant. When he rode it the saddle tilted forward and the plaintiff was injured. The defendant was in breach both of the contract of hire and of his duty of care in the tort of negligence reasonably to maintain the bike. A clause in the contract said 'nothing in this agreement shall render the owners liable for any personal injury'.

Does the clause apply only to strict liability in contract, or does it extend to the tort of negligence?

The clause as it stood covered strict liability for breach of contract only and thus damages for negligence could be recovered.

So in order to exclude liability for negligence it is necessary specifically to refer to negligence in the clause **or** to use words which cover all types of liability, such as 'howsoever, caused', 'no liability whatsoever' or 'sole risk'. The danger of so doing is to frighten off the other party from entering into the agreement. A canny compiler of an exclusion clause must balance the problem caused by the application of the construction rule against the danger of being too blunt and thus finishing without any contract!

A particularly extreme example of the application of the rule can be found in the next case:

Hollier v *Rambler Motors (AMC) Ltd* [1972] 1 All ER 399
The plaintiff left his car at the defendant's garage for repair. The garage was negligent and the car was badly damaged by fire. An exclusion clause said, 'the company is not responsible for damage caused by fire to customers' cars on the premises'.

The exclusion clause was not incorporated into the contract as insufficient notice had been given; but also, it would not have protected the defendant anyway.

The court said that a reasonable person would interpret the clause as excluding liability for non-negligently caused fire only, as no reasonable person would believe that the garage could totally avoid liability no matter how extreme their negligent conduct. Thus, since the clause covered non-negligently caused fire, and the car was damaged by negligently caused fire, the plaintiff could recover compensation as the clause did not cover the damage.

'It is arguable that this case has crossed the line between legitimate strict construction and illegitimate hostile construction.' (*Cheshire, Fifoot and Furmston's Law of Contract*, 12th ed., p. 165).

It surely would not be too difficult to argue that it was obvious that the defendant would not be liable in the absence of negligence and that, therefore, a reasonable person would interpret the clause as necessarily covering negligence.

To complicate things even further, if the only possible liability present is liability in negligence, then an exclusion clause may exclude liability for negligence **even if** it does not specifically mention negligence or use wider words covering negligence. This occurred in *Alderslade* v *Hendon Laundry Ltd* [1945] KB 189, where the plaintiff left articles with the defendant to be laundered. The defendant lost them. When the plaintiff claimed compensation the defendant wished to rely on a limitation clause which said: 'The maximum amount allowed for loss or damaged articles is 20 times the charge made for laundering.' It was held that the defendant's only liability here was in negligence; therefore the clause was valid and liability was limited.

SAQ 47

Is it possible to reconcile the decision in *Alderslade* with *Hollier* v *Rambler Motors*?

These decisions are difficult to reconcile. Perhaps a major difference between the cases is that *Alderslade* deals with a limitation clause rather than an exclusion clause and at least, therefore, **some** liability is being accepted.

If a party contracts to take reasonable care or to exercise reasonable care and skill etc., he can break the contract only by failing to take reasonable care, i.e. negligently, and he thus commits a negligent breach of contract. So the only basis of liability is negligence, and any exclusion clause can only apply to negligence.

It is important to remember that most students find the rules of construction difficult to comprehend and many of the decisions in the different cases difficult to reconcile. Despite having said that the **reasonableness** of the clause should not be relevant in deciding its validity, the common thread running through the decisions is that the more unreasonable the clause is, the more likely it is that it will be construed very strictly and so as not to be valid.

A clue as to the thinking of the judiciary on this matter is to be found in the judgment of Lord Denning MR in the Court of Appeal hearing of *Mitchell (George) (Chesterhall) Ltd v Finney Lock Seeds Ltd* [1983] 1 All ER 108. This was Lord Denning's very last judgment and it is essential reading. He said:

> Faced with this abuse of power, by the strong against the weak, by the use of the small print of the conditions, the judges did what they could to put a curb on it. They still had before them the idol, 'freedom of contract'. They still knelt down and worshipped it, but they concealed under their cloaks a secret weapon. They used it to stab the idol in the back. This weapon was called 'the true construction of the contract'. They used it with great skill and ingenuity. They used it so as to depart from the natural meaning of the words of the exemption clause and to put on them a strained and unnatural construction. In case after case, they said that the words were not strong enough to give the big concern exemption from liability, so that in the circumstances the big concern was not entitled to rely on the exemption clause. . . . But when the clause was itself reasonable and gave rise to a reasonable result, the judges upheld it, . . .

You can read a fuller version of this judgment in *Cases and Materials* (**4.1.2.1**).

4.3.2.2   Third parties and exclusion clauses

In addition to covering the damage, a clause must cover the person wishing to claim its protection if it is to be enforceable by that person. Under the doctrine of privity of contract, only a party to a contract can incur rights or obligations under it. Thus a third party to a contract may not be able to take the protection of an exclusion clause contained within that contract even if the clause purports to protect that person.

Adler v *Dickson & Another* [1955] 1 QB 158
The plaintiff was travelling as a first class passenger on board a ship. When the ship was in dock she walked up the gangplank which collapsed. She fell 16 feet down to the wharf below and was injured. A clause in the contract said, 'the Company will not be responsible for any injury whatsoever to the person of any passenger arising from or occasioned by the negligence of the Company's servants'. She sued the captain and the boatswain for negligence.

On its wording, the clause excluded only the liability of the Company. Thus the plaintiff could recover damages from the two defendants. However, the majority of the Court (Denning LJ dissenting) said that even if the clause **had** included the crew they could not have gained its protection because they were not parties to the contract between Mrs Adler and the Company.

This majority view was followed subsequently by the House of Lords in *Scruttons Ltd v Midland Silicones Ltd* [1962] 2 All ER 1, Denning LJ again dissenting, although it is arguable that this is not the *ratio* of the case, i.e. the American cases relied upon are decided on the ground that the clause did not purport to extend its benefit to strangers to the contract.

Third parties were held entitled to rely upon an exclusion clause contained in a contract to which they were not parties in *New Zealand Shipping Co. Ltd v Satterthwaite & Co. Ltd (The Eurymedon)* [1974] 1 All ER 1015. However, the decision of the Privy Council seems to rest heavily upon agency principles and the special facts of the case.

4.3.2.3 Fundamental breach

Even if the exclusion clause **is** incorporated and seemingly covers the damage, its validity may be affected where the person wishing to rely on the protection of the clause commits a fundamental breach of the contract. In such cases the clause may be declared ineffective.

It would be ludicrous, for example, if a person who had contracted to supply a motor car supplied a bicycle instead and then sought to rely on an exclusion clause to avoid any liability. The classic example used over the years is that a person is in fundamental breach if he contracts to supply peas and instead supplied beans.

Karsales (Harrow) Ltd v Wallis [1956] 2 All ER 866
The defendant examined a car at a dealers and decided to buy it. A clause in the written contract said, 'no condition or warranty that the vehicle is roadworthy or as to its condition or fitness for any purpose is given by the owner or implied therein'. Subsequently, a vehicle was delivered to the defendant which resembled the one which he had examined. However, when he tried to start it he discovered that the engine had major defects. The cylinder head was broken, as were two pistons, and all the valves were burnt out. He refused to pay the instalments on the car and was sued. In defence he pleaded the state of the car, but the plaintiffs claimed reliance on the exclusion clause.

The vehicle which was delivered was essentially different from that which was contracted for and therefore the exclusion clause could not be relied upon.

The major problem inherent in the application of the rule is establishing whether a breach is fundamental. It seems that a breach of condition is not necessarily sufficient – the doctrine requires a more serious breach amounting to non-performance. Partly because of this problem the courts adopted the doctrine with different degrees of enthusiasm.

One judge who enthusiastically applied the rule was Lord Denning. Throughout the 1960s and 1970s he evolved the doctrine into **a rule of law**, i.e. a fundamental breach automatically nullified the validity of an exclusion clause as a rule of law.

The House of Lords was more cautious. In *Suisse Atlantique Société d'Armement SA v NV Rotterdamsche Kolen Centrale* [1967] 1 AC 361, it declared, *obiter*, that the doctrine was a rule of construction only and not a rule of law. It further held that a very clearly worded clause that intended to exclude liability for a particular breach would do so even if the breach was fundamental. Despite this, the Court of Appeal, inspired by Lord Denning, throughout the 1970s continually treated the doctrine as a rule of law.

As *Cheshire, Fifoot and Furmston* says, 'this indiscipline was firmly corrected' in the case of *Photo Productions Ltd v Securicor Transport Ltd* [1980] 1 All ER 556. The defendants offered several contracts giving different standards of protection provided by security visits to the plaintiff's premises. The plaintiff accepted a contract at a particular price for specified protection. An exclusion clause in the contract said that Securicor would not 'be responsible for any injurious act or default by any employee . . . unless such act or default could have been foreseen and avoided by the exercise of due diligence' by the defendant.

During a security visit an employee of Securicor started a small fire. This rapidly spread and burnt down the whole factory, causing about £615,000 damage. You may consider that this was definitely a fundamental breach!

Securicor wished to rely on the exclusion clause, but the Court of Appeal said (not surprisingly) that the clause was ineffective because of the fundamental breach. However, on appeal the House of Lords said it is a question of construction as to whether an exclusion clause is nullified by a fundamental breach. Lord Wilberforce said that between parties of **equal bargaining power** 'there is everything to be said . . . for leaving the parties free to apportion the risks as they think fit, and for respecting their decisions'.

Thus it is clear that the doctrine of fundamental breach is a **rule of construction**, and that in construing the clause the intention of the parties is of paramount importance.

SAQ 48

What factors can you think of which the House of Lords might have found relevant in determining the intentions of the parties?

In determining the intentions of the parties, the court found two factors to be particularly relevant. First, the parties had equal bargaining power and could easily have negotiated an agreement without the clause, but chose not to do so. In fact, subsequent to the case, they negotiated a new agreement without the clause (presumably also without the particular employee!). Secondly, the insurance factor was introduced. It is far easier to fix the premium on property insurance than on employer liability insurance, and thus in allocating the risk it would be normal for property owners to accept liability, as was held to be the case here.

You might think that where the parties have unequal bargaining power then a different approach to construction might be adopted. However, the whole issue has now been superseded by the passing of the Unfair Contract Terms Act 1977. Under this Act many exclusion clauses are either void or are subject at least to a test of reasonableness. It is highly unlikely that a court will find it reasonable to exclude liability for fundamental breach except in exceptional circumstances such as those in the *Photo Productions* case.

It is widely believed that since the enactment of the Unfair Contract Terms Act 1977 fundamental breach is no longer very significant. Why is this so?

The answer centres on reasonableness. When faced with a truly oppressive clause the court is not likely to spend its time on matters of 'strained construction' when the validity of the clause can be dealt with quite readily under the reasonableness test laid down by the Unfair Contract Terms Act 1977.

4.4   The Unfair Contract Terms Act 1977

Despite its name the Act does not apply to unfair terms generally but only to exclusion clauses. Furthermore, it is not confined to contract terms; it also extends to non-contractual notices containing provisions exempting from liability in tort.

4.4.1   AIMS AND SCOPE OF THE ACT

The first thing you should notice is that the Act does not purport to affect the basis of liability. Thus, the first question you should ask is whether the person seeking to exclude liability is actually under any liability for breach of contract or for the tort of negligence. Therefore, prior to using the Act, you must apply the common law rules, viz. is the clause a term of the contract? If so, precisely construed, does that clause cover that for which it purports to exclude liability?

If the Act applies the clause may be rendered **void** or subject to the **reasonableness** test. In general the Act applies only to attempts to exclude **business liability**. We shall see what this means shortly.

Some of the provisions overlap, i.e. certain situations are covered by more than one section. You will need to examine the relevant sections and identify which one puts the 'innocent party' in the best position.

Students often find the Act difficult to understand, but the key to mastering it is to have a good working knowledge of **ss. 2, 3, 6, 7, 11, 12** and the **sch. 2 guidelines**, and to know the difference between dealing as a consumer and business dealing.

Sections 2 and 3 are general sections covering many types of contract, whereas ss. 6 and 7 cover only contracts under which goods change hands.

Where the Act does not apply, for example where one consumer deals with another consumer, then the clause will be valid subject to the application of the common law rules discussed above.

4.4.2   VARIETIES OF EXEMPTION CLAUSES

In general the Act applies only to terms which 'exclude or restrict' liability. However, s. 13 extends the ambit of the Act to terms, for example, which make the liability or its enforcement subject to restrictive or onerous conditions, or which, though not excluding or restricting liability themselves, make reference to words which do. An example of this would be terms requiring a party to make a claim within a certain time limit; or statements that an architect's certificate shall be conclusive evidence that building work has been properly carried out.

4.4.3   BUSINESS LIABILITY

As we noted above, substantially the Act applies only to **business liability**.

Section 1(3) defines 'business liability' as liability for things done or to be done in the course of a business, and liability arising from the occupation of business premises.

Section 14 defines 'business' broadly (not an exhaustive definition). It includes not only the normal meaning of commercial activity, but also activities of the professions, government departments and local or public authorities.

4.4.3.1   Liability for negligence

Section 2 covers liability for negligence, which includes liability both in the tort of negligence and also breach of an obligation to take reasonable care in the performance of a contract (s. 1).

Section 2(1) states that business liability for death or personal injury resulting from negligence **cannot** be excluded or restricted by any contract term or notice.

What would be the effect of s. 2(1) upon cases like *Thompson* **v** *LMS* **or** *Thornton* **v** *Shoe Lane Parking*?

You might say that it follows that exclusion clauses similar to those in *Thompson* v *LMS* or *Thornton* v *Shoe Lane Parking* would immediately be invalid under s. 2(1).

Section 2(2) states that in the case of 'other loss or damage' caused by negligence the clause must satisfy the test of **reasonableness**. This subsection covers damage to property or financial loss. Clauses similar to those in *McCutcheon* v *MacBrayne* and *Olley* v *Marlborough Court* would be subjected to a test of reasonableness to determine their validity (if they had been validly incorporated in the first place).

4.4.3.2 Liability for breach of contract

Section 3 applies to liability for breach of contract which does not fall within the ambit of ss. 6 and 7. It applies in two situations only:

(a) where one of the parties deals as a consumer; or

(b) where one of the parties deals on the other's written standard terms of business.

You may be able to see that these two possibilities frequently overlap. Consumer' is defined in s. 12.

If s. 3 applies the clause is subject to the **reasonableness** test.

Therefore, the section covers business/consumer contracts and business/business contracts made on one party's written standard terms. It follows that clauses similar to those in *Olley* v *Marlborough Court* (if incorporated) and *Photo Productions* v *Securicor* would each respectively be covered by s. 3 and therefore be subject to the reasonableness test.

Assuming that the above prerequisites are satisfied, s. 3(2)(a) is very wide and deals with attempts to exclude liability for **breach** of contract. Section 3(2)(b), however, deals with what might be described as 'disguised' exclusion clauses where there is **no apparent breach** of contract. It deals with attempts to reserve the right to vary contractual performance or to render no performance at all, which are treated by the Act as exclusion clauses.

It follows from this that a party cannot claim, by reference to any contract term, to be entitled:

(a) to render a contractual performance substantially different from that which was reasonably expected; or

(b) in respect of the whole or any part of the contractual obligation, to render no performance at all.

But s. 3(2)(b) goes on to provide a caveat (which applies to both s. 3(2)(a) and s. 3(2)(b)) in the following terms: 'Except in so far as . . . the contract term satisfies the requirement of reasonableness.'

SAQ 51

Can you think of any practical examples of this type of clause inserted into contracts which you have made? Write them down below.

You may have found s. 3(2)(b) in contracts often favoured by holiday tour operators: 'Steamers, Sailing Dates, Rates and Itineraries are subject to change without prior notice' (*Anglo-Continental Holiday* v *Typaldos (London) Ltd* [1967] 2 Lloyd's Rep 61). Also, they are often present in contracts for sporting events, e.g., no refunds if there is more than 30 minutes' play at a cricket match.

4.4.3.3   Contracts for the sale of goods and hire purchase contracts

Section 6 covers contracts for the sale of goods and hire purchase contracts. It relates to liability for breach of those terms implied into a contract by the Sale of Goods Act 1979, ss. 12 to 15, and similar legislation. (See **Chapter 3**.)

The implied condition that the seller has the right to sell (s. 12) can **never** be excluded.

The implied conditions as to description, satisfactory quality, fitness for purpose and corresponding to sample (ss. 13 to 15) can **never** be excluded as against a person dealing as a **consumer**. As regards **persons other than consumers**, clauses excluding such liability are subject to a test of **reasonableness**. We can conclude that whereas **consumers** have **total protection, business people** have **reasonable protection**.

4.4.3.4   Contracts which are not for the sale of goods

Section 7 applies to **miscellaneous contracts under which goods change hands** but which are **not** contracts for the **sale** of goods, e.g., a contract for work to be done and for materials to be supplied to do the work.

By virtue of the Supply of Goods and Services Act 1982, such contracts are to contain implied terms similar to those implied into contracts for sales of goods. The provisions of s. 7 therefore are identical to those of s. 6, and as against a **consumer**, liability for breach of those implied terms can **never** be excluded. However, as against **persons other than consumers**, clauses excluding such liability are subject to a test of **reasonableness**.

The exclusion clause position has been explained here where loss is caused by defective goods supplied under the contract. To which section would you turn to determine the validity of an exclusion clause where the loss has been caused by the provision of defective services? Before you answer, read s. 13 of the Supply of Goods and Services Act 1982 in *Cases and Materials* (4.2).

Section 13 of the Supply of Goods and Services Act 1982 implies a term that the services shall be carried out with reasonable care and skill. Thus, such an implied term can be breached only negligently. Therefore, you should turn to the relevant subsection of s. 2.

4.4.3.5 Summary

Sections 2, 3, 6, and 7 are then the most important provisions of the 1977 Act prior to the application of the reasonableness test and it is essential to 'know them backwards'. To apply them to a problem situation we need only answer some simple questions:

Do goods change hands under the contract?

If the answer is yes, then we immediately look at ss. 6 and 7. We then need to know whether the contract is a **sale** of goods or hire purchase (s. 6), or a **miscellaneous** contract under which goods are supplied (s. 7). Lastly, to decide whether the clause is void or subject to a test of reasonableness, we need to know whether the contract is business/consumer or business/business.

If the answer is no, then we ask the next question:

Is there negligence involved?

If the answer is yes, then we look at the provisions of s. 2. If the damage is death or personal injury then the clause is **void**. If other damage is suffered then it is subject to a test of **reasonableness**.

If the answer is no, then we ask our final question:

Is there liability for breach of contract?

If the answer is yes, then we look at the provisions of s. 3. This section only applies in two situations – business/consumer and business/business on written standard terms. If the section does apply then the clause is subject to a test of reasonableness.

If the answer to this final question is also no, then the provisions of the 1977 Act do not apply.

You will find it helpful to look at the flow-chart in **Figure 2** at the end of this chapter.

4.4.4 DEALING AS A CONSUMER

In the application of the provisions of the Act, you will find that it will be necessary to decide whether a person is dealing as a consumer. The definition is to be found in s. 12, and we examine that now.

A person deals as a consumer if:

    (a)   he neither makes the contract in the course of a business nor holds himself out as doing so; **and**

    (b)   the other party does make the contract in the course of a business; **and**

    (c)   in the case of a contract involving the sale or hire of goods, the goods passing under or in pursuance of the contract are of a type ordinarily supplied for private use or consumption.

The burden of proof is on the person who claims that the other party is **not** a consumer.

It would appear that a transaction will be a consumer transaction unless it is made in the course of a business, and is an integral part of the business itself and not merely incidental thereto.

R & B Customs Brokers Co. Ltd v *United Dominions Trust* [1988] 1 All ER 847
The plaintiff company's business was that of freight forwarding and shipping agent. It purchased a second-hand Colt Shogun car for the personal and business use of its directors. There was a breach of the term implied by s. 14(3) of the Sale of Goods Act 1979, in that the roof had an incurable leak and the upholstery became 'sodden with water, mouldy and evil smelling'. The contract contained an exclusion clause.

Was this a consumer or a business transaction? Give reasons for your decision.

The clause did not apply since the transaction was a consumer transaction. There was an insufficient degree of regularity of dealing to make the transaction an integral part of the company's business.

4.5   The Reasonableness Test

The problem with any reasonableness test is uncertainty and unpredictability, so that we will find it difficult to predict with any degree of certainty whether a particular clause would be deemed reasonable or not. What you can expect to be able to do is to follow the appropriate procedure, identify the relevant matters and to weigh the pros and cons of reasonableness or otherwise in the context of whatever factual situation confronts you. You should bear in mind that under s. 11(5) the burden of proof in respect of reasonableness lies on the party seeking to rely upon the exclusion clause, and that under s. 11(1) the clause must be a fair and reasonable one to have included **at the time of entering into** the contract.

You should be aware that we are not concerned with the actual damage suffered and the circumstances of the breach, but with the fairness of the bargain when actually struck. Accordingly the potential loss sufferable and potential circumstances in which breach might occur as contemplated by the parties are much more relevant.

Section 11(2) refers the court to the Sch. 2 guidelines on reasonableness when the contract is one covered by s. 6 or s. 7 of the 1977 Act. Even in that context the guidelines are not exhaustive, being matters to which the court must give first regard. However, it seems likely that the courts will refer to the guidelines in all cases when applying the reasonableness test and not limit them to s. 6 or s. 7 contracts.

4.5.1 SCHEDULE 2 GUIDELINES

The issues to which a court will have regard are as follows:

(a) The relative strength of the bargaining position of the parties, and alternative means by which the customer's requirements could have been met. The second part of this is geared to the issue of how far the supplier is in a monopolistic position.

(b) Whether an inducement was given to agree to the term and whether a similar contract could have been made with another person without the term. In *RW Green Ltd* v *Cade Brothers Farms* [1978] 1 Lloyd's Rep 602, a limitation clause relating to uncertified seed potatoes was upheld because the purchasers could have bought certified seed at a higher price.

(c) Whether the customer knew or ought reasonably to know of the existence and extent of the term. Clearly there is a connection with the incorporation test here, and therefore most clauses which are actually incorporated will probably be reasonable under this guideline. However, reasonableness might be more debatable where the incorporation test operates harshly, e.g., incorporation by previous dealing on the basis of constructive notice or cases of signed contracts like *L'Estrange* v *Graucob Ltd*.

(d) Where the term excludes or restricts liability if some condition is not complied with, the issue is whether compliance with that condition was practicable. In *RW Green Ltd* v *Cade Brother Farms* (above) it was held unreasonable to require any claim to be notified within three days since the potato virus could not be detected until the crop started to grow.

(e) Whether the goods were manufactured etc. to the special order of the customer. If a customer lays down the specification to which the product must be manufactured, it is probably reasonable for the manufacturer to exclude most obligations other than conformity with specification.

Section 11(4) provides two factors which are particularly relevant to the reasonableness of **limitation** clauses:

(a) The resources available to the party limiting the liability. Clearly the smaller his resources the more reasonable the limitation of liability.

(b) How far it was open to him to cover himself by insurance. The cases show that the availability and cost of insurance are important factors generally, not only in relation to limitation clauses.

4.5.2 CASE LAW ON REASONABLENESS

There are not many reported cases on the reasonableness test, because the test consists of a large element of fact marshalled by a few legal rules. According to Lord Bridge in *George Mitchell (Chesterhall) Ltd* v *Finney Lock Seeds Ltd* [1983] 2 All ER 737, 'the appellate court should treat the original decision with the utmost respect and refrain from interference with it unless satisfied that it proceeded on some erroneous principle or was plainly and obviously wrong'. Furthermore, the Court of Appeal in *Phillips Products Ltd* v *Hyland* [1987] 2 All ER 620 (following the remarks of Lord Bridge in *George Mitchell*) stated that such decisions should not be of precedental value because each case depends upon its own particular circumstances, i.e. although the clause may be similar the evidence of surrounding circumstances may be very different.

On the other hand, in *Smith* v *Eric S Bush* [1989] 2 All ER 514, the House of Lords seems deliberately to have sought to lay down a general rule on the unacceptability of exclusions of liability by professional surveyors towards purchasers in domestic housing transactions, whilst reserving its position with regard to exclusions involving surveys of business property.

A good illustration of the reasonableness test in operation is found in the following case:

George Mitchell (Chesterhall) Ltd v *Finney Lock Seeds Ltd* [1983] 2 All ER 737
The respondent farmers purchased from the appellant seed merchants a quantity of Dutch winter white cabbage seed, described as 'Finney's Late Dutch Special' for a price of £201. The appellants supplied seed of a variety of autumn cabbage and of very inferior quality. The respondent's crop failed causing a loss of approximately £61,500. When sued, the appellants argued that they were protected by a clause in their standard conditions of sale limiting liability to the replacement of the defective seeds or refunding payment.

The clause was unreasonable.

ACTIVITY 17

Read Lord Bridge's speech in *George Mitchell* v *Finney Lock Seeds Ltd*. List under (a)–(d) below the factors deemed by him to be relevant in determining the reasonableness of the clause. Answers in *Cases and Materials* (4.3).

(a)

(b)

(c)

(d)

An interesting case on the reasonableness test follows:

St. Albans City & District Council v *International Computers Ltd* [1996] 4 All ER 481
The defendants, a computer firm, supplied the plaintiff local authority with a database for the community charge register. A clause in the contract limited the defendants' liability for loss to £100,000. When the plaintiffs extracted the population figures from the database to be returned to the Department of the Environment the population was overstated by 2,966 owing to an error in the software. The consequences were disastrous. The community charge rate was set too low, which was recouped by setting a higher rate in the following year, and there were other, more serious financial consequences. The total loss amounted to £1,314,846. The defendants purported to rely upon the limitation clause.

The clause fell within the ambit of s. 3 of the Unfair Contract Terms Act 1977 because of the defendant's 'written standard terms of business' and also within s. 6 or s. 7. Consequently, the reasonableness test applied.

In an application of both s. 11(4) and the sch. 2 guidelines Scott Baker J concluded that the determining factors were:

(a)   the parties were of unequal bargaining power;

(b)   the defendants had not justified a figure of £100,000, which was small both in relation to the potential risk and the actual loss;

(c)   the defendants were insured in an aggregate sum of £50 million worldwide; and

(d)   the practical consequences.

In relation to factor (d):

(i)   it was better that the loss fell on an international computer company, which was well able to insure and was insured, and which could pass on the premium to its customers than

(ii)   on the local authority where ultimately the loss would be borne by the local population by increased taxes or reduced services

(iii) he who makes the profit should carry the risk.

These factors were said to outweigh the facts:

(iv)   that bodies such as computer companies and local authorities should be free to make their own bargains

(v)   the plaintiffs contracted with their eyes open

(vi)   such limitations were commonplace in the computer industry and

(vii) the software involved was in an area of developing technology.

The approach to the limitation clause was upheld by the Court of Appeal, though damages were reduced by some £484,000 on another ground.

4.6   The Unfair Terms in Consumer Contracts Regulations 1994

4.6.1   BACKGROUND

The Unfair Terms in Consumer Contracts Regulations came into force on 1 July 1995, and were enacted in response to a Directive from the European Commission designed to produce a common set of rules for assessing the fairness of standard form clauses in consumer contracts throughout the European Union.

The European Commission Directive was based upon German legislation and covers much of the ground covered in the Unfair Contract Terms Act 1977. There are, however, significant differences, both in scope and in approach.

The government had two options when deciding upon implementation: it could have amended the Unfair Contract Terms Act 1977 or enacted the Directive by regulations, leaving the Unfair Contract Terms Act 1977 untouched. In choosing the latter approach a can of worms has been opened in that both sets of rules must be considered where both apply.

4.6.2 SCOPE

The 1994 Regulations prohibit the use of unfair terms in consumer contracts which have not been individually negotiated. They apply to contracts between a consumer and a seller or supplier (of goods or services). Regulation 2 defines a consumer as a natural person, contracting for purposes outside his trade, business or profession. Sellers and suppliers are those who are dealing for purposes related to their trade, business or profession, whether publicly or privately owned.

Return to *R & B Customs Brokers* **v** *UDT* **above at 4.4.4. Write down below how the interpretation of consumer for the purposes of the Unfair Contract Terms Act 1977 differs from the definition of consumer in the 1994 Regulations.**

The definition in the 1994 Regulations (natural person) is narrower than the 1977 Act which could protect companies acting outside their normal business.

The 1994 Regulations do not apply to employment contracts, contracts relating to succession, family law, or the incorporation and organisation of companies and partnerships. They do apply to all other consumer contracts (including insurance contracts, which are excluded from the scope of the Act) and including contracts for the sale of land between a builder and a domestic purchaser.

WHICH CONTRACTS ARE COVERED?	
In addition to contracts for the sale of goods or supply of services the following categories of contract are covered by the 1994 Regulations:	The following types of contract are specifically excluded from the 1994 Regulations:
■ Contracts for the sale of land. ■ Contracts of insurance. ■ Contracts for the provision of financial services. ■ Take over bids. ■ Foreign exchange transactions. ■ Tenancy agreements. ■ Mortgages and other legal charges.	■ Contracts of employment. ■ Contracts relating to family law rights. ■ Contracts relating to rights of succession. ■ Contracts relating to the incorporation and organisation of companies or partnerships. ■ Terms in insurance contracts defining the insured risk and the insurer's liability.

4.6.3 TERMS TO WHICH THE 1994 REGULATIONS APPLY (TERMS NOT INDIVIDUALLY NEGOTIATED)

Under reg. 3 a term shall always be regarded as not having been individually negotiated where it has been drafted in advance and the consumer has not been able to influence the substance of the term. The burden of proof is on the seller/supplier to show that a term has been individually negotiated.

If an overall assessment of the contract indicates that it is a pre-formulated standard contract, it is no defence to claim that some of the terms in the contract have been negotiated, if the term in question has not. So the fact that in a hire-purchase agreement the parties negotiate the precise repayment period and thus the instalments will not prevent other non-negotiated terms being treated as unfair.

A term will not be subject to attack under the 1994 Regulations if it is a term incorporated in order to comply with a statutory provision; the statute prevails.

4.6.4 UNFAIR TERMS

Under reg. 4 'unfair term' means any term which contrary to the requirement of good faith causes a significant imbalance in the parties' rights and obligations under the contract to the detriment of the consumer.

There is no presumption of unfairness. The court must consider all the circumstances, including the nature of the transaction and the other terms of the contract.

The most important feature here is the concept of 'good faith' which in English law is not an established, well-defined and generally used concept. It is hardly a surprising concept to be included since the Directive was based on the German statute. The meaning to be attached to 'good faith' is of considerable significance. The 1994 Regulations give little guidance on the matter. Schedule 2 provides that in making an assessment of good faith, regard shall be had in particular to:

- the strength of the bargaining position of the parties;

- whether the consumer had an inducement to agree to the term;

- whether the goods or services were sold or supplied to the special order of the consumer;

- the extent to which the seller or supplier has dealt fairly and equitably with the consumer.

Where have you seen similar guidelines before? If a similar approach were adopted to the area in which you have seen the guidelines before what would the test be?

Yes, the guidelines are very similar to those contained in the Unfair Contract Terms Act 1977, and perhaps, on this view, 'good faith' can be equated to 'reasonableness' under the 1977 Act.

However, the preamble to the Directive makes reference to good faith involving 'an overall evaluation' of the different interests involved. 'Good faith' is capable of a much wider definition, which would springboard the desire to tackle the notion of the unconscionability of unfair contracts. English law so far has policed this area by a variety of doctrines such as duress, undue influence, restraint of trade and illegality. What we could see here is a move away from *caveat emptor* (let the buyer beware; see **Chapter Six**) towards a regulation of behaviour during the bargaining process, and the establishment of a duty to deal openly and fairly, or a duty to trade fairly.

The concept of 'significant imbalance' also lacks precision. It could well be argued that a large number of contracts quite naturally contain an imbalance between the parties' rights and obligations but which are not detrimental. The addition of the word 'significant' adds a useful qualification, but it is still possible for a contract to contain 'significant imbalance' which may be 'reasonable' under the 1977 Act, but still fail the wider interpretation of 'good faith' under the 1994 Regulations.

In addition, in assessing whether a term is unfair, the following factors must be taken into account:

(a)   the nature of the goods or services for which the contract was concluded;

(b)   the circumstances surrounding the conclusion of the contract;

(c)   all the other terms of the contract or of any other contract on which it is dependent.

These factors are relevant as guidelines only and any particular term in any particular contract will have to be assessed on its own merits. In contrast to the Unfair Contract Terms Act 1977, where the burden of proof of reasonableness rests upon the person seeking to reply upon the term, the 1994 Regulations require a consumer to show that a term is unfair.

The Regulations provide some assistance by including in sch. 3 an indicative and illustrative list of terms which **may** (but not necessarily must) be regarded as unfair. There are 17 examples in the list in all, all expressed in very general language.

EXAMPLES OF POTENTIALLY UNFAIR TERMS	
Terms included in sch. 3	**Examples**
Excluding/limiting liability of a seller/supplier for death/personal injury of a consumer due to negligence of seller/supplier.	Excluding/limiting liability for negligent servicing of an electrical tool which electrocutes the consumer upon usage.
Requiring the consumer to perform all his obligations where the seller/supplier does not perform his.	Obligations to pay a maintenance or service fee, but with exclusions for interruptions in or failure to provide a service by the supplier.
Enabling seller/supplier to alter contractual performance unilaterally without a valid reason specified in the contract.	Tour operator reserving the right to switch hotels/resorts for unspecified reasons.
Irrevocably binding the consumer to terms with which he had no real opportunity of becoming acquainted before the conclusion of the contract.	Clauses in service agreements requiring compliance with terms which are not delivered to the consumer until after the contract has been concluded.

4.6.5 CORE PROVISIONS

In accordance with reg. 3 the unfair term must not be the definition of the main subject matter of the contract, nor may the adequacy of the price and remuneration, on the one hand, as against the services or goods supplied in exchange, on the other be assessed, so long as these are expressed in plain, intelligible language.

Apart from the interesting issue of what is to be treated as the main subject-matter of the contract (the CD player only or the accessories too?) other questions can be asked here.

Can the fairness of core provisions ever be called into question? Write your answer in the space below.

Yes, the clear implication is that where core provisions are not in plain, intelligible language even their fairness can be called into question.

Is the unfairness test relevant to whether the consumer is getting 'value for money'?

No, normally the test does not relate to questions of 'value for money' provided that the contract explains what is being provided and the price in plain, intelligible language.

4.6.6 THE CONSEQUENCES OF UNFAIRNESS

If a term is deemed to be unfair, it will not be binding on the consumer. However, it is the individual term which is invalid, not the contract as a whole. The contract itself is to continue to bind the parties, so long as it is capable of continuing in existence without the unfair term (reg. 5).

Can you devise a test which might be adopted to determine whether the contract is capable of continuing in existence without the unfair term?

Unfortunately, the Regulations themselves provide no guidance whatsoever. Have a look at the doctrine of severance as applied to contracts in restraint of trade in **Chapter Six**, which provides a possible approach.

Regulation 6 requires the seller/supplier to ensure that any written term of a contract is expressed in plain, intelligible language. If there is any doubt about the meaning of a written term, the interpretation most favourable to the consumer shall prevail. Most insurance companies are rapidly redrafting!

4.6.7 PREVENTION OF CONTINUED USE OF UNFAIR TERMS

Regulation 8 provides that the Director General of Fair Trading shall consider any complaint made to him about the fairness of any contract term drawn up for general use.

He may, if he considers it appropriate to do so, seek an injunction to prevent the continued use of that term or a term having like effect in contracts drawn up for general use by a party to the proceedings. In addition, the Director General is given the power to arrange for the dissemination of information and advice concerning the operation of the Regulations.

4.6.8 INTERRELATIONSHIP BETWEEN THE REGULATIONS AND THE UNFAIR CONTRACT TERMS ACT 1977

As was pointed out earlier (**4.6.4**) there is considerable overlap between the two at least as far as exclusion/limitation clauses are concerned. A particular exclusion/limitation clause may fall foul of both pieces of legislation, or may satisfy the reasonableness test under the 1977 Act but not the good faith and significant imbalance test under the Regulations, or vice-versa.

Can you draft a table illustrating clauses or contracts to which the 1977 Act applies and the Regulations do not, and vice-versa? Use the space below or draft your table on a separate sheet of paper.

Hopefully, you will have come up with something like this:

A Comparison of the 1994 Regulations and the 1977 Act	
The 1994 Regulations	**The 1977 Act**
■ Apply to all clauses (other than core provisions drafted in plain and intelligible language).	■ Applies only to exclusion/limitation clauses.
■ Apply to contracts with individual consumers only.	■ Can apply to contracts with companies and partnerships.
■ Apply only to non-individually negotiated clauses.	■ Can apply to negotiated clauses.
■ Apply to contracts for the sale of land and insurance contracts.	■ Doesn't apply to contracts for the sale of land and insurance contracts.

4.6.9 APPLYING THE 1994 REGULATIONS

You may find the following flow-chart to be of considerable assistance in your voyage of discovery through turbulent waters:

Figure 1   Applying the Unfair Terms in Consumer Contracts Regulations 1994

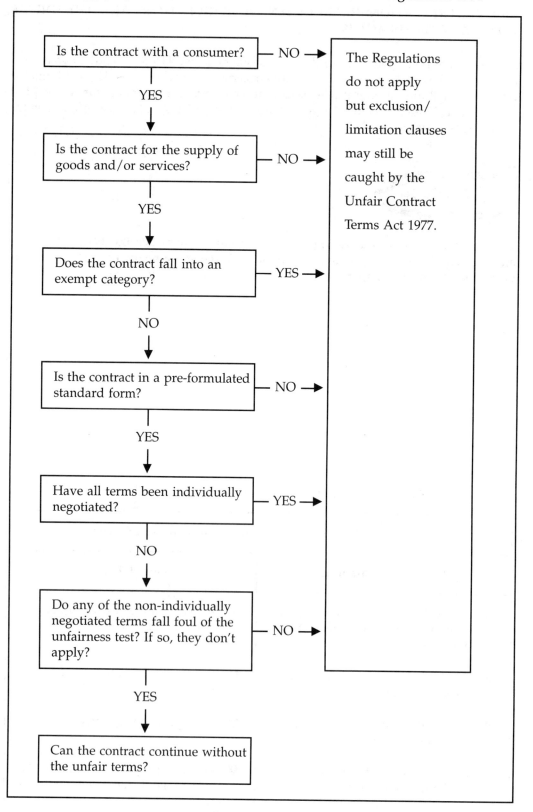

4.7 Conclusion

An exclusion/limitation clause should always be examined initially from a common law perspective. You should ask yourself the following questions:

(a) Has the clause been incorporated into the contract by some reasonable form of notice?

(b) Does the clause, construed strictly *contra proferentem*, cover the type of liability in question?

(c) Is the person seeking to rely upon the clause a party to the contract containing the clause?

If there is any possibility that the answers to the three questions above may be affirmative, the impact of the Unfair Contract Terms Act 1977 must be considered. Dependent upon the type of contract and the type of clause in question, the effect of the Act will be to render the clause invalid or to subject it to the reasonableness test. If the Unfair Terms in Consumer Contracts Regulations 1994 apply the term in question will not bind the consumer but he will continue to be bound by the rest of the contract if it is capable of continuing in existence without the unfair term.

It is hoped that you will find reference to **Figure 2** to be of some assistance in navigating the difficult waters of the Unfair Contract Terms Act 1977.

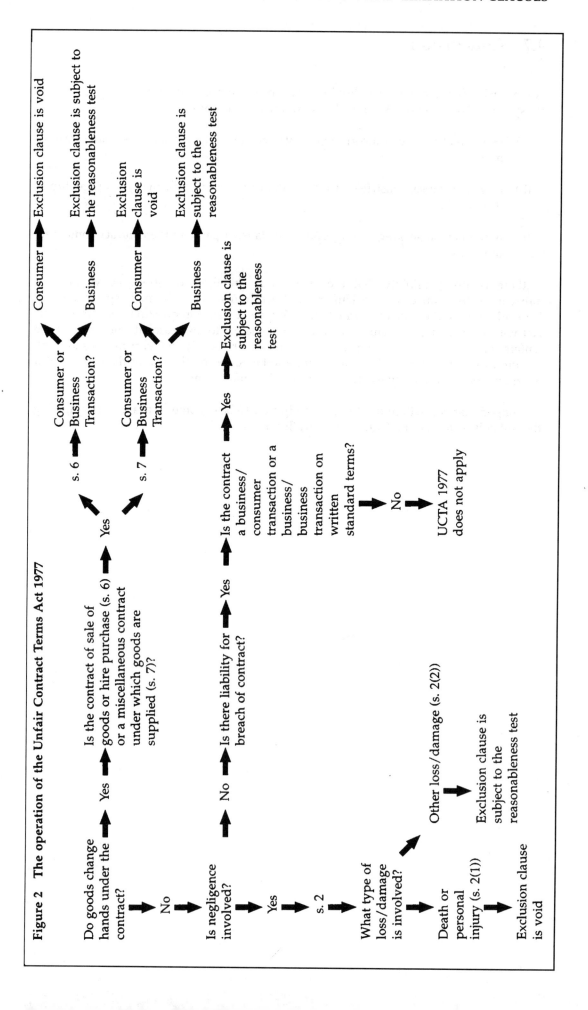

Figure 2   The operation of the Unfair Contract Terms Act 1977

4.8 End of Chapter Assessment Question

Janet, a 20-year-old law student, went to the Albert Bus Station to catch a coach home to Doncaster. She had made this journey from time to time in the past. Above the ticket-office window of the Trentshire Bus Company was a sign which stated that all tickets were issued subject to conditions displayed inside the coaches. Janet purchased a ticket which made no reference to any conditions.

While boarding the coach the driver carelessly knocked Janet's camera from her hand and the lens was broken.

One of the terms displayed inside the coach was as follows:

Passengers travel with goods at their own risk. Neither the company nor its servants accept any liability for damage or loss to passengers' goods. The company's servants are parties to this contract.

Advise Janet.

See *Cases and Materials* (**4.6**) for the complete answer.

CHAPTER FIVE

DISCHARGE OF LIABILITY

5.1 Objectives

By the end of this chapter you should be able to:

■ identify and synthesise the law relating to performance and breach;

■ synthesise the law relating to performance and breach with **Chapter 3** on terms;

■ explain the significance of the historical development of the doctrine of frustration;

■ identify and explain the relationship between common law frustration and the Law Reform (Frustrated Contracts) Act 1943;

■ apply the law relating to discharge to problem situations;

■ evaluate critically the doctrine of frustration and the Law Reform (Frustrated Contracts) Act 1943.

5.2 Introduction

In this chapter we are concerned with the various ways in which the parties may become discharged (released) from their contractual obligations. We shall consider the following four areas:

(a) Performance.

(b) Breach.

(c) Agreement.

(d) Frustration.

The difficulty of exposition of discharge by performance or by breach is that performance and breach are in reality mirror images of each other. Anson says they are 'two sides of the same coin'. By way of example, suppose X contracts to build a shed for Y for £800. X carries out the work, feels that he has performed his obligations, has no further obligation under the contract, and claims the £800 contract price. However, Y may claim that X's performance is defective, i.e. that X is in breach of contract, and that he, Y, is released from his contractual obligation to pay, or at least that X should remedy the defect or make a deduction from the contract price because of the defective work. X may claim the work is not defective.

We should conclude that, in fact, performance and breach should be considered at one and the same time. In addition, of course, the extent of one party's contractual obligations is to be discovered from the terms of the contract. They will provide the answer to the question of what performance is to be required.

Conversely, if performance is defective, i.e. there is breach of a term, we need to know what sort of term it is (condition, warranty or intermediate term) in order to ascertain whether or not the innocent party has any right to repudiate the contract, i.e. to regard himself as discharged from his contractual obligations. We considered this in **Chapter 3** and if you do not remember it, have another look at it now.

We need to bear all of this in mind, and to explain situations in such terminology, whenever appropriate, in undertaking an examination of the legal rules relating to performance and breach.

Throughout this chapter the innocent party will be referred to as Good and the party in breach as Bad.

5.3 Performance

An historical approach is useful. The original rule at common law was always that performance must be precise and exact. In other words, the obligation under the contract was entire, and only an entire performance would entitle the defendant to payment under the contract. This was well illustrated by *Cutter* v *Powell* (1795) 6 Term Reports 320, where the defendant agreed to pay Cutter 30 guineas provided he executed his duties as second mate on a voyage from Kingston, Jamaica to Liverpool. Cutter began the voyage but died when the ship was 19 days short of Liverpool. Cutter's wife sought a proportion of his wage equivalent to the amount of the voyage for which Cutter had acted as second mate. It was held that she failed because Cutter had not performed his entire contractual obligation.

Similarly, in *Bolton* v *Mahadeva* [1972] 2 All ER 1322, the plaintiff agreed to install a central heating system in the defendant's house for a lump sum of £560. He installed a system which failed to heat the house adequately and gave off fumes. The defendant refused to pay. The Court of Appeal held that it was a lump sum contract and the obligation entire; the plaintiff could recover nothing.

You may consider that the above decisions are harsh because the defendant either receives a benefit, or makes a profit without having to pay anything. Consequently, the courts have developed certain doctrines in order to achieve justice between the contracting parties.

5.3.1 SUBSTANTIAL PERFORMANCE

If the contract has been substantially performed, though not necessarily literally or exactly, Good cannot treat himself as discharged from his obligation to pay, though he will have a counterclaim or a right of set-off for any loss sustained by reason of the incomplete performance. In other words, Good has no right to repudiate for breach of condition but does have a right to compensation for breach of warranty.

What constitutes substantial performance is a question of degree in the circumstances of each particular case. It is usually established if the actual performance is not far short of the required performance and the cost of remedying the defects is not too great in proportion to the overall contract price.

Dakin & Co. Ltd v *Lee* [1916] 1 KB 566
The plaintiff builders contracted to carry out certain repairs to the defendant's house for £1,500. The plaintiff sought the contract price and the defendant resisted on three grounds: the underpinning of a wall was two feet thick instead of four feet; four inch solid columns instead of five inch hollow ones had been used; the joists over a bay window were not bolted as stipulated. All defects could have been rectified at a cost of £80.

Had the plaintiff substantially performed the contract? What kind of term had been breached by the plaintiff?

The plaintiff was entitled to the contract price less an amount in respect of the part of the work which had been carried out contrary to specification, i.e. the plaintiff had committed a breach of warranty only.

Our conclusion must be that whether entire performance is a condition precedent or not to any payment is a question of construction of the terms of the contract in each particular case. Clearly the court construed the contracts as requiring entire performance in both *Cutter* v *Powell* and *Bolton* v *Mahadeva*. In modern times such construction is not uncommon in cases involving contracts of sale of goods, but is very much the exception in other cases.

5.3.2   ACCEPTANCE OF PARTIAL PEFORMANCE

The usual rule is that if Bad partly performs a contract (i.e. there is no substantial performance, and thus a breach of condition is committed) he is not entitled to recover anything. However, a claim to remuneration may arise if Good accepts the partial performance.

In sale of goods cases this is recognised by the **Sale of Goods Act 1979, s. 30(1)**, which provides that: 'Where the seller delivers to the buyer a quantity of goods less than he contracted to sell, the buyer may reject them, but if he accepts them he must pay for them at the contract rate.'

In other cases any such claim rests upon a *quantum meruit* basis (a reasonable sum in respect of the benefit conferred by the partial performance). The basis of the liability here is that if Good accepts Bad's partial performance, both parties by implication mutually release one another from the original contract and agree to a new contract to pay for the work done or the goods supplied.

However, the doctrine of partial performance applies only if Good has a genuine choice either to accept or to reject partial performance.

Sumpter v *Hedges* [1898] 1 QB 673

The plaintiff agreed to erect certain buildings on the defendant's land for £565. He did part of the work and then abandoned the contract. The defendant completed the buildings himself, using materials left on the site by the plaintiff. The plaintiff sued to recover the value of the work done and of the building materials used.

What kind of term had been breached by the plaintiff? Can the plaintiff recover either the value of the work done or that of the materials used?

The plaintiff had committed a breach of condition. The plaintiff could not recover for the work he had done because the defendant had no option but to accept the partly erected buildings. Conversely, he could recover the value of the materials used because the defendant did have a choice whether or not to use them in completion of the building.

5.3.3 PREVENTION OF PERFORMANCE

If Good is prevented from completing his contractual obligations by the default of Bad, Good can either recover damages for breach of contract, or alternatively may seek reasonable remuneration on a *quantum meruit* basis for work already done. In *Planché* v *Colburn* (1831) 8 Bing 14, the plaintiff had agreed to write a book on costume and ancient armour for a series published by the defendants called 'The Juvenile Library'. He was to receive £100 on completion of the book, to which end he collected materials and wrote part of the book. The defendants then abandoned the series. The plaintiff was held to be entitled to recover 50 guineas on a *quantum meruit* basis.

5.3.4 DIVISIBLE COVENANTS

Many of the partial/substantial performance difficulties may be avoided if the court discovers the contract to consist of a number of severable obligations rather than one entire obligation. Whether this is so is a question of construction of the intention of the parties in each particular case. Suppose, for example, that Bad agrees to sell to Good 120 tons of wheat for £12,000, to be delivered 10 tons per month between January and December. There is no specification of time of payment. Bad makes appropriate 10 ton deliveries in January, February and March, but fails to make any further deliveries.

If the contract is one entire obligation then Bad is entitled to nothing until he makes all 12 deliveries. If the obligations are severable then payment is due each month upon delivery, and Bad can recover for the January, February and March deliveries.

5.3.5 SUGGESTED APPROACH TO PERFORMANCE DIFFICULTIES

Problems involving performance revolve around construction of the contract. The suggested approach is as follows:

(a) Is the contract an entire obligation requiring precise performance? If it is, nothing less will do, e.g., *Re Moore & Co. and Landauer & Co.* [1921] 2 KB 519. This will be unusual except in sale of goods cases.

(b) If precise performance is not required, are the contractual obligations divisible?

(c) If not, has there been substantial performance, acceptance of partial performance or prevention of performance?

Figure 3   Assessing difficulties of performance

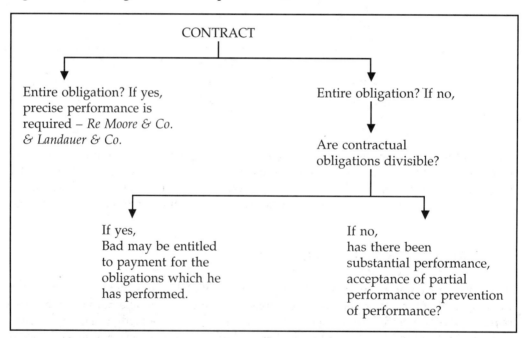

There remain for consideration two further aspects relating to performance:

5.3.5.1 Time of performance

(a) When the contract does not stipulate a time within which the contractual obligations must be performed, performance must be within a reasonable time.

(b) When there is a time stipulation in the contract then that is the time for performance.

(c) In either case, what is the effect of late performance? The answer depends upon whether time is of the essence of the contract, i.e. in the nature of a condition, or not. In *United Scientific Holdings Ltd* v *Burnley BC* [1977] 2 All ER 62, the House of Lords stated that time is of the essence of the contract if such is the genuine intention of the parties, and such intention may be expressly provided for, or inferred from the nature of the subject matter or the surrounding circumstances.

An interesting consideration of the problem can be seen in the next case:

Charles Rickards Ltd v *Oppenheim* [1950] 1 All ER 420
The defendant purchased a Rolls Royce chassis from the plaintiffs who contracted to build a body to go on the chassis, the work to be completed by 20 March at the latest. It was not completed by that date, but the defendant continued to press for delivery. However, on 29 June the defendant wrote to the plaintiffs and said that he would not take delivery after 25 July. The plaintiffs did not deliver by 25 July and the defendant treated the contract as repudiated.

Was the defendant entitled to repudiate the contract? If so, why?

The defendant was entitled to repudiate the contract. The original date of 20 March had been of the essence of the contract, but the defendant had waived it by his conduct. But he had given reasonable notice of a new date, 25 July, as being of the essence of the contract.

5.3.5.2 Tender of performance

If Good makes a valid tender of performance and Bad refuses to accept it, Good is freed from liability for non-performance provided that the tender is made under such circumstances that Bad has a reasonable opportunity of examining the performance tendered in order to ascertain conformity with the contract.

Startup v *MacDonald* (1843) 6 Man & C 593
The parties contracted for the sale of 10 tons of linseed oil to be delivered 'within the last 14 days of March'. The plaintiff delivered the oil at 8.30 pm on Saturday, 31 March and the defendant refused to accept delivery because of the lateness of the hour. It was held that the tender of the oil in the circumstances was equivalent to performance and the plaintiff was entitled to damages for non-acceptance.

5.4 Breach

When can Good terminate the contract and regard himself as discharged from his contractual obligations because of Bad's breach?

It is always possible to sue for damages for breach of contract (i.e. for breach of condition or warranty), but the right of Good to treat the contract as discharged arises only where there has been a breach of condition, or a repudiatory breach in the case of an intermediate term, viz:

(a)   where Bad repudiates the contract either before performance is due (anticipatory breach) or before the contract has been fully performed; or

(b)   Bad has committed breach of a term of major importance.

5.4.1   REPUDIATION BEFORE OR DURING PERFORMANCE

Such repudiation may be either express or implied, and it must be established that Bad has made it clear beyond reasonable doubt that he no longer intends to perform his part of the contract.

Breach before performance becomes due is known as **anticipatory breach**.

5.4.1.1   Anticipatory breach

In this situation Good has options. He may accept the breach and immediately sue for breach of contract, or he may refuse to accept the breach and wait until the due date for performance, hoping the other party will change his mind. In *Hochster* v *De La Tour* (1853) 2 E & B 678, the defendant agreed in April to engage the plaintiff as a courier during a foreign tour starting on 1 June. On 11 May the defendant wrote to the plaintiff informing him of a change of mind and that his services would no longer be required. The plaintiff sued for damages immediately and succeeded.

It may be dangerous for Good to wait for the due date for performance, as the contract continues at the risk of both parties. This happened in *Avery* v *Bowden* (1855) 5 E & B 714 where B chartered A's ship and agreed to load it with cargo at Odessa within 45 days. After a while, B told A that he had no cargo and advised him to leave. Instead, A waited at Odessa hoping B would find a cargo. Before the end of the 45 days the Crimean War broke out between England and Russia, and performance of the contract became illegal.

B's refusal to provide a cargo was an anticipatory breach and A could have sued immediately. When he chose not to do so the contract remained on foot until performed. However, in the meantime both parties were discharged from the contract by frustration (subsequent illegality in this case) due to the outbreak of war. Thus, B was not liable to A for breach of contract.

It should be noted that there are some problems surrounding the relationship between anticipatory breach and damages due to the decision in *White & Carter (Councils) Ltd* v *McGregor* [1961] 3 All ER 1178. These will be considered in **Chapter 7**.

5.4.1.2 Breach occurring during performance

Apologies for converting Good and Bad briefly to X and Y. However, who is Good and Bad in these cases depends upon the decision of the court!

Such breach raises a difficult question of construction of the contract for the court, which has to decide whether an act alleged by one party to be a repudiatory breach in fact amounts to such in law.

SAQ 60

X breaches a contract. Y treats this breach as a breach of condition and repudiates. The breach turns out to be a breach of warranty only. What are the consequences for Y?

In the general law of contract, if X breaches the contract and Y repudiates, alleging a breach of condition by X, then, if the court agrees, Y has acted perfectly properly. However, if the court finds X's breach to be of warranty only, then Y also will be in breach of contract due to wrongful repudiation. This point is illustrated in *Cases and Materials* (**5.2.2**) by *Mersey Steel & Iron Co.* v *Naylor Benzon & Co.* (1884) 9 App Cas 434.

Some guidance as to the test of construction to be applied, at least in sale of goods cases, was given by the Court of Appeal in *Maple Flock Co. Ltd* v *Universal Furniture Products (Wembley) Ltd* [1934] 1 KB 148, where Lord Hewart CJ said that the relevant factors were: 'First, the ratio quantitatively which the breach bears to the contract as a whole, and secondly, the degree of probability or improbability that the breach will be repeated.'

In the case itself, the buyer was held not to be entitled to repudiate on the following facts. The contract was for 100 tons of rag flock; the first 15 deliveries were in order; the 16th was defective; deliveries 17–20 were in order. In total, only 12 tons of the deliveries had been defective, and the breach was unlikely to be repeated. On the other hand, in *Munro & Co. Ltd* v *Meyer* [1930] 2 KB 312, the buyer was held to be entitled to repudiate the whole contract for 1,500 tons of meat and bone meal, when more than half of the total quantity delivered was found to be seriously defective.

5.4.2   BREACH OF A TERM OF MAJOR IMPORTANCE

You will have discovered how to identify a term of major importance earlier on in **Chapter 3** (a condition or an intermediate term which has been breached giving rise to serious consequences).

5.4.3   CONSEQUENCES OF REPUDIATION OF THE CONTRACT OR BREACH OF A MAJOR TERM

There are two possibilities here. Good will either:

(a)   treat the contract as still operative; or

(b)   treat the contract as terminated.

5.4.3.1   Contract still operative

Breach in itself does not discharge Good from his obligations – he must first accept the breach. So if he refuses to accept the breach, the contract remains in being for the future on both sides. In *Howard* v *Pickford Tool Co.* [1951] 1 KB 417, Asquith LJ said that 'An unaccepted repudiation is a thing writ in water and of no value to anybody; it affords no legal rights of any sort or kind.'

A breach is accepted either by expressly communicating acceptance or by performing an unequivocal act consistent with acceptance, of which the party in breach is aware: *Vitol SA* v *Norelf Ltd* [1996] 3 All ER 193.

It follows that in the case of breach of a major term, Good cannot repudiate or sue for damages until he accepts the breach; and in the case of an unaccepted anticipatory breach, Good cannot sue for damages until the due date for performance arrives.

5.4.3.2   Contract treated as terminated

The contract will be terminated for the future as from the moment the acceptance of the breach is communicated to Bad. However, it is clear from the House of Lords decision in *Johnson* v *Agnew* [1979] 1 All ER 883 that the breach does not operate retrospectively, i.e. Bad will be liable in damages both for any earlier breaches and also for the breach leading to the discharge of the contract, but will be excused any further performance.

5.5   Agreement

Just as a contract is formed by agreement, so it can be discharged or varied by agreement. But just as consideration is essential to agreement, so it is substantially necessary for discharge or variation, unless the release is executed by deed. The process is known as **accord and satisfaction**; the accord is the agreement and the satisfaction the consideration.

There are two forms of discharge by agreement: bilateral and unilateral.

5.5.1   BILATERAL DISCHARGE BY AGREEMENT

This applies to executory agreements, as where X and Y mutually release one another from their obligations.

5.5.2 UNILATERAL DISCHARGE BY AGREEMENT

If X has performed his part of the contract, a promise from him to release Y from further performance will not bind X unless Y provides consideration. We have already seen this in *Pinnel's Case* (1602) (see **2.4.2.3**).

What defence might Y be able to set up even though he has not provided any consideration?

Of course, even if Y has not provided consideration, he may be able to set up promissory estoppel by way of defence. (We examined this issue in **Chapter 2** and you may wish to refresh your memory.)

5.6 Frustration

Frustration occurs whenever a contract, without default of either party, after its formation, becomes impossible to perform. The doctrine is often called subsequent or supervening impossibility, and its effect is that the parties are released from their contractual obligations.

Until the nineteenth century the common law adopted a doctrine of absolute obligation to perform a contract. So, in *Paradine* v *Jane* (1647) Aleyn 26, a tenant was sued for arrears of rent and in defence pleaded that for the last three years he had been dispossessed of his farm by the King's enemies. The court rejected his plea and the tenant was liable for the rent, even though he was unable to take the benefit of the lease.

The basic principle of frustration was formulated by Blackburn J, to alleviate the harshness of the absolute obligation doctrine, in *Taylor* v *Caldwell* [1863] 3 B & S 826. The defendant agreed to hire to the plaintiff a music hall and Surrey Gardens for the purposes of entertainment. Before the day of the performance, due to the default of neither party, the music hall was destroyed by fire and the plaintiff sued the defendant for breach of contract. The court held the defendant not liable, the contract being frustrated by the fire.

5.6.1 UNDERLYING THEORIES

There are two underlying theories:

    (a) the implied term theory; and

(b)   the just solution theory.

Some cases base their approach upon (a), others upon (b).

5.6.1.1   The implied term theory

The contract will be discharged only where the court can imply a term into the contract that the contract shall come to an end upon the occurrence of the events in question. This view was expressly supported by Lord Loreburn in *Tamplin Steamship Co. Ltd* v *Anglo-Mexican Petroleum Products Co. Ltd* [1916] 2 AC 397.

5.6.1.1.2   The just solution theory

The contract is discharged by operation of law; otherwise the parties would have to perform a contract radically different from that originally undertaken. This view was expressly supported by (amongst others) Lord Radcliffe in *Davis Contractors Ltd* v *Fareham UDC* [1956] AC 696.

5.6.2   THE CIRCUMSTANCES IN WHICH FRUSTRATION MAY APPLY

5.6.2.1   Destruction of the subject matter of the contract

See *Taylor* v *Caldwell* at **5.6**.

5.6.2.2   The non-occurrence of a particular event which forms the basis of the contract

This invites a comparison of two of the 'Coronation cases' arising out of the postpone-ment of the coronation of Edward VII due to his sudden illness:

Krell v *Henry* [1903] 2 KB 740
The defendant agreed to hire a flat from the plaintiff for 26 and 27 June 1902. The contract contained no reference to the coronation processions, but they were to take place on those days and were to pass the flat. The processions were cancelled due to the illness of Edward VII and the plaintiff sued to recover rent not already paid.

The plaintiff failed; the processions and the location of the flat were the foundation of the agreement and the contract was frustrated.

Herne Bay Steamboat Co. v *Hutton* [1903] 2 KB 683
The defendant chartered the *SS Cynthia* from the plaintiff for 28 and 29 June 1902 for the express purpose of taking paying passengers to see the coronation naval review by Edward VII at Spithead, and to tour the assembled fleet. The review was cancelled due to Edward VII's pneumonia but the fleet remained assembled.

The contract was not frustrated. Vaughan-Williams and Romer LJJ felt that neither the review nor the tour were at the foundation of the contract (they were matters of importance to the charterer only and not to the owner); Stirling LJ felt that both the review and the tour were objects of the contract, and the tour could still be effected.

Can you see why the decision in *Krell* v *Henry* has often been criticised? The answer is that potentially it opens the floodgates to contractors to escape from contracts which have become less profitable due to changed circumstances. Consequently, it has rarely been followed in subsequent cases. (*Amalgamated Investment & Property Co. Ltd* v *John Walker & Sons Ltd* [1976] 3 All ER 509) (see **Cases and Materials (5.4.1)**).

ACTIVITY 21

Read the judgments of Vaughan-Williams LJ in *Krell* v *Henry* and *Herne Bay Steamboat Co.* v *Hutton* (*Cases and Materials*, 5.4.1). How does he distinguish between the two cases? Is the distinction he makes justifiable? Answer in *Cases and Materials* (5.4.1.1).

You should have discovered that what is deemed to be at the foundation of the contract must be fundamental as far as *both* parties are concerned and not merely one of them.

5.6.2.3 Non-availability of one of the parties due to death, illness or other circumstances

This applies to contracts for personal services such as contracts of employment. In *Condor* v *Barron Knights Ltd* [1966] 1 WLR 87, Edward Lottian Condor, a talented drummer, was contracted to play seven nights per week with the Barron Knights pop group, when he had a minor nervous breakdown. He was advised by a doctor that to continue the demanding schedule might well lead to a major breakdown, and the contract was held to be frustrated.

It appears that even contracts of employment determinable by notice on either side can be frustrated by long-term illness: *Notcutt* v *Universal Equipment Co. (London) Ltd* [1986] NLJ Reps 393.

5.6.2.4 Frustration of the common adventure

FA Tamplin Steamship Co. Ltd v *Anglo-Mexican Petroleum Products Co. Ltd* [1916] 2 AC 397
A steam ship was chartered for a period of five years, 1912–1917. In 1915, the government requisitioned the ship for use as a troopship. The charterers were willing to continue paying the agreed freight, but the owners claimed the charterparty to be frustrated as they wished to obtain a larger amount by way of compensation from the Crown.

There was no frustration, the interruption being of insufficient duration and insufficiently continuous to make it unreasonable for the parties to continue.

On the other hand, in *Jackson* v *Union Marine Insurance Co. Ltd* (1874) LR 10 CP 125, the interruption was of sufficient duration for the contract to become frustrated. (See *Cases and Materials* (5.4.3)).

5.6.2.5 Building contracts

Metropolitan Water Board v *Dick, Kerr & Co. Ltd* [1918] AC 119
DK contracted with MWB to build a reservoir within six years. After two years the Minister of Munitions required DK to cease work, and to remove and sell its plant. MWB claimed the contract subsisted on the basis of a contract provision allowing a time extension in the event of difficulties.

The contract was frustrated on the basis that if it were resumed after such interruption it would effectively be a different contract.

5.6.2.6   Supervening illegality

We have seen an example of this in *Avery* v *Bowden* at **5.4.1.1**.

5.6.2.7   Leases

It was for some time uncertain whether the doctrine of frustration can apply to leases. Leases create proprietary rights which usually receive special treatment in English law. However, the House of Lords in *National Carriers Ltd* v *Panalpina (Northern) Ltd* [1981] AC 675 held that frustration can apply, but the circumstances of its operation would be very rare. Perhaps it might apply, for example, where a holiday flat which has been rented for a month is destroyed by fire.

Can you identify a unifying thread running through the cases referred to in 5.6.2.1 to 5.6.2.7?

You might find such a thread in that the contract will not be frustrated unless its foundation has been destroyed so that performance becomes impossible or fundamentally different from what was agreed. It is not enough that the contract has become more onerous or expensive to perform. This issue arose in the next case:

Tsakiroglov & Co. Ltd v *Noblee & Thorl GMBH* [1962] AC 93
The appellants agreed to sell ground nuts to the respondents and to ship them from Sudan to Hamburg in November/December 1956. However, on 2 November the Suez Canal was closed, and remained closed for five months. The price of the nuts had been calculated on the basis of shipment via the canal, which was the normal route, though there was no term in the contract designating it the exclusive route. The appellants refused to perform the contract.

Do you think the contract was frustrated? Would it have made any difference had the goods been perishable?

There was no frustration. It was still possible to ship the nuts via the Cape of Good Hope, a journey some 3,000 miles longer. The journey would not be commercially or fundamentally different from that by the canal, merely much more expensive. However, the outcome may well have been different had the goods been perishable.

Davis Contractors Ltd v *Fareham UDC* [1956] 2 All ER 145
The appellants contracted with the respondents to build 78 houses for £94,000. Due to unexpected strikes and materials shortages, the contract took 22 months to perform instead of eight months and cost £115,000. The appellants claimed that the contract was frustrated, and that they were entitled to their actual costs on a *quantum meruit* basis.

This was not so. The contract had merely become more onerous and expensive, not radically different.

5.6.3 THE INCIDENCE OF RISK

Before the doctrine of frustration can apply, the court must be satisfied that neither party has agreed to run the risk of the event in question. The court construes the contract to see if the risk is expressly provided for (a **force majeure** clause), or if there is evidence of intention to run such risk. Indeed, force majeure clauses are common in modern commercial contracts so that the parties know where they stand from the outset.

Let us consider the circumstances in which this question of risk is particularly relevant.

5.6.3.1 Express provision

If the contract expressly provides for the risk in question, that provision will usually apply and the doctrine of frustration will not. Such provision must, however, be full and complete, and embrace totally the nature of the risk in question. In *Jackson* v *Union Marine Insurance Co. Ltd* (1874) LR 10 CP 125, a provision to the effect, 'dangers and accidents of navigation excepted' did not apply when a tanker's availability under a charterparty was delayed for eight months after it ran aground. It was deemed not to cover an accident causing injury of such an extensive nature.

Similarly, in *Metropolitan Water Board* v *Dick, Kerr & Co.* (see **5.6.2.5**), a proviso to the effect that if the work should be 'unduly delayed or impeded' an extension of time for completion was to be granted was deemed inapplicable to a delay causing a radical change in the obligation.

5.6.3.2 Can a contract be frustrated by events which are foreseeable by both parties?

An obvious answer would be that if the event was foreseeable, the parties should have provided for it in the contract. Indeed, many of the cases refer to frustration applying to 'unexpected' or 'uncontemplated' events, and many *obiter dicta* express the view that a contract cannot be frustrated by foreseen or foreseeable events.

However, the point remains undecided, and there is support for the opposite view in the *obiter dicta* of Lord Denning MR in *The Eugenia* [1964] 1 All ER 161, and the strange decision of Goddard J in *W. J. Tatem Ltd* v *Gamboa* [1938] 3 All ER 135, where he held a charterparty to be frustrated by the ship's foreseeable seizure, because it was not foreseeable that it would be seized for such a lengthy period of time. This indicates that a very high degree of foreseeability is required to exclude frustration!

5.6.3.3 Event foreseen by one party only

A party cannot rely, as a basis for frustration, on an event foreseen by him but not by the other party. This is illustrated by the following case:

Walton Harvey Ltd v *Walker & Homfrays Ltd* [1931] 1 Ch 274
The plaintiffs were granted the right by the defendant to display an advertising sign on the defendant's hotel during a seven-year period. Within this period the hotel was compulsorily acquired and demolished, a risk of which the defendant was aware and the plaintiffs were not.

The defendant was liable in damages, the contract not being frustrated since the defendant could have provided for such risk in the contract.

5.6.3.4 Lack of common assumption

A contract cannot be frustrated by an event which prevents performance in a manner contemplated by one of the parties only.

Blackburn Bobbin Co. Ltd v *Allen & Sons Ltd* [1918] 2 KB 467
The defendants agreed to sell and deliver to the plaintiffs a quantity of Finnish timber. They found it impossible to fulfil the contract because the outbreak of war cut off their source of supply from Finland. The plaintiffs did not know that Finnish timber was normally imported direct from Finland and that timber merchants did not hold stocks of it in England.

The contract was not frustrated. Frustration would have applied only if the continuance of the normal mode of shipping the timber from Finland was a matter which **both** parties regarded as essential for the fulfilment of the contract. Since this was not the case, the defendants bore the risk.

5.6.3.5 Self-induced frustration

Frustration **cannot** apply where the alleged frustrating event arises from a deliberate act or choice of one of the parties.

Maritime National Fish Ltd v *Ocean Trawlers Ltd* [1935] AC 524
The respondents chartered to the appellants a steam trawler fitted with an otter trawl. Both parties knew that it was illegal to use an otter trawl without a licence from the Canadian government. The appellants applied for five licences for the trawlers they were operating, including the respondents' trawler. They were granted three licences only, which they used for their own vessels, and proceeded to repudiate the charterparty on grounds of frustration.

There was no frustration since the failure of the charterparty was the result of the appellants' own election.

There is uncertainty as to whether a negligent act can amount to self-induced frustration, though the House of Lords has suggested (*obiter*) that it might in *Joseph Constantine Steamship Line Ltd* v *Imperial Smelting Corpn Ltd* [1942] AC 154. The burden of proof of self-induced frustration rests upon the party alleging it.

5.6.4 THE EFFECTS OF THE DOCTRINE OF FRUSTRATION

5.6.4.1 At common law

At common law the contract was terminated automatically and immediately, and both parties were released from their future obligations under the contract. They were, however, required to fulfil any obligations which fell due before the occurrence of the frustrating event. It is said that the loss lay where it fell.

In other words, we could say that the contract was not void from the outset, but only from the occurrence of the frustrating event. (We can contrast the effect of mistake, which overrides the contract right from the beginning.)

This led to unfortunate consequences in the next case:

Appleby v *Myers* (1867) LR 2 CP 651
The plaintiffs undertook to erect machinery on the defendant's premises, the work to be paid for on completion. When the work was almost completed, both the premises and the machinery already erected were destroyed by fire.

Can the plaintiff recover anything for work done prior to the occurrence of the frustrating event?

The contract was frustrated, and the plaintiff could recover nothing for the work done since the obligation to pay did not arise until completion.

Chandler v *Webster* [1904] 1 KB 493
The plaintiff agreed to hire from the defendant a room in Pall Mall to watch King Edward VII's coronation procession. The price was £141, payable immediately. The plaintiff paid £100, but before he could pay the balance the procession was cancelled and the plaintiff sought to recover the £100 paid.

Can the plaintiff recover his £100, or is he liable to pay the entire £141?

Not only did the plaintiff fail to recover his £100, but also he was liable to pay the balance of £41, an obligation which fell due before the occurrence of the frustrating event. (This is because the contract is valid until the occurrence of the frustrating event.)

As discussed below *Chandler* v *Webster* has been partly overruled. When you have studied the Law Reform (Frustrated Contracts) Act 1943, you should return to this point and explain the relevance of *Chandler* v *Webster* to the modern law of frustration. Compare your conclusions with the paragraph at the end of 5.6.4.2.

Chandler v *Webster* in particular provoked much judicial criticism, and was eventually partly overruled in:

The Fibrosa [1942] 2 All ER 122
The respondents contracted with the appellants, a Polish company, to manufacture certain machinery and to deliver it to Gdynia. Part of the price was to be paid in advance, and the appellants paid £1,000. The contract was frustrated by the occupation of Gdynia by hostile German forces in September 1939. The appellants requested the return of the £1,000, but this was refused on the basis that considerable work had already been done on the machinery.

You should be able to see that if *Chandler* v *Webster* had been followed, then the £1,000 would have been irrecoverable because it had already been paid at the time of the frustrating event. However, the House of Lords held that the appellants could recover the £1,000. The basis for this was not the contract, which had ceased to exist, but an action in what is known as quasi-contract for the restitution of money paid where there has been total failure of consideration. Consideration in quasi-contract does not have the same meaning as the consideration necessary to formation of contract which we considered in **Chapter Two**. So if the party paying the money has received no part of the performance for which he bargained (i.e. none of the machinery had been delivered), there is total failure of consideration.

The result of *The Fibrosa* was that the position was improved, but it was still unsatisfactory for two reasons:

SAQ 66

Can you work out from the account of *The Fibrosa* above, why, despite the improvement in the legal position which it introduced, the parties might still be unjustly treated in this type of situation?

First, the party who had to return the pre-payment might have incurred expenses but would be entitled to nothing (as in *The Fibrosa*). Secondly, if the party seeking to recover the pre-payment had received any part of what he bargained for, no matter how small, e.g., 1 per cent of the machinery in *The Fibrosa*, there would be no total failure of consideration.

An attempt to deal with these difficulties led to statutory reform.

5.6.4.2   The Law Reform (Frustrated Contracts) Act 1943

The Act applies to all contracts governed by English law except:

(a)   contracts for the carriage of goods by sea or charterparties (other than a time charterparty or charterparty by way of demise);

(b)   contracts of insurance;

(c)   contracts for the sale of specific goods where the goods have perished (Sale of Goods Act 1979, s. 7).

In modern times it is the 1943 Act which must be applied to ascertain the position of the parties upon the occurrence of frustration, and not the common law (unless the contract falls within the exempted categories).

What is the effect of the 1943 Act?

The right to recover money paid and the right to set off expenses against pre-payment

Section 1(2) provides that:

All sums paid or payable to any party in pursuance of the contract before the time when the parties were so discharged . . . shall, in the case of the sums so paid, be recoverable from him as money received by him for the use of the party by whom the sums are paid, and, in the case of sums so payable, cease to be so payable:

Provided that, if the party to whom the sums were so paid or payable incurred expenses before the time of discharge in, or the purpose of, the performance of the contract, the court may, if it considers it just to do so having regard to all the circumstances of the case, allow him to retain or, as the case may be, recover the whole or any part of the sums so paid or payable, not being an amount in excess of the expenses so incurred.

Did I hear you say: 'Please explain'?

There are three main points to be made about s. 1(2):

(a)   It applies only when there has been a pre-payment or agreement to make a pre-payment.

(b)   It embodies the rule in *The Fibrosa* case in terms of recovering pre-payments, but it is not now necessary to prove total failure of consideration.

(c)   It goes further than *The Fibrosa* case in that it gives the court a discretionary power to permit the payee to set-off against the sum paid or payable a sum not exceeding the value of any expenses incurred in performing the contract before frustration occurred.

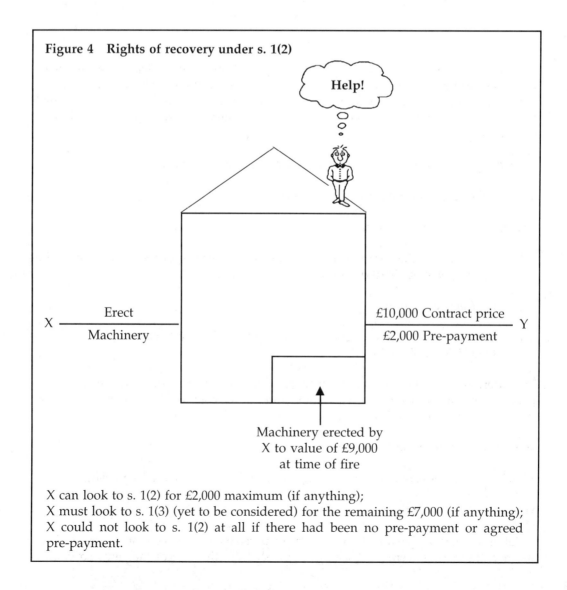

Figure 4   Rights of recovery under s. 1(2)

Help!

X ———— Erect / Machinery ————

£10,000 Contract price / £2,000 Pre-payment — Y

Machinery erected by
X to value of £9,000
at time of fire

X can look to s. 1(2) for £2,000 maximum (if anything);
X must look to s. 1(3) (yet to be considered) for the remaining £7,000 (if anything);
X could not look to s. 1(2) at all if there had been no pre-payment or agreed pre-payment.

Restitution of benefits other than money where there has been partial performance

Section 1(3) represents an attempt to deal with the difficulties created by cases like *Appleby* v *Myers* (see **5.6.4.1**). It provides that:

> Where any party to the contract has, by reason of anything done by any other party thereto in, or for the purpose of, the performance of the contract, obtained a **valuable benefit** (other than the payment of money) before the time of discharge, there shall be recoverable from him by the other party such sum (if any), not exceeding the value of the said benefit to the party obtaining it, as the court considers just, having regard to all the circumstances of the case and in particular:
>
> (a) the amount of any expenses incurred before the time of discharge by the benefited party in, or for the purpose of, the performance of the contract, including any sums paid or payable by him to any other party in pursuance of the contract and retained or recoverable by that party under section 1(2), and
>
> (b) the effect, in relation to the said benefit, of the circumstances giving rise to the frustration of the contract.

(Emphasis added.)

The effect of this is that either party may be awarded compensation in respect of any non-monetary valuable benefit conferred by him upon the other party in pursuance of the contract.

This involves a two-stage process:

Identification and valuation of the valuable benefit   This is very difficult and controversial, for, if we take a case like *Appleby* v *Myers*, there are two alternative arguments. First, that no valuable benefit has been obtained because the completed work has been totally destroyed; or, secondly, on a more liberal interpretation, that a valuable benefit was obtained by the owner in that work had been done on his land as per contract immediately before discharge.

Perhaps, in an *Appleby* v *Myers* situation, the second interpretation is preferable in that the Act does speak of a valuable benefit being obtained **before** the time of discharge, and the owner is more likely to be insured against fire than the builder. On the other hand, even a liberal interpretation of the Act would not cover all situations, e.g., in *Krell* v *Henry*, Krell would not be able to claim that he conferred a valuable benefit on Henry by arranging to have his furniture stored away while Henry was in the flat.

Section 1(3) was considered by Robert Goff J, in a judgment affirmed by the Court of Appeal and House of Lords

BP Exploration Co. (Libya) Ltd v *Hunt (No. 2)* [1982] 1 All ER 125
Hunt, who owned an oil concession in Libya, contracted for its development with BP Exploration, who were to provide the capital and expertise if and when the oil was developed and sold. BP would be repaid from Hunt's share of the oil. After BP had done considerable work and incurred great expense in developing the oil field successfully, the Libyan government withdrew the concession and the contract was frustrated. BP claimed under s. 1(3).

BP had incurred expenditure under the contract, and consequently a valuable benefit had been conferred on Hunt in the form of the increased value in his share of the concession.

In *BP* v *Hunt*, Robert Goff J identified and valued the benefit immediately after the occurrence of the frustrating event. What problems would this approach create in an *Appleby* v *Myers* situation?

The problem would be that there would be no valuable benefit immediately after the occurrence of the frustrating event (the machinery has been destroyed by fire) so no award can be made under s. 1(3). If the identification and valuation takes place before the event (when the machinery exists), some award can be made, though no doubt the 'just sum' awarded would be considerably less than the value of the benefit because calculation of the 'just sum takes into account circumstances after the occurrence of the frustrating event.

Calculation of the 'Just Sum'   The second stage is for the court to assess what sum (not exceeding the value of the benefit) it considers just to award (if anything). In accordance with s. 1(3) it must consider any sum received by the plaintiff under s. 1(2) and the circumstances giving rise to the frustration of the contract, in other words the position **after** the frustrating event. In *Appleby* v *Myers*, that was the fact that the owner's valuable benefit no longer existed!

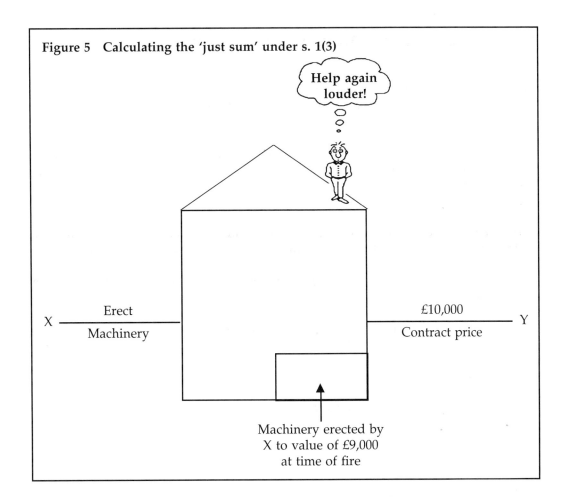

Figure 5 Calculating the 'just sum' under s. 1(3)

X can look to s. 1(3) to the extent of £9,000, if he is deemed to have conferred a valuable benefit upon Y immediately before discharge (a big if!). The court will take account of the destruction of the machinery in the calculation of the 'just sum'. Section 1(2) does not apply because there is no pre-payment.

Any loss or expenditure not covered by the Law Reform (Frustrated Contracts) Act, 1943 which does not fall within the ratio of *The Fibrosa* decision is still subject to *Chandler* v *Webster*. Consequently, the loss will lie where it falls. For example, the expenses incurred by the owner of the flat in putting his furniture into storage in *Krell* v *Henry* would be irrecoverable.

5.7 Conclusion

When someone is sued for breach of contract they may be able to plead the doctrine of frustration by way of defence. Should frustration be established, the parties' respective financial positions will usually be worked out under the provisions of the Law Reform (Frustrated Contracts) Act 1943, falling back upon the common law to the extent that the Act does not deal with the situation.

However, if frustration cannot be established there will be a breach of contract. Issues will then arise concerning performance and breach. Has there been substantial or partial performance (is the breach of a minor or major nature)? The rights of the parties to sue for damages, or to repudiate the contract or to receive payment for anything carried out towards performance of the contract will have to be determined.

5.8   End of Chapter Assessment Question

In order to promote tourism in the town of Accrington, Stanley, a prominent business-man, organises a 'May Day Marathon' running race to be held on the May Day national holiday .

Stanley agrees to purchase 20,000 sheets of foil (to be used to wrap around the runners at the end of the race) from Tin Ltd at a price of £20,000. He pays £10,000 immediately and is to pay the remaining £10,000 after the race. Tin Ltd subsequently delivers 15,000 sheets 'with 5,000 to follow'.

Parliament then passes an Act which states that May Day will no longer be a national holiday. As a result, the vast majority of the runners withdraw their entries for the race.

Stanley cancels the race and claims repayment from Tin Ltd of his £10,000, saying that the contract is frustrated.

Alf, an enthusiastic jogger, who had paid his £10 entry fee in order to run in the race, claims compensation from Stanley for his 'loss of enjoyment'.

Advise Stanley.

See *Cases and Materials* (5.6) for the complete answer.

CHAPTER SIX

VITIATING FACTORS

6.1 Objectives

When you have completed this chapter you should be able to:

■ distinguish terms from representations;

■ identify the essential ingredients of an actionable misrepresentation;

■ distinguish between fraudulent, negligent and innocent misrepresentation, the necessary burdens of proof in each case, and the remedies available in each case;

■ distinguish duress from undue influence and the circumstances in which they operate;

■ identify the essential ingredients of duress, particularly economic duress;

■ distinguish actual undue influence from presumed undue influence;

■ recognise the relevance of manifest disadvantage to the doctrine of undue influence;

■ explain the distinction between void and voidable contracts;

■ identify the essential ingredients of each category of operative mistake;

■ apply the rules relating to contracts in restraint of trade.

6.2 Introduction

Even where it is established that the essential elements of a legally binding contract are present, and the terms can clearly be identified, the agreement may not be legally enforceable because of the presence of some vitiating factor. Thus where fraud is present, or a fundamental mistake as to the contract has been made by one or both parties, the contract may be either totally **void** or **voidable** at the option of the innocent party. (The distinction between void and voidable is explained in the **Introduction** to this book.)

The main vitiating factors which we will examine are misrepresentation, duress and undue influence, mistake and illegality (with particular reference to restraints of trade).

Once again, for purposes of illustration we are back with our old friends Good and Bad.

6.3   Misrepresentation

6.3.1   SCOPE OF MISREPRESENTATION

An action for misrepresentation is the remedy for a party who has entered into a contract in reliance on a false statement (representation) of fact by the other party, but the statement has not become incorporated in the contract as a term, i.e. the statement is not part of the bargain that the parties have made. Where the statement has become a term the remedy will be an action for breach of contract.

Let us consider an example. Good, wishing to buy a used car privately, enters into negotiations with Bad who has advertised his car for sale. The odometer of the vehicle in question is turned back to nought. In the course of negotiations Bad makes a number of statements including a (false) statement that the car has a very low mileage. A few days later Good returns and agrees to buy the car. The written note of the transaction makes no statement as to the mileage of the car. The remedy in this instance will normally be an action for misrepresentation and not an action for breach of contract.

Where there is an actionable misrepresentation it renders the contract **voidable**, i.e. valid until avoided at the instance of the innocent party (Good).

We will deal first with the distinction between representations and terms, then with the concept of actionable misrepresentation and the remedies available, and conclude by looking at clauses which purport to exclude liability for misrepresentation.

6.3.2   REPRESENTATIONS AND TERMS

This section constitutes a brief reminder of an area already covered in greater detail in **Chapter 3**.

As we have seen, statements made by the parties in the course of negotiations leading up to the formation of a contract are classified as either representations or terms.

Whether a statement is a representation or a term is primarily a question of intention. If the parties have indicated that a statement is to be regarded as a term, the court will implement their intention. In other cases, the following guidelines may be applied:

6.3.2.1   Manner and timing of statement

A statement is not likely to be a term if the person making the statement asks the other party to check or verify it, as where the seller of a boat stated that it was sound but asked the buyer to have it surveyed: *Ecay* v *Godfrey* (1947) 80 LL LR 286. If the statement is made with the intention of preventing the other party from finding a defect, and succeeds in this, the court may consider it to be a term. Thus in *Schawel* v *Reade* [1913] 2 IR 64, the vendor of a horse said to the buyer, 'you need not look for anything, the horse is perfectly sound' and the House of Lords held that the statement was a term.

Where there is a distinct interval of time between the making of the statement and the conclusion of the contract, this may indicate that the parties do not intend the statement to be a term: *Routledge* v *McKay* [1954] 1 WLR 615.

6.3.2.2   Importance of statement

A statement is likely to be a term if it is such that the injured party would not have entered the contract had it not been made. In *Bannerman* v *White* (1861) 10 CB NS 844, a prospective purchaser of hops asked whether they had been treated with sulphur, adding that if they had, he would not even trouble to ask the price. The seller's (erroneous) statement that sulphur had not been used was held to be a term.

6.3.2.3 Special knowledge and skill

Where one of the parties possesses superior knowledge and skill relating to the subject matter, the court may conclude that any statement made by such a party is a term. In *Dick Bentley Productions Ltd v Harold Smith (Motors) Ltd* [1965] 1 WLR 623, a car dealer gave a false statement as to the mileage of a Bentley. The Court of Appeal held the dealer's statement to be a term, thus distinguishing *Oscar Chess Ltd v Williams* [1957] 1 WLR 370, where, on a part-exchange deal, a private car owner falsely (but honestly) stated the age of the car to the dealer. The statement was held to be a representation; the dealer was in at least as strong a position as the owner to verify the truth of the statement.

6.3.2.4 Statement reduced to writing

Where the agreement has been reduced to a written document, statements appearing in the written contract will normally be regarded as terms. Subject to the matters discussed above, statements excluded from the written contract are likely to be regarded as representations. Nevertheless, the court will look to the intention of the parties to see whether they intended that the contract, as a whole, should be partly written and partly oral: *J. Evans and Son (Portsmouth) Ltd v Andrea Merzario Ltd* [1976] WLR 1078.

6.3.3 ACTIONABLE MISREPRESENTATION

An actionable misrepresentation is **a false statement of fact** made during pre-contractual negotiations by one party which **induces** the other party to enter into a contract. The words emphasised in the previous sentence will now be examined.

6.3.3.1 False statement of fact

To be actionable, the statement must be one of some specific existing fact or past event. Thus the vendor who states that 'the drains are in good working order', or 'the car's engine has been re-conditioned' is clearly making a statement of fact which would be actionable if manifestly false.

However, the position is rarely so straightforward, and it is necessary to distinguish between statements of fact, which are actionable if false, and statements of opinion or belief; statements of future conduct or intention; statements of law; and cases of silence or non-disclosure, which are not in general actionable.

Statements of opinion or belief

Such statements, if false, do not constitute actionable misrepresentation. In *Bisset v Wilkinson* [1927] AC 177, the owner of a farm, **which had never been used as a sheep farm**, stated that he believed it would support a certain number of sheep. The court held the statement to be one of opinion not fact.

Of course, very often, the makers of such statements are dealers or agents who have special knowledge or skill in relation to the subject matter, or who are in a stronger position to know the truth. Here the court may infer an implied representation of fact. Examples can be found in *Smith v Land and House Property Corporation* (1884) 28 Ch D 7 and *Esso v Mardon* [1976] QB 801.

Clearly, many (but not necessarily all) statements made by advertisers are classed as 'mere puff' and are not actionable because they have no factual basis (e.g., 'we take the drama out of a crisis').

ACTIVITY 22

Read *Bisset* v *Wilkinson* and *Smith* v *Land & House Corporation* in *Cases and Materials* (6.1.1.1). Write down three essential distinguishing factors between the two cases.

You may have chosen the following distinguishing factors:

(a)   In *Bisset* the statement was made honestly; in *Smith* it was not.

(b)   The statement in *Bisset* was incapable of verification (the land had never before been used for sheep farming); the statement in *Smith* was clearly verifiable.

(c)   The maker of the statement in *Smith* was in a stronger position to know the truth; such was not the case in *Bisset*.

Statements of future conduct or intention

A statement by a person as to what he will do in the future is not a statement of fact, e.g., 'over the next five years, our investment plans amount to five million pounds'. But even here a person who wilfully lies about his intentions may be guilty of a (fraudulent) misrepresentation of fact, as illustrated by *Edgington* v *Fitzmaurice* (1885) 29 Ch D 459. A company raised money from the public by saying that it would be invested in the expansion of the business. The directors' real intention was to use the money to pay off the company's debts. The statement was held to be a fraudulent misrepresentation of fact. Bowen LJ, in a famous judicial pronouncement, said:

> There must be a mis-statement of an existing fact; but the state of a man's mind is as much a fact as the state of his digestion. It is true that it is very difficult to prove what the state of a man's mind at a particular time is, but if it can be ascertained, it is as much a fact as anything else. A misrepresentation as to the state of a man's mind is, therefore, a mis-statement of fact.

The same principle would also apply to a dishonest statement of opinion or belief, which we have covered above.

Statements of law

If a person makes a false statement as to what the law is, that is not an actionable misrepresentation. An example would be if X says 'a valid contract of hire purchase does not need to be in writing'. In practice, such bold statements are rarely made and statements containing legal propositions may be related to the subject matter in such a way that they are really statements of fact. For example, in *Solle* v *Butcher* [1950] 1 KB 671, a statement that a flat was 'new', and therefore not subject to the Rent Acts, was held to be one of fact.

Silence or non-disclosure

The general rule here is that to remain silent does not amount to misrepresentation. Thus a commercial traveller who kept quiet, at a job interview, about the fact that he had serious motoring convictions was not guilty of misrepresentation: *Hands v Simpson Fawcett* (1928) 44 TLR 295. Obviously, if he had been asked directly whether he had such convictions and had denied it, he would have been liable.

On the other hand, as Lord Campbell LC observed in *Walkers v Morgan* (1861) 3 D F & J 718,

> although simple reticence does not amount to a legal wrong . . . a single word or a nod or a wink or a shake of the head or a smile from one party might amount to misrepresentation.

And, of course, misrepresentation **by conduct** is possible. Thus, deliberately physically to conceal dry rot in a building may amount to misrepresentation. In *R v Barnard* (1837) 7 C & P 784, the defendant wore a cap and gown in Oxford in order to persuade shopkeepers to let him have goods on credit. The fact of appearing so dressed was held to amount to a false pretence, and although this was a criminal case, there is no reason to suppose that the same principles would not apply to civil proceedings.

The rule that silence does not amount to a misrepresentation is subject to four exceptions:

(a) **The statement is a half-truth**   A statement that is partial, i.e. fails to present the whole truth, can constitute misrepresentation: *Tapp v Lee* (1803) B & P 367. So if a vendor of property states that the property has planning permission for business purposes, but fails to add that the permission is a temporary one and is shortly due to expire, he is guilty of misrepresentation.

(b) **Change of circumstances**   A duty of disclosure may arise where the circumstances have changed – a statement which was true when made has become false by the time it is acted upon. An example of this is *With v O'Flanagan* [1936] Ch D 575. A doctor, negotiating the sale of his practice, correctly stated that it produced an income of £2,000 per annum. By the time the contract was signed four months later the practice had declined so that it was worth no more than £5 per week. It was held that the failure of the vendor to disclose this state of affairs was an actionable misrepresentation.

(c) **Contracts *uberrimae fidei* (of the utmost good faith)**   These are a type of contract which require full disclosure of all material facts. The most important example of such contracts is contracts of insurance.

(d) **Parties in a *fiduciary* relationship**   Where the parties are in a relationship based on good faith (e.g. principal and agent, solicitor and client, doctor and patient), a duty of disclosure will arise.

6.3.3.2   Inducement

To amount to an actionable misrepresentation, a false statement of fact must be material in the sense that it **induces** the misrepresentee to enter the contract. If the misrepresentee relies on his own judgment or investigations, there will be no liability on the part of the misrepresentor.

Attwood v Small (1838) 6 Ch & Fin 232
The vendors of a mine made exaggerated statements as to its earning potential and the purchaser instructed a firm of expert surveyors to check the veracity of the statements. The surveyors reported that the vendors' statements were correct.

The vendors were not liable – the purchasers had been induced to enter the contract by the expert's report and not by the vendors.

Is the purchaser in *Attwood* v *Small* left entirely without a remedy?

The purchaser in such a situation would, of course, nowadays have an action against the surveyors for negligence: *Hedley Byrne & Co. Ltd* v *Heller & Partners* (see **6.3.4.2**).

Redgrave v *Hurd* (1881) Ch D 1, introduces a complication to the above principle. The plaintiff, a solicitor, wished to take a partner and negotiated with Hurd. The plaintiff told Hurd that the income of the practice was £300–£400 per annum and Hurd was shown papers purporting to prove this. If Hurd had read these documents carefully he would have seen that the practice was virtually worthless. He did not read them, but the court nevertheless held the misrepresentation to be actionable, and the plaintiff's action for breach of contract failed. It made no difference that a prudent purchaser would have discovered the true position.

Why do you think the case was decided this way? The answer is that the misrepresentation was material to Hurd's decision to enter into the contract. However, if the plaintiff is **unaware** of the misrepresentation at the time of the contract, there can be no liability (*Horsfall* v *Thomas* (1862) 1 H & C 90), and the position is the same if he is aware of it but it is proved that it cannot possibly have affected his judgment: *Smith* v *Chadwick* (1884) 9 AC 187.

The misrepresentation does not have to be the sole inducing factor. If it was clearly one inducing cause it is irrelevant that it was not the only inducing cause. For example, in *Edgington* v *Fitzmaurice* (**6.3.3.1**), the plaintiff's action succeeded when he was induced to take debentures in a company, partly by a mis-statement in the prospectus, and partly because of his own incorrect assumption that debenture holders would have a charge (a type of security interest) over the company's property.

6.3.4   TYPES OF MISREPRESENTATION

In the modern law, misrepresentation is classed as fraudulent, negligent or wholly innocent, and we shall now consider these terms.

6.3.4.1   Fraudulent misrepresentation

'Fraudulent' in this sense was defined by Lord Herschell in *Derry* v *Peek* (1889) 14 App Cas 337, as a false statement that is 'made (i) knowingly, or (ii) without belief in its truth, or (iii) recklessly, careless as to whether it be true of false'. The essence of fraud is the absence of honest belief. In *Derry* v *Peek*, a share prospectus falsely stated that the company had the right to use mechanical power to draw trams, without explaining that government consent was required for this. In fact, the directors honestly believed that obtaining consent was a pure formality, although it was ultimately refused. The House of Lords held that there had been no **fraudulent** misrepresentation.

6.3.4.2 Negligent misrepresentation

Negligent mis-statement at common law

Until 1963, damages could be claimed for misrepresentation only where it was fraudulent. All non-fraudulent misrepresentations were classed as 'innocent' and damages were not available for them. In 1963, the House of Lords stated, *obiter*, in *Hedley Byrne & Co. Ltd* v *Heller & Partners Ltd* [1964] AC 465, that in certain circumstances damages may be recoverable in tort for negligent mis-statement causing financial loss. The liability depends on a duty of care arising from a 'special relationship' between the parties. It is now clear that a party can claim damages under the principle in *Hedley Byrne* where a negligent mis-statement has induced him to enter a contract: *Esso Petroleum Co. Ltd* v *Mardon* [1976] QB 801. Broadly speaking, the special relationship will arise only where the maker of the statement possesses knowledge or skill relevant to the subject matter of the contract and can reasonably foresee that the other party will rely on the statement.

Negligent misrepresentation under the Misrepresentation Act 1967

Section 2(1) of the 1967 Act introduced a statutory claim for damages for non-fraudulent misrepresentation. It provides that where one party (Good) has entered a contract after a misrepresentation has been made to him by another party (Bad), and as a result thereof Good has suffered loss, then, if Bad would be liable to damages in respect thereof had the misrepresentation been made fraudulently, Bad shall be so liable notwithstanding that the misrepresentation was not made fraudulently, unless Bad proves that he had reasonable grounds to believe and did believe up to the time the contract was made that the facts represented were true.

SAQ 69

It has been said that after 1967 the distinction between representations and terms is no longer of such great significance. Do you agree? Justify your answer and list your reasons below.

You should be aware that the subsection assumes all non-fraudulent statements are negligent and puts the burden on the maker of the statement to disprove negligence.

The main effect of the Misrepresentation Act 1967 is to provide a remedy in damages for negligent misrepresentations. The pressing need which existed before 1967 to show that the statement was a term of the contract no longer applies (damages are not generally available for wholly innocent misrepresentation).

6.3.4.3   Wholly innocent misrepresentation

We have seen that before 1963, the word 'innocent' was used to describe all misrepresentations that were not fraudulent. In the light of *Hedley Byrne* and s. 2(1) of the 1967 Act, the word may now be used to refer to a statement made by a person who **has** reasonable grounds for believing in its truth. To avoid confusion, 'wholly innocent' is a better description.

6.3.5   REMEDIES FOR MISREPRESENTATION

Let us assume that an actionable misrepresentation has occurred. We now need to consider the remedies available to Good.

6.3.5.1   Rescission

Rescission is available whether the misrepresentation is fraudulent, negligent or innocent.

Rescission means setting aside the contract. This may be done by Good applying to the court for an order rescinding the contract, or he may rescind by notifying Bad or by any other act indicating repudiation of liability. Depending on the facts, this could take the form of, say, notifying the police or a Justice of the Peace.

The effect of rescission is to terminate the contract *ab initio*, i.e. the parties are put back in the position they would have been in had the contract never been made. In order to achieve this position, an order of rescission may be accompanied by the court ordering an **indemnity**. This is a money payment by the misrepresentor which is designed to restore the parties to their original positions. It is limited to payments in respect of obligations necessarily created by the contract and is to be distinguished from damages. The distinction is illustrated by *Whittington v Seale Hayne* (1900) 82 LT 49. Poultry breeders took a lease of premises as a result of an innocent misrepresentation that the premises were sanitary. They were not and the contract was rescinded. It was held that an indemnity could be recovered in respect of rent, rates and repairs as these were obligations necessarily created by taking the lease. The indemnity would not, however, cover loss of business profits, loss of stock and medical expenses etc. as these were losses related to the plaintiffs' business and the plaintiffs were not obliged to carry on a business under the terms of the contract. Such items, had they been awarded, would have amounted to damages.

In what circumstances do you think that this remedy remains particularly significant after the Misrepresentation Act 1967? Write them down below.

An indemnity may still be awarded after the Misrepresentation Act 1967, although it will not be appropriate where damages are in fact awarded, either under that Act or at common law. This means that the remedy remains particularly significant where the contract is rescinded for a wholly innocent misrepresentation.

There are certain 'bars' to rescission, i.e. situations in which Good may lose the right to rescind. These are:

Affirmation

Affirmation occurs where Good, with full knowledge of the misrepresentation, states (expressly or impliedly) that he intends to continue with the contract. Thus if Good, having bought a vehicle from Bad as a result of a misrepresentation as to its condition, subsequently agrees to share with Bad the cost of necessary repairs and continues to use it, he may be said to have affirmed the contract: *Long* v *Lloyd* [1958] 1 WLR 753.

Lapse of time in seeking a remedy may be evidence of affirmation. In the case of non-fraudulent misrepresentation, rescission may be barred where, even though there is no delay in seeking a remedy, Good does not become aware of the misrepresentation until a period of time has elapsed since the contract: *Leaf* v *International Galleries* [1950] 2 KB 86. In that case the plaintiff bought a picture as a result of an innocent misrepresentation that it was a Constable, and five years later discovered it was not genuine. The Court of Appeal held that rescission was barred.

In *Peyman* v *Lanjani* [1985] Ch 457, the Court of Appeal held that the right to rescind will be lost by affirmation only where the plaintiff not only knows the facts but is also aware of his **right** to rescind.

Impossibility of restitution

Good will lose the right to rescind if the parties cannot be restored to their original position. In *Clarke* v *Dickson* (1858) E B & E 148, the plaintiff invested money in a partnership to exploit a lead mine (as a result of a misrepresentation by the defendants). Later the partnership was in financial difficulty and, with the plaintiff's consent, it was converted into a limited company with the partnership capital converted into shares. On discovering the false representations, the plaintiff sought rescission of the contract. It was held that rescission could not be granted because the partnership was no longer in existence, having been replaced by the company. It was not possible to restore the parties to their original positions.

In this case the property had totally changed in nature, but where the property has merely deteriorated the court may rescind with a cash adjustment: *Erlanger* v *New Sombrero Phosphate Co.* (1878) 3 App Cas 1218 (a case involving a phosphate mine which had been worked in the period between entering into the contract and recission).

Third party rights

Rescission is not available where an innocent third party has acquired rights to the subject matter of the contract. This bar to rescission also operated in *Clarke* v *Dickson* (above) as creditors had acquired rights over the company.

Two further bars to rescission were **abolished** by s. 1 of the Misrepresentation Act 1967. These were, first, where the misrepresentation had become incorporated as a contractual term, and secondly, where, after a non-fraudulent misrepresentation, the contract had been executed. You should bear this in mind when looking at some of the older cases.

6.3.5.2   Damages for misrepresentation

Damages for misrepresentation may be claimed or, as the case may be, awarded under the following heads:

Damages for fraudulent misrepresentation

This is essentially a claim for compensation in the tort of deceit. The object is to restore the plaintiff to the position he would have been in had there been no misrepresentation, i.e. the amount by which he is out of pocket by entering the contract. In *McConnel* v *Wright* [1903] 1 Ch 546, the plaintiff was induced to buy shares by a fraudulent misrepresentation. He recovered the difference between the purchase price and the actual value of the shares, assessed at the time of the contract.

How does this outcome differ from what the result would have been if the plaintiff had been able to sue for breach of contract where damages are awarded on a loss of bargain basis? Please list your anticipated differences below.

You should see that the 'out of pocket' rule does not necessarily preclude a claim for loss of profits, as illustrated by *East* v *Maurer* [1991] 2 All ER 733, where the plaintiff purchased a hairdressing salon on the basis of a fraudulent misrepresentation. Damages were awarded for the profit the plaintiff might have made had he bought a different salon in the same area – he could recover for the 'lost opportunity cost' of relying on the misrepresentation. However, this was a smaller sum than the plaintiff would have recovered had the defendant warranted the value of the salon (damages for breach of contract).

Damages for **breach of contract**, on the other hand, are normally on the 'loss of bargain' basis, i.e. the injured party is put in the position he would have been in if the contract had not been breached. Thus if in *McConnel*, the shares had been **warranted** as having a certain value, then the plaintiff could have recovered (in an action for breach of contract) that value. In practice the difference can be striking and an example will show you this:

Let us suppose the vendor of a business makes certain misrepresentations which, if true, would mean the business was worth £100,000. The purchaser puts down a deposit of £50,000, the balance to be paid at a later date. In fact the business is really worth £25,000. Can you work out the damages on the tortious basis? What would they be on the contractual basis? The answers are that damages on the tortious basis (i.e. for misrepresentation) would amount to £25,000; on the contractual basis to £75,000.

However, in *Doyle* v *Olby (Ironmongers) Ltd* [1969] 2 QB 158, it was held that in a fraudulent misrepresentation action the plaintiff may recover for all the **direct** loss incurred as a result of the misrepresentation, regardless of foreseeability. This is a more generous basis than either contract (reasonable contemplation) or negligence (reasonable foreseeability) and can, in practice, bring the damages up to the contractual level, or even exceed it, as happened in *Doyle*.

We can see an interesting (and expensive for the defendant!) application of *Doyle* in *Smith & New Court Securities Ltd* v *Scrimgeour Vickers (Asset Management) Ltd* [1996] 4 All ER 769. The defendants, who owned shares in F Ltd, offered them for sale to the plaintiffs, fraudulently claiming that other bids had been received. On the faith of this the plaintiffs increased their offer from 78p per share to 82.25p per share. The defendants accepted this offer and sold in excess of 28 million shares to the plaintiffs at a price of just over £23 million. Unfortunately, F Ltd had been duped by another unrelated fraud, and its share price went down dramatically. The plaintiffs managed to sell the shares at a loss of over £11 million, which they claimed by way of damages from the defendants. The defendants argued that damages should be limited to the difference between the price which the plaintiffs would have been prepared to pay without the fraud (78p per share) and the price actually paid (82.25p per share).

The House of Lords held that an application of *Doyle* entitled the plaintiffs to recover their full consequential loss. They would never have entered into the contract at all were it not for the fraud, and as a result of the fraud they were 'locked into the property'.

The House (*obiter*) also expressed scepticism as to whether the deceit test should apply to an award of damages under s. 2(1) of the Misrepresentation Act 1967, but gave no conclusive view. *Royscott Trust Ltd* v *Rogerson* remains goods law for the time being (see below).

Damages for negligent misrepresentation

Good may elect to claim damages under *Hedley Byrne* provided the ingredients of the tort are established. The measure of damages will be on the same basis as deceit (i.e. the 'out of pocket' rule discussed above), but the remoteness test will be one of reasonable foreseeability.

As an alternative Good may base his claim for damages on s. 2(1) of the Misrepresentation Act 1967. As explained later, where Good has entered into a contract, s. 2(1) will be the normal remedy, not *Hedley Byrne*.

Under s. 2(1), the maker of the statement, Bad, is deemed to have been negligent and bears the burden of disproving negligence. The wording of the subsection (which is not a model of clarity) appears to introduce what has been called a 'fiction of fraud'. This apparently requires Good to establish that Bad would have been liable in damages if the statement had been made fraudulently. The main consequence is that the measure of damages under s. 2(1) is on the same basis as damages for deceit, i.e. the out of pocket rule. Similarly, the remoteness test will be the same as that laid down in *Doyle* v *Olby* (above). This was affirmed by the Court of Appeal in *Royscott Trust Ltd* v *Rogerson* [1991] 3 All ER 294. Despite earlier cases (e.g. *Watts* v *Spence* [1976] Ch 165) placing damages under s. 2(1) on the contractual basis, it would now seem to be established, as a result of the *Royscott* decision, that damages under s. 2(1) are indeed awarded on the same basis as in the tort of deceit.

The following case, which you should study carefully, is the leading decision on s. 2(1):

Howard Marine and Dredging Co. Ltd v *Ogden and Sons* [1978] QB 574
Negotiations took place for the hire of certain sea-going barges and the owner's negotiator misrepresented their capacity. He relied on Lloyds Register which was in fact incorrect, the correct information being on file at the owner's head office.

There was liability under s. 2(1). The presumption of negligence had not been rebutted and the burden on the misrepresentor is a heavy one.

It is clear that the reasonable grounds of belief must continue up to the time when the contract was made, and so the statute imposes an absolute obligation on the representor not to state facts which he cannot prove he had reasonable grounds to believe. (Such an obligation does not necessarily exist under *Hedley Byrne*.)

ACTIVITY 23

Write down below all of the advantages and disadvantages you can think of concerning an action under s. 2(1) vis-à-vis an action under *Hedley Byrne & Co.* v *Heller & Partners*. If you need more space use a separate sheet of paper.

You should have compiled a list something like this:

(a) Section 2(1) applies only 'where a person has entered into a contract', so if there is an operative mistake and the contract is **void**, no action for damages under s. 2(1) would be possible since there is no contract.

(b) Under *Hedley Byrne* you do not have to prove that a misrepresentation has been made, i.e. it could be a statement of opinion or law.

(c) An action may be brought under *Hedley Byrne* where the misrepresentation was made by a third party to the contract because privity of contract does not apply to the law of torts.

(d) *Hedley Byrne* may be applicable where negotiations do not result in a contract between Good and Bad, but Good nevertheless suffers loss in reliance on the misrepresentation.

(e) The great advantage of s. 2(1) is the fact that it provides Good with an assumption of negligence on the part of Bad; under *Hedley Byrne* there is a far greater burden of proof.

(f) Damages awarded under s. 2(1) are not subject to a reasonable foreseeability test.

Nevertheless, in all cases where Good **has entered into a contract** as a result of negligent misrepresentation, an action under s. 2(1) will be the normal remedy.

6.3.5.3   Damages in lieu of rescission

You should by now have become aware that damages may not be claimed for a wholly innocent misrepresentation, i.e. one that is neither fraudulent nor negligent. The remedy for wholly innocent misrepresentation is rescission, which may, as we have seen, be accompanied by an indemnity.

However, s. 2(2) of the Misrepresentation Act 1967 gives the court a **discretion,** where Good would be entitled to rescind, to award damages in lieu of rescission. Damages under s. 2(2) cannot be **claimed** as such, they can only be **awarded** by the court. The power of the court under the subsection can be used only in the case of non-fraudulent misrepresentation (i.e. negligent and wholly innocent misrepresentation) and presumably, you might have thought, cannot be used where one of the bars to rescission exist. However, in *Thomas Witler Ltd* v *TBP Industries Ltd, The Independent*, 15 July 1994, Jacob J decided that the power to award damages depended only upon the right to rescind having existed in the past.

Where damages are awarded under s. 2(1) the court must (by virtue of s. 2(3)) take into account any damages awarded in lieu of rescission under s. 2(2).

6.3.6   EXCLUSION OF LIABILITY FOR MISREPRESENTATION

You may have wondered whether a party can attempt to exclude liability for misrepresentation, and attempts are not uncommon, e.g., by estate agents. The law on this is to be found in s. 3 of the Misrepresentation Act 1967, which provides, that if a contract contains a term which would exclude or restrict:

(a)   any liability to which Bad may be subject by reason of any misrepresentation made by him before the contract was made; or

(b)   any remedy available to Good by reason of such a misrepresentation,

that term shall be of no effect except in so far as it satisfies the requirement of reasonableness as stated in s. 11(1) of the Unfair Contract Terms Act 1977; and it is for those claiming that the term satisfies that requirement to show that it does.

We need to consider one or two points in connection with s. 3. The first is that it cannot be evaded by the contract term in question deeming that statements of fact are not representations: *Cremdean Properties Ltd* v *Nash* (1977) 244 EG 547. On the other hand, a term which stated that an auctioneer had no **authority** to make any representation was held to fall outside s. 3 as it was not an exclusion clause at all but a limitation on the apparent authority of the auctioneer: *Overbrooke Estate Ltd* v *Glencombe Properties Ltd* [1974] 3 All ER 511.

6.3.7   SUMMARY

Misrepresentation is one of the most difficult topics in the law of contract, involving as it does a mixture of common law, equity and statutory rules. If you are faced with a problem involving pre-contractual negotiations you may find the 'action guide' in **Fig. 6** helpful.

Figure 6   Action guide to misrepresentation

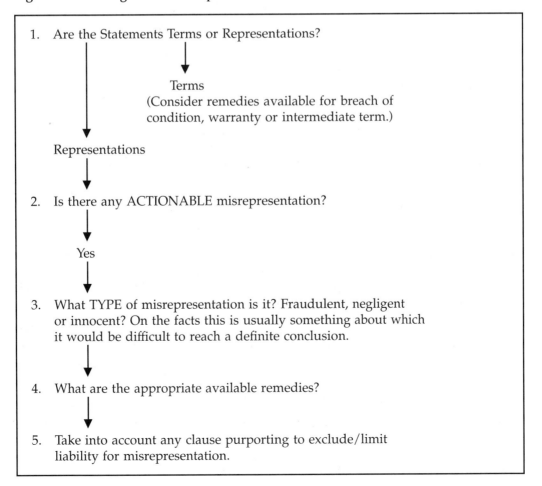

1.   Are the Statements Terms or Representations?

Terms
(Consider remedies available for breach of
condition, warranty or intermediate term.)

Representations

2.   Is there any ACTIONABLE misrepresentation?

Yes

3.   What TYPE of misrepresentation is it? Fraudulent, negligent
or innocent? On the facts this is usually something about which
it would be difficult to reach a definite conclusion.

4.   What are the appropriate available remedies?

5.   Take into account any clause purporting to exclude/limit
liability for misrepresentation.

6.4   Duress and Undue Influence

Suppose we have a concluded agreement but that Good says it was obtained as the result of some improper and excessive pressure exerted by Bad. The problem is dealt with by the common law doctrine of **duress** and the equitable doctrine of **undue influence.** These will be discussed in turn.

6.4.1   DURESS

Duress is a common law concept which, if established, renders the contract **voidable**. The scope of duress at common law was originally very narrow and confined to actual or threatened unlawful physical violence or constraint of the other party. In the Australian case of *Barton* v *Armstrong* [1975] 2 All ER 465, A threatened to have B killed if he did not buy A's shares in a company of which B was the managing director. The majority of the Privy Council held that the agreement was vitiated by duress.

Originally the courts refused to recognise 'duress of goods', i.e. a threat to damage a person's property as constituting duress. However, it is now recognised that the doctrine extends to goods. In *The Siboen* [1976] 1 Lloyd's Rep 293, Kerr J said, *obiter*, that a person coerced into a contract by the threat of having his house burned down or a picture slashed could plead duress.

It would seem that the basis of duress is an unlawful threat amounting to 'coercion of the will'. In *Pao On* v *Lau Yiu Long* [1979] 3 All ER 65, Lord Scarman said that in determining whether there was coercion of the will such that there was no consent, it is material whether the person alleged to have been coerced, Good, (i) did or did not protest, (ii) whether at the time he did or did not have an alternative course open to him such as an adequate legal remedy, (iii) whether he was independently advised, (iv) whether after entering the contract he took steps to avoid it. These are all matters relevant in considering whether Good acted voluntarily or not.

There are a number of cases in which the courts have recognised a doctrine of 'economic duress'. This may occur where parties are already in an existing contractual relationship and Bad takes advantage of the plight of Good to renegotiate the contract on terms advantageous to himself.

North Ocean Shipping Co. Ltd v *Hyundai Construction Ltd* [1978] QB 705
A contract was made to build an oil tanker for an agreed price. The dollar was devalued and the shipbuilders refused to complete unless the buyer promised to pay a further 10 per cent. The buyer agreed and made the payment as the ship was urgently needed to fulfil a charter. (At this point you will notice that the facts resemble *Stilk* v *Myrick* (which we considered at **2.4.2.2.**) However, here the judge, Mocatta J, found a technical consideration in the fact that the shipyard had increased a letter of credit.

Nevertheless, the payment could **in principle** be recovered on the ground of duress, although the buyers had lost their right to rescind. They had paid the money and made no further protest until several months after taking delivery of the ship. This was held to constitute an affirmation. In effect the buyers had complained too late.

The parties need not already be in an existing contractual relationship for economic duress to arise. In *Universe Tankships of Monrovia* v *ITTF* [1983] 1 AC 366, the plaintiff's ship was 'blacked' by a trade union, and, in order to secure its release from blacking, the plaintiffs paid a sum of money into the union's welfare fund. A majority of the House of Lords held that the agreement was vitiated by economic duress.

There is a dividing line between economic duress and what has been called 'hard and fair bargaining' or mere commercial pressure, and it will always be difficult to draw. It will turn on detailed findings of fact by the court as, for example, in *Atlas Express Ltd* v *Kafco (Importers and Distributors) Ltd* [1989] 3 WLR 389.

ACTIVITY 24

Read *Atlas Express* v *Kafco* in *Cases and Materials* (6.2). Is lack of consent the best approach to the establishment of economic duress? Can you discover a better approach in Tucker J's judgment? Explain below.

You may have said that lack of consent is not terribly helpful because the coerced party always consents to the contract into which he enters. Whether this consent is genuine or not is much better determined by examining whether the coerced party had any real, practical alternative to entering into the contract. As Tucker J said, the defendant felt that he was 'over a barrel'.

We have discovered that so far duress requires an unlawful threat. This could be a threat to commit a crime, a tort or, as is often the case where economic duress is involved, a breach of contract. However, in *CTN Cash & Carry Ltd* v *Gallaher* [1994] 4 All ER 714 the Court of Appeal took the view that it is possible, in principle, for duress to be based on a lawful threat.

CTN Cash & Carry Ltd v *Gallaher* [1994] 4 All ER 714
The plaintiff company ran a cash and carry business. The defendants in error sent a delivery of cigarettes to the wrong place of business for the plaintiffs. The plaintiffs agreed to remedy the situation, but before the cigarettes could be moved they were stolen. The defendants **genuinely but mistakenly** believed that the cigarettes had been stolen at the plaintiff's risk, and refused to continue to supply the plaintiffs on a credit basis unless they paid for the stolen cigarettes, a lawful threat. The plaintiffs paid in order to retain their credit facilities, but then attempted to recover the payment on grounds of economic duress.

The Court of Appeal found that no economic duress had been established on the facts of the case, but did not rule out a possible finding of economic duress based on a lawful threat in an appropriate case.

SAQ 72

Can you envisage circumstances in which economic duress might have been established had the facts of the case been slightly different? The words in bold type might give you a clue.

The Court of Appeal emphasised that the defendants had acted in good faith (bona fide), i.e. they genuinely believed that they were entitled to the money which they demanded. Presumably, had their belief not been genuine, economic duress might have been established on the basis of their lawful threat.

Last, you should note that (as with misrepresentation) duress need not be the only or main reason for the plaintiff entering the contract in order for the contract to be vitiated: *Barton* v *Armstrong* (above).

6.4.2   UNDUE INFLUENCE

The narrow scope of the common law doctrine of duress led to the development, in equity, of the doctrine of undue influence. The doctrine applies to certain situations where improper pressure (not amounting to duress at common law) was brought to bear on a party to enter a contract.

The effect of undue influence is to render the contract **voidable**.

Explain the difference between a *void* contract and a *voidable* contract below.

A **void** contract is void from the outset (*ab initio*) and no rights or obligations can be transferred under it. A **voidable** contract is valid until the innocent party takes steps to avoid it. Thus, rights and obligations can be transferred under it prior to its being set aside.

There are two classes of case which fall within the doctrine. First, where there is no special relationship between the parties, in which case undue influence must be proved. Secondly, where, because of the relationship between the parties, there is a 'presumption' of undue influence.

6.4.2.1   No special relationship (actual undue influence)

Where there is no special relationship between the parties, Good must establish that Bad exerted dominating influence over him which he used to extract an advantageous bargain.

Williams v *Bayley* (1866) LR 1 HL 200
A young man forged his father's signature on some promissory notes and presented them to a bank, who discovered the forgery. At a meeting between the bank, the father and the son, the bank threatened to prosecute the son unless some satisfactory arrangement could be arrived at, and the possible penalty of transportation for life was referred

to. As a result, the father entered into an agreement to mortgage his property to pay for the notes.

The House of Lords set aside the agreement on the grounds of undue influence – the father could not be said to have entered the agreement voluntarily.

SAQ 74

Why was *Williams* v *Bayley* not a case of duress? List your reasons below.

The reason the bank's act in *Williams* v *Bayley* did not amount to duress is because the **threat** here is not **in itself** unlawful, i.e. to report a person for a criminal offence.

It would seem that in this type of case, Good must establish actual coercion or that Bad exercised such domination or control that Good's independence of decision was substantially undermined. Many of the cases under this heading involve gifts, not contracts, although the legal principles are the same.

6.4.2.2 Where there is a special relationship (presumed undue influence)

A transaction may be set aside on the ground that a **presumption** of undue influence arises from the nature of the **relationship** between the parties.

The presumption applies to the following relationships: parent and child; guardian and ward; solicitor and client; trustee and beneficiary; religious adviser and disciple; principal and agent. It will be noticed that in all these relationships, trust or confidence is reposed by one party in another to such a degree that the former becomes dependent on the latter. (In spite of this, or perhaps because of it, it seems that the presumption does not apply between a husband and wife!)

The list of such special or 'fiduciary' (based on good faith) relationships is not closed, and even where the relationship does not fall into one of recognised classes above, it is possible to establish that the presumption arises from the particular facts. Atiyah says that

> . . . in any case where one person turns to another for advice, or assistance, and the court thinks that the relationship of the parties, for example, their relative ages, or experience, or blood relationship, is such as to require confidence and good faith, the duty not to abuse that confidence may be imposed.

In *Lloyds Bank* v *Bundy* [1975] QB 326, the Court of Appeal applied these principles to a transaction between a bank and one of its customers. An elderly farmer gave the bank a guarantee in respect of his son's overdraft and mortgaged the farmhouse to the bank as security. It was clear that the farmer had placed himself entirely in the hands of the assistant bank manager and had been given no opportunity to seek independent advice.

On the particular facts of the case, the transaction was set aside. In *National Westminster Bank v Morgan* [1985] AC 686, the House of Lords made it clear that the presumption of undue influence does not arise merely from the relationship of banker and customer (see further below).

What, then, is the effect of establishing that a presumption of undue influence arises? The position is that unless the presumption is rebutted, the transaction is liable to be set aside. The orthodox view is that the presumption may be rebutted by showing that there was no undue influence. However, the cases show that a transaction falling into this category may be set aside even though the conduct of the defendant falls well short of 'domination' or 'undue influence'. Thus in *Goldsworthy v Brickell* [1987] 1 All ER 853, the plaintiff, an 85-year-old farmer, who owned a valuable farm, came to trust and depend on the defendant, a neighbouring farmer, for help and advice. There was no personal domination as the plaintiff was fit and active with a strong personality. Nevertheless, it was held that there was a presumption of undue influence in the relationship between them. An agreement whereby the plaintiff let his farm to the defendant on very favourable terms was set aside.

In practice the cases show that there are three ways in which the presumption may be rebutted:

Transaction not manifestly disadvantageous (relevant to presumed undue influence only)

If it can be established that the transaction was not disadvantageous or unfair to the plaintiff then it will be upheld.

National Westminster Bank v Morgan [1985] AC 686
A husband and wife were faced with losing their home because the building society was seeking possession for non-payment of the mortgage. The bank agreed to refinance the house purchase by granting a bridging loan to cover a short period until the husband expected to have the money. The husband being an enthusiastic but unsuccessful businessman, the bank required a charge on the house for the loan. The bank manager visited the Morgans' home with the relevant papers, where he mistakenly assured the wife that the charge would not extend to her husband's business liabilities to the bank. The bank's documents did, in fact, extend to her husband's business liabilities and the wife signed them. The husband died and the bank sought possession of the house. The wife did not raise the misrepresentation issue but claimed that the charge should be set aside for undue influence.

The relationship did not raise the presumption. The manager had explained the charge to the wife but she had not sought the manager's advice on the wisdom of entering into the transaction. She had signed the charge because she knew it was the only way to preserve the family home. Additionally, the transaction was not manifestly disadvantageous to the Morgans since it enabled them to stay in the family home on terms not inferior to those enjoyed under the building society mortgage.

Independent advice obtained

If the plaintiff received competent advice from an independent third party adviser then this may be sufficient to rebut the presumption. But the mere existence of independent advice may not be enough. In *Inche Noriah v Sheik Allie Bin Omar* [1929] AC 127, an aged widow who gave away almost the whole of her property to her nephew had consulted a solicitor, but the solicitor was not fully aware of the circumstances, nor did he advise her that she could equally well have benefited her nephew by will.

Spontaneous act of free will

It was established in *Goldsworthy v Brickell* (above) that if, despite the suspicious circumstances, the transaction was a truly spontaneous act of free will, this may rebut the presumption. It must be proved that the 'weaker' party fully understood and intended the transaction that was in fact entered into.

6.4.2.3 Rescission

The remedy for a plaintiff who has entered into a contract tainted by undue influence is rescission of the contract. The remedy may be lost in two ways:

Affirmation

If, after the undue influence has ceased, the influenced party expressly or impliedly affirms the transaction, the right to rescind will be lost. It seems that a private, secret mental reservation not to affirm will not suffice. The most significant factor will be the lapse of time after the termination of the influence. In *Allcard* v *Skinner* (1887) 36 Ch D 145, the plaintiff, under the influence of the defendant spiritual adviser, gave a large sum of money to the defendant. Six years after leaving the religious order in question the plaintiff sought to recover the money, but it was held that her claim was barred by delay.

Third party rights

If third party rights have intervened, for example by a resale of the property which is the subject matter of the contract, rescission will not be available. If the third party is actually aware of the undue influence then the transaction which he has entered into will be likewise tainted and will also be voidable: *Bridgeman* v *Green* (1757) Wilm 58.

6.4.3 INEQUALITY OF BARGAINING POWER

The cases just discussed on undue influence are part of a wider principle of fairness in contract bargaining. A similar type of case is the 'unconscionable bargain'.

In *Fry* v *Lane* (1888) 40 Ch D 312, it was held that where a purchase is made from a poor and ignorant person at a considerable undervalue, the vendor having had no independent advice, the court has an equitable jurisdiction to set the contract aside. In *Cresswell* v *Potter* [1978] 1 WLR 225, the doctrine was applied to a post office telephonist, who, being a member of the 'lower income group' and 'less highly educated', was held to be the modern equivalent of poor and ignorant!

In *Lloyds Bank* v *Bundy* (see **6.4.2.2**), Lord Denning MR had sought to establish a single doctrine whereby all the instances where the courts intervene to set aside unconscionable transactions (including duress and undue influence) **are** based on a single unifying principle, namely, 'inequality of bargaining power'. However, in *National Westminster Bank* v *Morgan* (**6.4.2.2**), the House of Lords refused to accept such a wide principle. Lord Scarman said: '. . . there is no precisely defined law setting limits to the equitable jurisdiction of a court to relieve against undue influence.'

Read the speech of Lord Scarman in *National Westminster Bank* v *Morgan*. **Why did he reject the introduction of a principle of inequality of bargaining power? Answer in** *Cases and Materials* (**6.3.2**).

You should have discovered that Lord Scarman regarded the introduction of such a sweeping principle as the function of Parliament and not of the judiciary.

6.4.4   PARTY TAINTED BY UNDUE INFLUENCE USED BY A THIRD PARTY

This situation has arisen in the circumstances set out in **Figure 7.**

Figure 7   Party tainted by undue influence

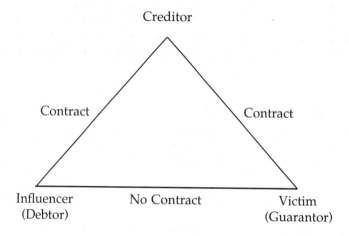

Normally, the influencer has persuaded the victim by undue influence or misrepresentation to guarantee a loan to the influencer using the matrimonial home by way of security. The issue is whether the victim can set up the undue influence/misrepresentation of the influencer to set aside the guarantee entered into with the creditor, i.e. can the creditor be tainted by the influencer's undue influence/misrepresentation?

In a number of cases this type of situation was dealt with by one or the other of two approaches:

6.4.4.1   Agency

The debtor/influencer was deemed to be the agent of the creditor. Any undue influence exerted upon the victim was deemed to be used on behalf of the creditor (even if the creditor was unaware of it!).

6.4.4.2   Special equity

This was an approach applied to married women, who were regarded as requiring special protection because of the likelihood of their being subjected to undue influence by their husbands in business matters. The creditor was obliged to ensure that steps were taken to avoid the risk of undue influence by the husband when the wife was providing security for the husband's debts.

Subsequently, the House of Lords has rejected the special equity argument and declared the agency approach to be of limited value. Situations such as this are now to be dealt with under the next doctrine.

6.4.4.3   Notice

Barclay's Bank v *O'Brien* [1993] 4 All ER 417

Mr O'Brien wished to increase the overdraft facility available to a company in which he had an interest to £135,000, and offered the matrimonial home, which was in his and his wife's joint names, as security. Mr and Mrs O'Brien executed the legal charge on the house at the bank.

Mrs O'Brien was given no explanation of the effect of the documents. She signed the legal charge without reading the documents. Mr O'Brien had told her the charge was to secure only £60,000 and would be released in a short time. The company's indebtedness grew and the bank sought to enforce its charge.

Mrs O'Brien was entitled to set aside the legal charge on the matrimonial home.

The findings and principles underlying this decision are as follows.

(a)   Mrs O'Brien was an 'intelligent and independent minded' woman who had not been unduly influenced by her husband.

(b)   However, she had been misled by her husband's misrepresentation of the amount of the guarantee, and would not have entered into the guarantee had she known of its true extent.

(c)   Such cases, whether involving misrepresentation or undue influence, are best dealt with by applying the doctrine of 'notice'.

This means that:

(a)   if the creditor had **actual** knowledge of the undue influence/misrepresentation the contract will be avoided; and

(b)   the same result will ensue where the circumstances should put the creditor on enquiry, i.e. **constructive** notice.

Constructive notice will arise where the transaction is of a type where there is a substantial risk of misconduct by the debtor (e.g. a wife guaranteeing her husband's business debts) **and** the transaction on the face of it is not to the financial advantage of the victim.

According to Lord Browne-Wilkinson the approach is not limited to husband and wife relationships, it extends to cohabitees, whether heterosexual or homosexual; furthermore the creditor can avoid the effects of the doctrine by informing the victim of the true nature of the transaction (in the absence of the debtor) and by advising the victim to take independent legal advice.

Interestingly, the Court of Appeal in *Massey v Midland Bank plc* [1995] 1 All ER 929 was prepared to apply the doctrine to a couple who had a long-term sexual and emotional relationship, and had children, but did not cohabit.

Furthermore, the test laid down by Lord Browne-Wilkinson as to how the creditor can avoid the effect of the doctrine of constuctive notice has not been regarded as exhaustive in subsequent cases. In both the *Massey* case (above) and in *Banco Exterior Internacional SA v Thomas* [1997] 1 WLR 221 the Court of Appeal found that the bank had discharged its obligation by ensuring that the victim had received legal advice, and had no duty to enquire further into the quality of the advice, even though in the *Massey* case the solicitor consulted was that of the influencer, i.e. the bank is entitled to assume that the solicitor will advise properly. Additionally, the test was deemed to have been satisfied in *Massey*, even though the bank did not explain the true nature of the transaction to the victim, because the solicitor consulted had explained the nature of the transaction to the victim in the presence of the influencer!

Conversely, in *Credit Lyonnais Bank Nederland NV v Burch* [1997] 1 All ER 144 the Court of Appeal adopted a much sterner approach. The case involved a relationship of presumed undue influence between an employer, who owned a business, and an employee. The employee was persuaded to offer her home as security for her employer's business bank overdraft facility of £270,000, the security being unlimited either as to time or amount. In these circumstances the Court of Appeal found that it was totally inadequate that the bank had encouraged her to seek legal advice. It should have explained to her the business's full financial position and overdraft facility, and ensured that she had received independent legal advice, before the transaction was entered into.

Can you see any way in which *Burch* can be distinguished from *Massey* and *Thomas*? If not, what reasons can you think of (expressed in terms of different priorities) to explain the divergent approaches adopted in the cases?

It may be possible to distinguish *Burch* from *Massey* and *Thomas* on the ground that the transaction was so massively disadvantageous, but this would seem to be a dubious principle for future advice. When does a transaction become sufficiently massively disadvantageous? The reality is that the approach in *Burch* puts the victim first, whereas *Massey* and *Thomas* are more concerned that the wheels of commerce should be allowed to run smoothly without imposing unreasonable burdens upon banks and similar institutions.

Whilst one would suspect that *Massey* and *Thomas* are likely to prevail, in *Royal Bank of Scotland* v *Etridge* [1997] 3 All ER 628 the Court of Appeal did at least place a duty upon the bank to ensure that the solicitor gave independent advice to the victim (in the absence of the influencer), when the solicitor had been appointed as the agent of the bank.

A contrast to the decision in *O'Brien*, demonstrating the significance of manifest disadvantage, can be seen in the House of Lords' decision in:

CIBC Mortgages v *Pitt* [1993] 4 All ER 433
CIBC Mortgages granted a joint loan of £150,000 secured on the matrimonial home to Mr and Mrs Pitt, having been told that the money was required for the purchase of a holiday cottage. Mr Pitt used the money to buy shares. He was initially successful with his investments, but later found himself in arrears in repaying the loan. CIBC brought proceedings for possession under the charge on the home. Mrs Pitt alleged that she was induced by Mr Pitt's undue influence to enter into the transaction.

CIBC could enforce the charge against Mrs Pitt. Although Mr Pitt had exercised actual undue influence over his wife (it being irrelevant as regards Mr Pitt that the transaction was not to Mrs Pitt's manifest disadvantage), CIBC was not tainted by this because it had no actual knowledge of the undue influence and the transaction appeared to be simply 'a normal advance to a husband and wife for their joint benefit'.

ACTIVITY 26

Read through 6.4.2 on undue influence again. How relevant now is the concept of 'manifest disadvantage' to each category of undue influence? List your reasons below.

You should have said something along the following lines:

(a) Manifest disadvantage is still required in cases of presumed undue influence: *National Westminster Bank* v *Morgan*.

(b) Manifest disadvantage is not required in cases of actual undue influence between **two** parties.

(c) Manifest disadvantage is relevant in **third party** cases (even where the influencer has used **actual** undue influence) in deciding whether the creditor should be deemed to have constructive notice of the undue influence.

6.4.5 SUMMARY

The most important aspect of duress is the relatively recently developed doctrine of economic duress, which remains difficult to identify and elusive to define. However, it seems best approached from a perspective of 'was a person's financial/economic position exploited unlawfully by threats by the other party in such a way as to leave him no practical alternative but to enter into the unfavourable contract in question?'

Undue influence is an equitable doctrine, not requiring threats, which has developed to deal with situations falling short of duress. Characteristically, the parties will enjoy a relationship of trust and confidence and one party's trust will have been abused by the other party to the transaction in question. A factor to isolate, particularly in the light of recent developments, is the relevance of 'manifest disadvantage'.

Duress and undue influence have moved closer together, and as long as undue influence continues to expand as necessary, there should be no need for a separate doctrine of 'inequality of bargaining power'.

6.5 Mistake

You may already be aware that an underlying principle of the law of contract is *caveat emptor* ('let the buyer beware'). This means that the situations in which a contract will be avoided on the ground that one or both parties have made a mistake will be somewhat limited. Nevertheless, the cases reveal that in certain circumstances a contract may be void at common law on the ground of a mistake; and in some cases, even where the contract is valid at law, it may nevertheless be voidable in equity on the ground of mistake.

A mistake which has the effect of rendering a contract void is described as an 'operative' mistake. Mistakes of law, as opposed to mistakes of fact, will not be operative.

6.5.1 COMMON MISTAKE

Here, the parties, although apparently in agreement, have entered into the contract on the basis of a false and fundamental assumption. It is called common mistake since both parties make the **same** mistake. The contract is not necessarily void at common law in these circumstances. The cases may be categorised as follows:

6.5.1.1 Mistake as to the existence of the subject matter (*res extincta*)

The contract will be void at common law if, unknown to the parties, the subject matter of the agreement does not exist or has ceased to exist. Thus, a cargo of corn, en route to London, had to be sold at a port of refuge as it had begun to ferment. Unaware of this, the respondents agreed a sale of the corn in London. It was held that the purchaser was not liable for the price: *Couturier v Hastie* (1856) 5 HLC 673.

Similarly, the parties may contract on the basis of a false assumption which underlies the contract, as in *Scott v Coulson* [1903] 2 Ch 249, where the plaintiff contracted to sell to the defendant a policy of life insurance on the life of a certain Mr Death. However, at the time of the contract, Death was already dead. The court set aside the transaction.

A statutory version of this principle is to be found in s. 6 of the Sale of Goods Act 1979, which provides that where there is a contract for the sale of specific goods which, without the knowledge of the seller, have perished at the time when the contract was made, the contract is void.

ACTIVITY 27

Read *Amalgamated Investment Co. Ltd* v *John Walker & Sons Ltd* in *Cases and Materials* (6.6.1). **What difference in approach to the case would there have been if the warehouse had been treated as listed at the time the contract came into existence?**

You might have answered that mistake applies where the contract is impossible at the time of entering into the contract. Thus, if the warehouse had been listed at the time the contract was made the argument would have to have been that the contract was void for mistake rather than frustrated. However, in neither scenario would the contract have been void, the purchasers being deemed to have taken on board the risk of the occurrence of such an event.

But even where the subject matter is not in existence, the contract is not automatically void. There are three possibilities which we may have to consider before the law of mistake comes into play:

Warranty

One party may have impliedly **warranted** the existence of the subject matter, as in *McRae v Commonwealth Disposals Commission* (1950) 84 CLR 377. The Commission invited tenders for the purchase of an oil tanker lying on the Journaund Reef. The plaintiff's tender was accepted. In fact there was no tanker lying anywhere near the longitude or latitude stated by the Commission and there was no such place as the Journaund Reef. However, the plaintiff did not discover this until he had incurred considerable expense in fitting out a salvage expedition. The High Court of Australia found that the Commission had acted carelessly rather than fraudulently, and that the plaintiff was entitled to damages as the Commission had implicitly warranted the existence of the tanker.

Misrepresentation

Rescission and/or damages may be available where one party has misrepresented the existence of the subject matter.

Assumption of risk

The true construction of the contract may be that one party has assumed the risk of the subject matter not being in existence. So if in *Couturier v Hastie* the purchaser had assumed the risk of the non-existence of the corn, he would have been liable for the price.

6.5.1.2 Mistake as to title (*res sua*)

The contract will be void at common law in the situation, rare today, where one party agrees to transfer property to the other which the latter already owns and neither party is aware of this fact. In *Cooper v Phibbs* (1887) LR 2HL 149, the court set aside an agreement whereby A had agreed to lease a fishery to B but, unknown to either, the fishery was already owned by B.

You will perhaps already have concluded that the explanation of both *res extincta* and *res sua* cases is impossibility; the parties are attempting to make an impossible contract.

6.5.1.3 Mistake as to quality

There is authority that a common mistake as to the **quality** of the subject matter, as opposed to its existence, is not operative at common law. In *Leaf v International Galleries* [1950] 2 KB 86, the Court of Appeal agreed that if A sells to B a painting which both parties mistakenly believe to be the work of the famous John Constable (and therefore very valuable), but which in fact is not his work (and therefore worth far less), the contract is valid at law, assuming the absence of actionable misrepresentation or the other matters outlined above. The mistake concerns the quality of the subject matter.

Leaf was based on the earlier and rather difficult case of *Bell v Lever Bros*:

Bell v Lever Bros [1932] AC 161
Bell was appointed to the Board of the Niger Company, a subsidiary of Lever Bros., under a service contract for five years at a salary of £8,000 per annum. As a result of company rationalisation, Lever Bros. needed to dispense with the services of Bell before the expiration of five years. A compensation agreement, negotiated in consideration of Bell's retiring within the service period, promised to pay Bell £30,000.

However, during his period of appointment, Bell had been involved in illicit cocoa pooling transactions, a course of conduct which would have given Lever Bros. the right to dismiss him without compensation had they been aware of it. At the time of entering into the compensation agreement Lever Bros. were unaware of Bell's conduct and Bell did not have in mind his breaches of duty. Thus, there was a common mistake as to the quality of Bell's service contract in the sense that both parties believed it to be terminable only upon the payment of compensation, whereas it was terminable without such payment.

The House of Lords (by a 3–2 majority) held that the compensation contract was not void for mistake.

The speeches in *Bell* are somewhat at variance with each other, but the orthodox interpretation of the case (and the one followed in most subsequent cases) is that a common mistake as to quality, however fundamental, can never render the contract void at common law. Nevertheless, there are *dicta* in the speeches which suggest that a contract may be void if the common mistake as to quality is sufficiently fundamental. This view was accepted by Steyn J in *Associated Japanese Bank* v *Credit du Nord* [1988] 3 All ER 902.

ACTIVITY 28

Read *Associated Japanese Bank* v *Credit du Nord* in *Cases and Materials* (6.6.1.3). Is this really a case of a common mistake as to quality as in *Bell* v *Lever Bros.*, or is some other fundamental fact being treated as crucial in reality?

Having read the case, you might say that Steyn J seems to be treating two separate transactions (the lease and the contract of guarantee) as one composite transaction intended to raise money on the security of the alleged machinery. Thus, he is emphasising that the fact that both guarantor and lessor believed the machinery to be in existence was much more fundamental to their state of mind than the legal effects of the fraud on the lease, i.e. the case is really analogous to cases of *res extincta*.

6.5.1.4 Common mistake in equity

Where a contract is void at common law on the ground of common mistake (i.e. in the two situations discussed above), the court, exercising its equitable jurisdiction, may refuse specific performance of the contract. Alternatively, the court may rescind any contractual document between the parties and, in order to do justice between them, impose terms. In *Cooper* v *Phibbs* (6.5.1.2), while setting aside the lease, the House of Lords imposed a requirement that the 'lessor' should have a lien on the fishery for such money as he had spent on improvements during the time he wrongly thought it belonged to him.

Where there is a common mistake as to **quality**, although the agreement is probably valid at common law, it is apparently **voidable** in equity. The case of *Solle* v *Butcher* [1950] 1 KB 671, broke new ground in that the Court of Appeal enunciated a new doctrine of common mistake in equity under which the courts have a discretionary jurisdiction to grant such relief as in the circumstances seems just. It will come as no surprise to learn that Lord Denning was involved in this decision.

In *Solle*, the plaintiff agreed to lease a flat from the defendant, both parties mistakenly believing that the premises were not subject to rent control. The Court of Appeal held that the mistake was as to the quality of the flat and would not render the lease void at common law, but the court set the contract aside in equity. To do justice, terms were imposed that the plaintiff should either give up the flat, or stay on at the maximum rent chargeable by law.

The approach in *Solle* v *Butcher* has never been adopted in the case of a contract of sale of goods. It could well be adopted, but what difficulties of legal principle would this raise? Make a list below.

Other examples of this equitable jurisdiction include *Grist* v *Bailey* [1967] Ch 532 and *Magee* v *Pennine Insurance* [1969] 2 QB 507. The precise relationship between the equitable jurisdiction to rescind and the common law position as stated in *Bell* v *Lever Bros*. remains uncertain. One view – Lord Denning's – is that Bell does not contain the whole law and must now be read with the equity cases.

However, in sale of goods cases, e.g., the sale of a painting believed to be a Constable, a finding at common law that the contract is not void upholds the principle of *caveat emptor* (let the buyer beware) and presupposes that the buyer has assumed the risk that the painting may not be a Constable. This is not easily reconcilable with equitable rescission of the contract.

6.5.2 MUTUAL MISTAKE

A mistake is said to be 'mutual' where the parties misunderstand each other's intentions and are at cross-purposes. Unlike common mistake, in this situation the parties do not both make the **same** mistake. Operative mutual mistake is illustrated by *Raffles* v *Wichelhaus* (1864) 2 H & C 906, where the defendants agreed to buy cotton from the plaintiffs ex the ship *Peerless* from Bombay. Two ships of that name were due to leave Bombay. It seems the defendants had in mind the ship leaving in October, while the plaintiffs had in mind the ship leaving in December. The court held that the transaction was too ambiguous to be enforced as a contract.

You should be able to see that the problem in the above case is essentially one of defective offer and acceptance, so the test applied by the court in this type of case is to ask what a reasonable third party would take the agreement to mean? Would he take the agreement to mean what one party, A, understood it to mean, or what the other party, B, understood it to mean? It is only when the transaction is totally ambiguous under this objective test that the contract is void for mutual mistake. The following cases are worth comparison.

Wood v *Scarth* (1855) 2 K & J 33

The defendant offered in writing to let a pub to the plaintiff at £63 per annum. After a conversation with the defendant's clerk, the plaintiff accepted by letter, believing that the £63 was the only payment under the contract. The defendant had intended that a £500 premium would also be payable and he believed that his clerk had explained this to the plaintiff.

The contract as understood by the plaintiff would be enforced and the court awarded him damages.

Scriven v *Hindley* [1913] 3 KB 564

At an auction, lots of hemp and also of tow (an inferior commodity) were up for sale. The defendants bid for a lot of tow and their bid was accepted. The defendants believed that they had bid for hemp. Their bid was about right for hemp but extravagant for tow, although the auctioneer was unaware of the true nature of the defendants' mistake (he thought they were ignorant of the value of tow). The catalogue and samples were misleadingly described and marked, and these factors, together with other circumstances, meant that a reasonable person could not say whether the contract was for hemp or tow.

The contract was void.

In another auction case, *Tamplin* v *James* (1880) 15 Ch D 215, where there was no misdescription in the particulars and the mistake was due to the plaintiff's carelessness, the contract was held to be valid.

In *Scriven*, the defendants were mistaken as to the nature of the plaintiff's promise (the plaintiff was promising to sell tow). In *Tamplin*, the plaintiff was mistaken only as to the quality of the subject matter.

6.5.2.1   Mutual mistake in equity

If the contract is void at law on the ground of a mutual mistake, equity 'follows the law'. Specific performance will be refused, and any contractual document the parties have entered into, e.g., a lease, will be rescinded. However, even where the contract is valid at law, specific performance will be refused if to grant it would cause hardship. Thus the remedy of specific performance was refused in a sequel to *Wood* v *Scarth* ((1858) 1 F & F 293).

6.5.3   UNILATERAL MISTAKE

Here one party is fundamentally mistaken concerning the contract and the other party is **aware** of the mistake, or the circumstances are such that he may be taken to be aware of it.

For a unilateral mistake to be operative, the mistake by one party must be as to a fundamental **term** of the contract itself, rather than an error of judgment as to the **quality** of the subject matter. The distinction is illustrated by the following pair of cases.

Hartog v *Colin and Shields* [1939] 3 All ER 566

The defendants offered goods to the plaintiffs at a certain price per pound, but had intended to offer them at the same price **per piece**. The value of a piece was one-third that of a pound.

The circumstances were such that the plaintiffs must have realised the defendants' error, which, as it concerned a term of the contract, rendered the contract void.

Smith v *Hughes* (1871) LR 6 QB 597

The plaintiff showed a sample of oats to the defendant who bought them in the belief that they were 'old' oats. He did not want 'new' oats, but that is what they were.

The court was of the view that the mistake was merely as to the **quality** of the subject matter and could not render the contract void, even if the plaintiff seller knew of the mistake. (But if the buyer mistakenly believed that the seller had **warranted** that the oats were old, and the seller was aware of this mistake, the mistake would be operative.)

6.5.3.1 Unilateral mistake in equity

As with mutual mistake, equity follows the law and will rescind a contractual document affected by operative unilateral mistake or refuse specific performance, as in *Webster* v *Cecil* (1861) 54 ER 812. Here the defendant, **having refused** to sell his property to the plaintiff for £2,000, wrote offering to sell it to him for £1,250. This offer was immediately accepted. The defendant had intended to write £2,250. It was held that the mistake was operative and specific performance was refused.

6.5.4 MISTAKES AS TO IDENTITY

If one party is mistaken as to the identity of the other party, can the contract be void at common law? The answer is that, in certain circumstances, it may be.

Almost all the decided cases of operative mistake in this area are in fact instances of unilateral mistake, as the non-mistaken party is aware of the mistake which he has engineered through his own fraud. Even where the contract is not void, it may be voidable for fraudulent misrepresentation and, if the goods which are the subject matter have passed to an innocent third party before the contract is avoided, that third party may acquire a good title. We shall see examples of this below. It would seem to be much easier to establish that identity was fundamental where the parties were not in one another's presence at the time of contracting than where they were face to face.

For the contract to be void, certain requirements must be satisfied.

6.5.4.1 The identity of the other party must be of crucial importance

This means that the plaintiff must prove that the person he believed the other party to be is the only person with whom he would have been prepared to contract.

Cundy v *Lindsay* (1878) 3 App Cas 459
The plaintiffs received an order for linen from a rogue, Blenkarn, who gave his address as 37 Wood Street, Cheapside. In the correspondence, he imitated the signature of a reputable firm, Blenkiron and Co., known to the plaintiffs, who traded at 123 Wood Street, Cheapside. The plaintiffs were thus fraudulently induced to send goods to Blenkarn's address, where he took possession of them and disposed of them to the defendants, innocent purchasers.

The contract between the plaintiffs and Blenkarn was void for mistake as the plaintiffs intended to deal **only** with Blenkiron and Co. No title in the goods passed to Blenkarn (because the contract was void), and therefore none passed to the defendants who were liable in conversion to the plaintiffs.

Do you think that identity would be crucial in *Phillips* v *Brooks* [1919] 2 KB 243? Here, a rogue called North entered the plaintiff's shop. Having selected some jewellery, he wrote a cheque and announced himself as Sir George Bullough of St James' Square, a man of means of whom the plaintiff had heard. The plaintiff, having checked this address in a directory, allowed North to take away a ring. North then pledged the ring with the defendants, who had no notice of the fraud. In an action by the plaintiff to recover the ring from the defendants, it was held that the contract between the plaintiff and North was not void for mistake, because the plaintiff had intended to contract with the person in the shop, whoever it was. The only mistake was as to the customer's credit-worthiness, not his identity. The contract was, however, voidable for fraud; but because the defendants had acquired the ring in good faith, before the contract was sought to be set aside, they acquired good title.

In the light of *Phillips* v *Brooks*, we can examine the issue of identity again in *Ingram* v *Little* [1961] 1 QB 31. The plaintiffs, elderly ladies, advertised their car for sale. A rogue, calling himself P. G. M. Hutchinson of an address in Caterham, offered to buy it. The plaintiffs would accept a cheque only when they had checked, from a directory, that there was such a person at that address. The cheque was worthless and the rogue disposed of the car to the defendant, who took it in good faith. It was held that the contract between the plaintiffs and the rogue was void for mistake. The grounds for the decision in this case are very difficult to distinguish from *Phillips* v *Brooks*.

Which decision do you think is correct in law? The decision in *Phillips* v *Brooks* was followed by the Court of Appeal in *Lewis* v *Averay* [1972] 1 QB 198, where the plaintiff, a postgraduate student, advertised a car for sale and was visited by a rogue posing as the actor Richard Greene, who offered to buy it. The rogue signed a cheque, but the plaintiff allowed him to take the car away only after being shown a forged studio admission pass. The cheque was worthless and the rogue sold the car to the defendant, an innocent purchaser. The Court of Appeal held that the contract, though voidable, was not void. The court took the view that, where the parties are face to face, there is a presumption that a person intends to deal with the person before him, as identified by sight and hearing. There was insufficient evidence in this case that the plaintiff intended to deal only with the well-known actor.

Phillimore LJ commented that if *Ingram* v *Little* is correctly decided then it must depend upon its own special and very unusual facts. So what could they possibly be? Apparently, that the rogue described himself as Hutchinson from the outset, that when credit was mentioned one of the ladies uttered the immortal words 'The deal's off', that the ladies went to a considerable degree of trouble in going to the post office to check the telephone directory in order to verify identity, and, a cynic might suggest, that the court felt a degree of sympathy for two little old ladies!.

SAQ 77

Why is it much more difficult to prove that identity was fundamental where the parties were face to face when contracting than where they were not?

Where the parties are face to face when contracting there is a strong presumption of intending to contract with the person standing in front of you, identified by sight and hearing, no matter what he might call himself. This presumption is not easily rebutted.

You should distinguish a mistake as to identity from a mistake as to the capacity in which a party deals.

Hardman v *Booth* (1863) 1 H & C 803
The plaintiffs, intending to sell cloth to Thomas Gandell & Co., negotiated with one Edward Gandell at the firm's offices. Edward, an employee and not a member of the firm, intended to take possession of the goods for his own use. Having obtained possession, he sold them to the defendant, an innocent third party.

The contract between the plaintiffs and Edward was void. The plaintiffs had believed he was a representative of the firm and never intended to deal with him personally.

It is sometimes stated that an additional requirement for the contract to be void is that the mistaken party must have taken reasonable steps to verify the identity of the other party. It may be that this is more in the nature of an evidential burden, helping to establish that the identity of the other party is crucial.

6.5.4.2 The mistaken party must have in mind an identifiable person with whom he intends to contract

This requirement was not satisfied in *King's Norton Metal Co.* v *Edridge Merrett Co. Ltd* (1897) 14 TLR 98. The plaintiffs received a letter purporting to be from 'Hallam and Co.' with an impressive letterhead. In fact Hallam was a fictitious firm consisting entirely of a rogue named Wallis. The plaintiffs despatched goods on credit to the bogus company. The court took the view that the plaintiffs had intended to contract with the writer of the letter, whoever it may be, and the contract was not void for mistake. The only mistake was as to the credit-worthiness of the other party and not as to his identity. You should compare this decision with *Cundy* v *Lindsay* (**6.5.4.1**) and you should note that there was no other person in existence with whom the plaintiffs could have intended to contract since Hallam & Co. and Wallis were one and the same person.

6.5.4.3 The other party must be aware of the mistake

In the cases discussed above, identity was fraudulently misrepresented and therefore this requirement was satisfied. An unusual case in this context is as follows:

Boulton v *Jones* (1857) 27 LJ Ex 117
The plaintiff was employed by Brocklehurst, a pipe hose manufacturer, with whom the defendants had had previous dealings. The plaintiff took over Brocklehurst's business and, on the same day, the defendants ordered hose from Brocklehurst. The plaintiff supplied the goods. The defendants refused to pay on the ground that they intended to contract, not with the plaintiff, but with Brocklehurst as they wished to enforce a set-off against him.

There was no contract, although the precise state of knowledge of the plaintiff was not made clear. If the plaintiff was unaware of the fact that the offer was not intended for him then, arguably, the contract was valid.

6.5.5 MISTAKE RELATING TO DOCUMENTS

6.5.5.1 *Non est factum*

As a general rule, a person is bound by his signature to a document, whether or not he has read or understood it: *L'Estrange* v *F. Graucob* [1934] 2 KB 394. Where he has been induced to sign a contractual document by fraud or misrepresentation, the transaction will be voidable. Similarly, if one of the other forms of mistake discussed in this chapter is present, the contract may be void.

In the absence of these factors, the plea of *non est factum* (not my deed) may be available. The plea is an ancient one and was originally used to protect illiterate persons. It eventually became available to literate persons who had signed a document believing it to be something totally different from what it actually was. In *Foster* v *Mackinnon* (1869) LR CP 704, the defendant, a senile man with poor eyesight, was induced to sign a document which he was told was a guarantee. In fact, it was a bill of exchange upon which the plaintiff ultimately became entitled. It was held that the plea of *non est factum* succeeded and that the defendant, who had not been negligent, was not liable on the bill.

One problem is that an unrestrained right to raise the plea would lead to abuse and uncertainty, so the courts have placed two restrictions on it:

(a)   the signer's mistake as to the nature of the document must be fundamental or radical; and

(b)   the signer must not have been careless in signing the document.

With regard to (a), the courts originally took the view that the plea was not available where the signer's mistake was merely as to the contents of the document rather than as to its character or class: *Howatson* v *Webb* [1908] 1 Ch 1. This test was not realistic and was substituted by the House of Lords in *Saunders* v *Anglia Building Society* [1971] AC 1004. The test is now that there must be a fundamental or radical difference between the document actually signed and what the signer believed it to be.

With regard to (b), the Court of Appeal had ruled in *Carlisle and Cumberland Banking Co.* v *Bragg* [1911] 1 KB 489 that negligence on the part of the signer defeated the plea only if the document was a negotiable instrument. The distinction was illogical and *Bragg's* case was overruled by *Saunders*. The position is now that the plea cannot be raised by a signer who has been careless.

Saunders v *Anglia Building Society* [1969] 2 Ch 17
An elderly widow wished to transfer the title of her house to her nephew by way of gift. Her nephew and a man named Lee prepared a document assigning the property to Lee and asked her to sign. She signed it unread as she had lost her spectacles and trusted her nephew. Lee mortgaged the property to the Building Society and disposed of the moneys raised for his own use. He defaulted on the repayments and the Building Society sought possession of the house. Saunders (the widow's executrix) sought a declaration that the assignment to Lee was void by reason of *non est factum*.

In the view of both the Court of Appeal and the House of Lords, the plea could not be raised because, (i) the transaction the widow had entered was not fundamentally different from what she intended at the time she entered it; and (ii) she had been careless in signing the document. She could at least have made sure that the transfer was to the person intended by her.

The effect of *Saunders* v *Anglia Building Society* is, if anything, to restrict the circumstances in which the plea of *non est factum* can be raised successfully.

Nevertheless, the defence was successfully raised in *Lloyds Bank plc* v *Waterhouse* [1991] Fam Law 23, where the signer , who was illiterate, signed a bank guarantee of his son's debt without either reading the document or indicating that he was unable to read. However, he had done his best, by asking questions to discover the nature and extent of his liability, and the bank's employees had misrepresented the nature of the document to him.

6.5.5.2   Rectification

Where the parties are agreed on the terms of the contract but, by mistake, record them incorrectly in a subsequent written document, the remedy of rectification may be available. The court can rectify the error and order specific performance of the contract as rectified.

The remedy is an exception to the parol evidence rule (see **3.3.1**) because, here, oral evidence is admissible to show that the written document is in error.

In order to obtain rectification the following must be established:

(a)   There must be a concluded antecedent agreement upon which the written document was based. The agreement need not necessarily be a finally binding contract: *Joscelyne* v *Nissen* [1970] 2 QB 86.

(b) The written document must fail to record what the parties had agreed. In *Frederick E. Rose (London) Ltd* v *William H. Pim Co. Ltd* [1953] 2 QB 450, the parties had contracted for the sale of a type of horsebean and the written contract referred to 'horsebeans'. The goods delivered were not of the type the parties had in mind. Rectification was refused since the written contract correctly recorded what the parties had **agreed**.

(c) The written document must fail to express the **common** intention of the parties. However, if one party mistakenly believes the document gives effect to that intention and the other party is aware of this mistake but nevertheless is guilty of sharp practice in allowing the contract to be executed, rectification may be ordered: *A. Roberts Co.* v *Leicestershire CC* [1961] Ch 555.

(d) It must be equitable to grant the remedy. In particular, it will be refused where third parties have acquired rights on the faith of the written contract.

6.5.6 SUMMARY

When approaching questions on mistake you are advised to remember that the law of mistake is often a last resort – there may have been an actionable misrepresentation or a warranty which will provide the plaintiff with a remedy.

SAQ 78

Is there a *general* doctrine of mistake in the law of contract? Write down your answer in the space below.

There is not really a single underlying principle governing all the cases where a contract is invalidated on the grounds of mistake. Operative mutual mistake is clearly an instance of defective offer and acceptance and could quite easily be dealt with under that heading.

The same might be said of unilateral mistake, although the emphasis on the concept of a 'fundamental' mistake has close parallels with common mistake. Indeed, it is only with common mistake that we have anything coming close to a 'doctrine', though here the equitable intervention of *Solle* v *Butcher* and the inconsistency of the common law has done much to cloud the issue.

6.6   Illegal and Void Contracts

As a general proposition, the courts will not enforce contracts whose purpose is illegal, and this includes not only agreements that are criminal in intent but also those that are injurious to society in the wider sense. In this area we shall focus our attention upon **contracts in restraint of trade** and this will be dealt with in depth shortly. In order to have an understanding of that topic, however, it will be necessary to look first at the question of illegality generally.

6.6.1   ILLEGAL CONTRACTS

Contracts may be illegal in one of two ways, either by statute or on the grounds of public policy. In the case of the former, a contract may be expressly forbidden by statute, or the prohibition may be implied. In *Cope v Rowlands* (1836) 2 M & W 149, a statute required that persons acting as stockbrokers must obtain a licence or forfeit £25. The plaintiff did brokerage work for the defendant without a licence. In the absence of an express prohibition, the brokerage contract was held impliedly illegal since the object of the licences was to protect the public.

A further group of contracts are illegal at common law on the grounds of public policy. It will come as no surprise to learn that one of these is a contract to commit a crime, a tort or a fraud, e.g., a contract by two highwaymen to ambush a coach: *Everet v Williams* (1725) unreported. Contracts promoting sexual immorality are likewise illegal. In *Pearce v Brooks* (1866) LR 1 Exch 213, a case which law students tend to remember, a prostitute hired a carriage 'of intriguing design' for the purposes of her trade. The contract was held illegal. The modern tendency is for the courts to look more benignly on agreements which contemplate stable extra-marital relations, so that in *Somma v Hazlehurst* [1978] 2 All ER 1011 (overruled but not on this issue) an unmarried couple rented a room but the contract was not struck down on the grounds of public policy.

Other contracts illegal on public policy grounds are those prejudicial to public safety or prejudicial to the administration of justice (e.g. stifling a prosecution), or those promoting corruption in public life, as well as contracts to defraud the revenue.

Where a contract is illegal, the consequences are **in general** as follows:

(a)   The contract is void and therefore neither party can sue upon it: *ex turpi causa non oritur actio* (no right of action arises from a base case).

(b)   Money paid or property transferred under the contract is normally not recoverable.

(c)   Related transactions will also be void. In *Fisher v Bridges* (1854) 3 E & B 642, the plaintiff sold land to the defendant for illegal purposes. The defendant, who still owed money to the plaintiff under the transaction, executed a deed promising payment of the outstanding sum. The deed was held to be unenforceable as it was tainted by the illegality of the main transaction.

6.6.2   VOID CONTRACTS

Certain contracts are expressly declared void by statute. The most notable examples are wagering contracts (rendered void by the Gaming Act 1845) and restrictive trading agreements (controlled by the Restrictive Trade Practices Act 1976). Individual resale price maintenance agreements are rendered void by the Resale Prices Act 1976.

In addition there are three categories of contract which are void at common law on the grounds of public policy:

(a)   contracts to oust the jurisdiction of the courts;

(b)   contracts prejudicial to the status of marriage; and

(c)   contracts in restraint of trade.

This last category will now be considered in greater detail.

6.6.3   CONTRACTS IN RESTRAINT OF TRADE

A contract in restraint of trade is an agreement by which one or both parties limit their freedom to work or pursue a trade or profession in some way. Much of the case law concerns clauses in contracts for the sale of a business or in written contracts of employment. In the former, the buyer of a business, e.g., a shop, will want an assurance that the seller will not immediately set up in competition next door and entice back his former customers. In the latter, an employee, on terminating his employment with a particular employer, will agree not to work for a competing employer or set up a competing business. Both types of agreement usually include some limits of area and duration.

The position at common law is that all contracts falling **within** the doctrine are contrary to public policy and prima facie void, unless they can be regarded as reasonable both as between the parties and as regards the public interest. The burden of proving that, as between the parties, the restraint is reasonable lies on the promisee; the burden of proving that, as far as the public interest is concerned, the restraint is unreasonable lies on the promisor. Reasonableness is considered as at the time of the agreement.

Why should the general rule be that all contracts in restraint of trade are prima facie void?

The rule is designed to protect freedom of competition, which is the cornerstone of our economic system. Thus, a valid restraint must be seen to be protecting some special right or interest belonging to the plaintiff which is more than mere freedom from competition.

The following transactions fall within the doctrine:

6.6.3.1   Agreements between employer and employee relating to the subsequent occupation of the employee

An agreement imposing a restriction on an employee after leaving an employer will be reasonable between the parties only if there is some proprietary interest of the employer meriting protection, which may be either **trade secrets** or **business connection**. The restriction must be no wider than reasonably necessary to protect such interest. The classic statement of these principles by Lord MacNaghten is to be found in *Nordenfelt* v *Maxim Nordenfelt* [1894] AC 535. Two cases illustrate these principles:

Forster v *Suggett* (1918) 35 TLR 87

The defendant was employed as the works manager of the plaintiff's glass works. He agreed that for five years after termination of employment with the plaintiff, he would not divulge any secret manufacturing process learnt during employment, nor would he work in the glass industry in the UK.

The restraint was reasonable to protect the plaintiff's legitimate interest and was enforceable.

Herbert Morris Ltd v *Saxelby* [1916] 1 AC 688

The respondent was employed by the appellants as a draftsman in their business of manufacturing lifting machinery. The company had its head office in Loughborough and branches in eight large cities. The respondent's contract of employment contained a clause that for seven years after leaving he would not become engaged anywhere in the UK in any similar business.

The clause was wider than reasonably necessary to protect the appellants' interest – they were merely trying to reduce competition. Lord Atkinson said that the clause would deprive the respondent 'for a lengthened period of employing, in any part of the United Kingdom, that mechanical and technical skill and knowledge which . . . his own industry, observation and intelligence have enabled him to acquire in the very specialised business of the appellants, thus forcing him to begin life afresh, as it were, and depriving him of the means of supporting himself and his family'.

The employer may protect his business connection only in respect of employees who are in a position to influence and subsequently entice away established customers. Thus restraints protecting business connection have been upheld in the case of a milk roundsman, a solicitor's clerk, a brewery manager and an estate agent's clerk. Restraints have been disallowed against a bookmaker's manager who had no personal contact with customers, and a grocer's assistant.

ACTIVITY 29

Do you think that a valid restraint could be imposed upon a hairdresser? Read *Marion White Ltd* v *Francis* [1972] 1 WLR 1423 in *Cases and Materials* (6.7.1) for the answer.

We have already seen that the restriction must be reasonable as regards both area and duration. Further examples from the cases are *Mason* v *Provident Clothing* [1913] AC 724, in which a restriction on a canvasser was held void as the area of restraint (within 25 miles of London) was one thousand times larger than the area of employment, and *Fitch* v *Dewes* [1920] 2 Ch 159, where a life-long restraint on a solicitor's managing clerk not to work within seven miles of Tamworth was held to be reasonable in the circumstances.

ACTIVITY 30

Before reading *Fitch* v *Dewes* **in** *Cases and Materials* **(6.7.1), try to envisage what circumstances would justify the upholding of a lifetime restraint.**

You might think that a lifetime restraint would be justifiable if the business in question had a strong family connection, and where the clientele were accustomed to use the same firm of solicitors from generation to generation.

From time to time the courts are prepared to recognise **other** interests apart from trade secrets and business connection as meriting protection. For example, in *Greig* v *Insole* [1978] 1 WLR 302 (arising out of the Packer cricket affair), it was held that the governing bodies of cricket had a legitimate interest in the administration of the game to justify the imposition of reasonable restraints on the players. However, it was also held that the bans in question, preventing players who had joined the Packer organisation from playing in test and county cricket, were too wide. In this case, however, it should be noted that there was no contract between the governing body and the players.

Exceptionally, agreements between an employer and an employee will be held unreasonable as regards the public interest. In *Wyatt* v *Kreglinger and Fernau* [1933] 1 KB 793, an employee (a wool broker) was promised a pension on his retirement, but it was agreed that he would not receive the pension if he competed against his employers in the wool trade. The Court of Appeal held the contract void. It was contrary to the public interest to deprive the community of a valuable skill. A particular feature of the case is that the services of wool brokers were in short supply at the time, and the plaintiff was being subjected to a lifetime restraint.

Construction of restraint clauses

It is clear that the court cannot redraft a restraint clause that is too wide, but it can, as a matter of construction, reach the conclusion that the parties intended to limit the clause to matters which are legitimate to protect. The following case is an illustration of this approach.

Littlewoods v *Harris* [1978] 1 All ER 1026
Harris was executive director of the mail-order firm of Littlewoods. He entered into a restraint clause whereby he agreed not to work for any company in the Great Universal Stores group for a period of 12 months after leaving Littlewoods. Harris had acquired a great deal of confidential information with regard to the catalogue which is the whole foundation of the mail-order business. Great Universal Stores were Littlewoods' main rival in the mail-order business, but Great Universal Stores operated worldwide and their business was not confined to mail-order. Littlewoods, on the other hand, operated only in the UK. Littlewoods sought an injunction against Harris to prevent him from working for Great Universal Stores.

The Court of Appeal held that although the clause, on its literal wording, was too wide, by construing the clause by reference to circumstances existing when the contract was made, it was possible to limit it to those matters it was clearly **intended** to protect, i.e. the mail-order business in the UK.

However, the approach to construction has not been at all consistent, and sometimes clauses have been given a literal interpretation and been declared to be void, even though it was possible to see what the parties probably intended. In *Gledhow Autoparts Ltd* v *Delaney* [1965] 3 All ER 288, for example, the defendant, a commercial traveller, was employed by the plaintiff company. His contract provided that for three years from the termination of his employment he would not 'solicit or seek to obtain orders from any person carrying on business' within the districts in which he had worked during his employment with the company. The restraint was held to be void even though the clause could have been construed as restricted to the same type of business as carried on by his employer.

Thus, the court may reach a different conclusion dependent upon whether it adopts a literal or a flexible approach to construction. This unsatisfactory situation has been perpetuated in subsequent cases. The Court of Appeal in *J A Mont (UK) Ltd* v *Mills, The Times*, 7 January 1993, adopted a literal approach where flexible interpretation would have been possible, whereas a differently constituted Court of Appeal adopted a rather more liberal approach in *Hanover Insurance Brokers Ltd & Christchurch Insurance Brokers Ltd* v *Schapiro* [1994] IRLR 82. In the latter case, dealt with in interlocutory proceedings, the Court indicated that *Littlewoods* v *Harris* and *J A Mont (UK) Ltd* v *Mills* required reconciliation in a full hearing.

ACTIVITY 31

Read *Greer* v *Sketchley Ltd* [1978] CAT 148 in *Cases and Materials* (6.7.2). **How does Shaw LJ distinguish *Greer* from *Littlewoods* v *Harris*?**

Having read *Greer* v *Sketchley Ltd*, you should see that Shaw LJ regarded the *Littlewoods* case as a special one involving a restraint in relation to a named competitor rather than a geographical area.

6.6.3.2   Agreements between the buyer and seller of a business

Restraints imposed on the seller of a business to restrict competition are more readily upheld than restraints on employees, but are generally subject to the same principles. In particular, there must be a proprietary interest meriting protection.

SAQ 80

What do you think that the proprietary interest meriting protection will usually be?

The answer is that:

(a) only the actual business sold is entitled to protection (see, for example, *British Reinforced Concrete Co.* v *Schelff* [1921] 2 Ch 563); therefore

(b) a restriction which purports to restrain a business not actually carried on will be void: *Vancouver Malt and Sake Co. Ltd* v *Vancouver Breweries Ltd* [1934] AC 181.

The proprietary interest meriting protection is usually goodwill, i.e. 'the benefit arising from connection and reputation' (*per* Lord Lindley). Thus, the purchaser will be imposing a restraint preventing the solicitation of customers or utilisation of business connection by the vendor. As a rule of thumb, the larger the amount paid for goodwill the more severe the restraint the purchaser may reasonably impose. *Nordenfelt* v *Maxim Nordenfelt* (**6.6.3.1**) illustrates this point.

6.6.3.3 Agreements between manufacturers to restrict output and fix prices

Such agreements are prima facie void at common law, but the courts have been prepared to uphold them where reasonable, e.g., to avoid a glut on the market: *English Hop Growers* v *Dering* [1928] 2 KB 174. Such agreements are now almost entirely subject to statutory control under the Restrictive Trade Practices Act 1976.

6.6.3.4 Exclusive dealing agreements

'Solus' agreements, whereby a garage agrees to purchase all its supply of petrol from one oil company, are within the doctrine of restraint of trade and are prima facie void.

Esso Petroleum Co. Ltd v *Harper's Garage (Stourport) Ltd* [1968] AC 269
The owner of two garages agreed, *inter alia*, to sell only Esso's petrol, in return for a rebate on the price per gallon. At one of the garages, the tie was to last for nearly four and a half years, and at the other it was to last for 21 years, being contained in this case in a mortgage of the premises to Esso.

The House of Lords upheld the four and a half year agreement, but the agreement for 21 years was held to be unreasonable and void as being longer than necessary to protect Esso's interests, i.e. the continuity and stability of their marketing operation.

However, if a trader, when purchasing or leasing new premises, covenants with the vendor or lessor (in the conveyance or lease) to buy only the latter's products, and then goes into possession, the exclusive dealing tie is outside the restraint of trade doctrine: *Harper's* case. This would apply to persons who buy or take a lease of a public house or garage subject to a tie, because they have surrendered no freedom previously enjoyed.

The approach of the courts to exclusive dealing ties is illustrated by the next case:

Alec Lobb (Garages) Ltd v *Total Oil Ltd* [1985] 1 WLR 173
The plaintiffs, whilst in financial difficulties, leased their garage to the defendant oil company for 51 years at a premium of £35,000. The defendants sub-leased it back to the plaintiffs for 21 years at an annual rent of £2,500, with a mutual right to break at seven or 14 years. The sub-lease contained a solus tie, whereby the plaintiffs agreed to sell only the defendants' petrol.

The lease and lease-back were subject to the restraint of trade doctrine but the tie was valid as being reasonable in the circumstances. The principal purpose of the agreement was as a financial rescue operation from which the plaintiffs benefited, as they received ample consideration (£35,000) for the lease and they were free to exercise the break clause after seven or 14 years.

Exclusive service agreements, such as where, for example, a songwriter agrees to provide his services to a music publisher for a period of time, are within the restraint of trade doctrine (i.e. prima facie void) if oppressive and one-sided:

Schroeder Music Publishing Co. Ltd v *Macaulay* [1974] 1 WLR 1308
M, a young and unknown song-writer, contracted with S, music publishers, to give them his exclusive services for five years. Under the contract M assigned to S the full, worldwide copyright in anything composed by him before or after entering into the contract. If M's royalties during the five-year period exceeded £5,000, the contract was to be automatically extended for a further five years. S reserved the right to terminate the contract by one month's notice; while M had no such right; and S was not obliged by the contract to publish anything composed by M at all.

Not surprisingly the House of Lords found the contract to be unreasonable and void. The contract required total commitment from M and virtually nothing from S, who could leave M's songs lying in a drawer if they wanted to.

A case of note in this area is *Panayiotou & Others* v *Sony Music Entertainment (UK) Ltd*, *Independent*, 24 July 1994 (the 'George Michael case'), in which it was held that where proceedings alleging that an agreement was in restraint of trade were genuinely compromised by the substitution of a new agreement, it is contrary to public policy to allow the doctrine of restraint of trade to apply to the new agreement or a renegotiated version of the new agreement.

6.6.4   EFFECTS OF THE CONTRACT BEING VOID

The effects discussed below relate to contracts void at common law, and will apply by analogy to contracts void by statute unless the statute in question has special provisions dealing with the matter.

6.6.4.1   The contract is void in so far as it contravenes public policy

In *Wallis* v *Day* (1837) 3 B & A 113, a contract of employment contained a provision which was alleged to be a void restraint of trade, but this did not prevent the plaintiff being able to recover arrears of salary. It follows from this that subsequent or collateral transactions are not necessarily void unless they relate solely to that part of the original transaction that is itself void.

6.6.4.2   Money paid or property transferred is recoverable

Authority for this proposition is to be found in *Herman* v *Charlesworth* [1905] 2 KB 123, where the plaintiff recovered a £52 fee paid under a marriage brokage contract, the contract being void as it undermined the status of marriage.

6.6.4.3 Severance

Severance is the power of the court to remove a void provision in a contract and enforce the remainder. The power exists in the case of void contracts and there is authority that an illegal contract may also be subjected to severance: *Carney v Herbert* [1985] AC 301.

Severance is not possible if it would eliminate the whole or substantially the whole of the consideration given by a party to the contract; *Wyatt v Kreglinger and Fernau* [1933] 1 KB 793.

It may be possible to sever in the sense of removing the void part of a promise and enforcing the rest. This will be possible provided the severance does not alter the meaning of the contract in any way:

Goldsoll v Goldman [1915] 1 Ch 292
The defendant sold a jewellery business to the plaintiff, the defendant covenanting that he would not deal in real or imitation jewellery in the United Kingdom or in other specified foreign places. The latter restraint was too wide in the circumstances, as was the reference to 'real' jewellery since the business dealt only in imitation jewellery in the United Kingdom.

The void restrictions were severed leaving a valid contract in restraint of trade.

Attwood v Lamont [1920] 3 KB 571
The defendant was employed as a tailoring cutter for the plaintiff, a general outfitter. The defendant covenanted not subsequently to engage in a number of trades carried on by the plaintiff's business, including tailor, milliner, draper, hatter and haberdasher, within a 10-mile radius.

The court refused to sever so as to leave the tailoring restriction valid. The covenant formed a single indivisible covenant for the protection of the plaintiff's entire business and not a series of covenants for the protection of each department of that business. The whole covenant was therefore void.

It should further be noted that the court will not re-draft the covenant in any way, thus applying the so-called 'blue pencil test'. The court will merely strike out the offending words; what is left must make sense without further additions.

6.6.5 SUMMARY

Contracts in restraint of trade do not require a knowledge of many legal principles. Once the basic test of reasonableness laid down in *Nordenfelt v Maxim Nordenfelt* has been mastered, most situations turn on the issue of reasonableness as between the parties. As in all areas where the issue is one of reasonableness, there is not much more that you can do other than to be aware of the kinds of things which have influenced the courts and be able to refer to illustrative cases. Each case turns on its own particular facts.

Restraints in contracts for the sale of a business are viewed rather more favourably than restraints in employment contracts, since it is assumed that there is less likely to be inequality of bargaining power and the purchaser has paid for the goodwill of the business.

In terms of construction of restraint clauses, the approach adopted by the court (literal or flexible) could well produce alternative outcomes to a given set of circumstances dependent upon which approach were adopted. Finally, there is often the possibility of severance.

6.7   Conclusion

Whereas operative mistake and illegality render contracts void, misrepresentation, duress and undue influence render contracts voidable. There is a strong interrelationship between the law on misrepresentation and the law on mistake, particularly when dealing with cases of mistaken identity. In this area a satisfactory remedy is often not provided by establishing that the contract is voidable for fraud, so the plaintiff will seek to establish that the contract is void for mistake.

Duress and undue influence continue to move closer together but are still clearly separate doctrines, duress being characterised as it is by the need for an unlawful threat.

6.8   End of Chapter Assessment Question

Gaspers Ltd of Nottingham, cigarette manufacturers, wished to buy a new cigarette-making machine. The production manager of Gaspers, Ash, contacted Rollem Ltd who sent their sales representative, Keen, to negotiate.

Keen said, 'I reckon our machine is capable of making upwards of 5,000 cigarettes per hour'. Keen also stated that it was the type of machine that did not require fencing under the industrial safety legislation. If Ash had consulted the literature that Keen had handed to him, he would have seen that the latter statement was untrue. Three months later, Gaspers Ltd entered into a written contract to purchase the machine and the price was paid. The written contract made no reference to the statements made by Keen during negotiations, but did include a term that Gaspers' acceptance of the machine should be conclusive evidence that it was 'in all respects fit for the intended and contemplated use' by them.

After delivery, it was discovered that the machine would make only 2,000 cigarettes per hour and that it needed fencing by law. When it was installed, Ash arranged for parts of the machine to be sawn off to allow for the welding on of a safety fence.

Advise Gaspers Ltd.

See *Cases and Materials* (**6.9**) for the complete answer.

CHAPTER SEVEN

REMEDIES FOR BREACH OF CONTRACT

7.1 Objectives

When you have completed this chapter you should be:

- aware of what remedies are available for breach of contract;

- able to identify the context in which such remedies operate;

- able to apply appropriate remedies and the rules relating thereto to problem situations;

- capable to explain what is meant by restitution;

- able to identify in what circumstances money can be recovered on the basis of restitution;

- competent to explain the circumstances in which there can be recovery for conferment of a benefit on the basis of restitution.

7.2 Introduction

The topic consists of:

- Common law remedies, i.e. damages. Damages are available to the plaintiff as of right.

- Equitable remedies of specific performance, injunction, rescission, rectification.

- Restitution (quasi-contractual remedies).

Equitable remedies are available only at the discretion of the court. The primary remedy for a party who suffers a breach of contract is an action for damages, which is the award of a sum of money to compensate the plaintiff for his loss. For historical and commercial reasons, the idea of compelling a party to perform his obligations (a decree of specific performance), or that of restraining him from breaking the contract (an injunction) are regarded largely as secondary remedies in English law. It is assumed that most breaches of commercial contracts can be adequately compensated by the financial equivalent of performance.

7.3 Damages

Damages are usually awarded to compensate the plaintiff for loss, though they can be awarded where no loss has been incurred and what is involved is the mere infringement of a legal right. In this case nominal damages are sometimes awarded, though in modern times declaratory judgments are more common.

Damages in contract are compensatory, not punitive, and are normally designed to put the plaintiff into the same financial position that he would have been in had the contract been performed correctly. However, in exceptional circumstances it is sometimes better to put the plaintiff into the position he would have been in if the contract had never been made. This distinction will be examined in due course at **7.3.1.2**.

7.3.1 REMOTENESS OF DAMAGE AND MEASURE OF DAMAGES

Remoteness of damage poses the question: 'For what kind of damage is the plaintiff entitled to recover compensation?' Measure of damages asks: 'On what principles must damage be quantified in monetary terms?'

7.3.1.1 Remoteness of damage

The plaintiff must satisfy an initial causation test by showing that his loss was caused by the defendant's breach of contract, i.e. that it would not have occurred but for the defendant's breach. However, the consequences of a breach of contract can be far-reaching and, for practical reasons, not all of them are compensatable. An example will illustrate this.

Suppose X breaks a contract with Y. Y consults a solicitor with regard to the legal position instead of returning home early to drive his son to tennis practice. Y's son cycles to tennis practice and is seriously injured in a collision with a lorry.

Is X liable in breach of contract for Y's son's injuries? On a simple 'but for' test, the causal connection is apparently clear, but X is not liable; the damage is too remote. By this expression, lawyers tend to mean that the injury or loss is not sufficiently proximate to the alleged 'causal' act to be seen as a consequence of it.

Can you construct a rule to be applied to discover whether loss incurred is too remote to be recovered?

The rule was first stated by Baron Alderson in 1854 in *Hadley* v *Baxendale* (1854) 9 Exch 341. Accordingly we can say that damages will not be too remote if they are:

(a) 'damages . . . such as may fairly and reasonably be considered as arising naturally, i.e. according to the usual course of things'; **or**

(b) 'such as may reasonably be supposed to have been in the contemplation of both parties, at the time they made the contract, as the probable result of the breach of it'.

Damages recoverable under (a) are often referred to as normal loss, whereas damages recoverable under (b) are usually referred to as abnormal loss and usually rest upon special facts made known to the defendant.

Let us examine the two branches of the rule in the context of the facts of *Hadley* v *Baxendale*: The plaintiffs were millers in Gloucester. The crankshaft of the steam engine which worked their mill broke and the mill came to a halt. The plaintiffs gave the shaft to the defendant, a carrier, to take to the manufacturer in Greenwich as a pattern for a new one. The defendant agreed to deliver the following day, but in fact took one week and the mill was idle unnecessarily. The plaintiffs sued for compensation for loss of profits during the delay.

SAQ 81

Give a reasoned explanation of the likelihood of success or failure of the plaintiffs' action.

On the facts, it was held that the plaintiff failed for two reasons:

(a) In the usual course of things no one would have expected the mill to have become idle; the defendant was entitled to assume that the mill owner had a spare crankshaft.

(b) The defendant had no knowledge of any special circumstance – he had not been informed that there was no spare.

The test was subsequently reformulated by the Court of Appeal in a later case giving a clearer illustration of its application.

Victoria Laundry (Windsor) Ltd v *Newman Industries Ltd* [1949] 1 All ER 997
The plaintiffs, who were launderers and dyers, wished to extend their business as they had certain very lucrative dyeing contracts lined up. To this end they contracted with the defendants for delivery of a new and larger boiler, stressing that time of delivery was of the essence. The agreed delivery date was 5 June, but the boiler was not delivered until 8 November. Consequently, the plaintiffs lost not only ordinary business profits from the extension of their business, but also the lucrative dyeing contracts and the profits therefrom. The plaintiffs claimed:

(a) £16 per week as loss of ordinary business profits; and

(b) £262 per week for loss of the special dyeing contracts.

Explain why you think that the plaintiffs' claim might succeed totally, partially or not at all.

The defendants, knowing what the plaintiffs' business was, should have known that some business profits would be lost, and therefore were liable for loss of ordinary business profits. However, because the defendants did not actually know of the lucrative dyeing contracts, the plaintiffs could not recover the full £262 per week. On the other hand, because some loss of profits from dyeing contracts was likely as part of the plaintiffs' ordinary business, the plaintiffs could recover some compensation for the loss of the dyeing contracts. The case was remitted to the Official Referee for assessment of compensation.

Unfortunately, in his judgment Asquith LJ said: 'The aggrieved party is only entitled to recover such part of the loss actually resulting as was at the time of the contract **reasonably foreseeable** as liable to result from the breach.' (emphasis added) This raised a problem, because the words **reasonably foreseeable** are the words applicable for the test of remoteness in the law of torts, and suggested that the remoteness test in contract and in tort was the same.

This suggestion was rejected by the House of Lords in *The Heron II* [1967] 3 All ER 686, where Lords Reid and Morris made it clear that the contractual test is **reasonable contemplation**, not reasonable foreseeability, and that Asquith LJ cannot have meant reasonable foreseeability in the tortious sense.

ACTIVITY 33

Can you devise a test to distinguish between reasonable forseeability and reasonable contemplation?

After consideration, you might have said that the difference between the two standards is that something can be reasonably foreseeable even if it is most unlikely to occur, e.g., suffering frostbite in England; whereas reasonable contemplation means 'not unlikely to occur' or there must be a 'serious possibility of occurrence'.

This interrelationship of the contractual and tortious tests for remoteness was further, if unsatisfactorily, considered by the Court of Appeal in *Parsons (H) (Livestock) Ltd* v *Uttley Ingham & Co. Ltd* [1978] 1 All ER 525. The defendant contracted to supply the plaintiff pig farmer with a hopper for storing pig nuts. The defendant installed a 28 feet high hopper but left the ventilator sealed, and consequently the nuts went mouldy. At first the plaintiff continued to feed the mouldy nuts to his top grade pig herd. Some pigs became ill. Although the plaintiff then ceased to feed the nuts to the pigs, 254 died from a rare intestinal infection. The plaintiff sued for breach of contract, claiming damages for the sickness and death of the pigs, and loss of profits on future sales of the pigs.

Lord Denning MR concluded that since *Hadley* v *Baxendale*, the *Victoria Laundry* case and *The Heron II* all dealt with economic loss, they could be regarded as establishing a principle to be applied only where the breach caused economic loss (loss of profits). Where there was physical harm, as in this case, the tortious test of reasonable foreseeability should apply, and the plaintiff recovered for the loss of the pigs. However, the claim for loss of profits on future sales failed on application of the reasonable contemplation test.

Scarman LJ (with whom Orr LJ agreed) approached the matter differently. He concluded that there was no difference in the test to be applied whether the loss was economic or physical, and that the test was reasonable contemplation. However, applying *Wroth* v *Tyler* [1974] Ch 30, it was not necessary to contemplate the precise nature of the damage which had arisen; it was sufficient if the loss was of a type which could reasonably have been supposed to have been in the contemplation of the parties as a serious possibility in the event of the breach which actually occurred. On the facts, since there was a serious possibility that the pigs would develop stomach trouble, the plaintiff recovered for loss of the pigs, even though the **actual** damage was more serious than mere stomach trouble, because the damage was of a similar **type**.

ACTIVITY 34

Write down any criticisms you can think of relating to the logic of the judgments of Lord Denning and Scarman LJ. Compare your answer with the criticisms listed at (a) and (b) on this and the next page.

Scarman LJ also found loss of profits to be irrecoverable without stating any reason therefor!

You should see that all three judges reached the same conclusion, but via different routes. This is most unsatisfactory, as both Lord Denning MR and Scarman LJ agreed that in principle there should be no difference between the contractual and tortious tests for remoteness.

SAQ 83

Is this view reconcilable with the view of Lord Reid in the *Heron II* (above)?

The view appears not to be reconcilable with the view of Lord Reid that the contract test should be stricter. Lord Reid recognises that contracts enable the parties to allocate the risks between themselves, and that such allocation works only if the parties are properly informed of the risks involved. The stricter contractual remoteness test encourages the provision of such information (special knowledge), and unless such information is provided the loss will not be recoverable.

The following criticisms may be made of the logic of the judgments of Lord Denning MR and Scarman LJ in the *Parsons* case:

   (a)   Lord Denning MR's view has no explicit support in the authorities. He is suggesting an approach which cuts across the traditional contract/tort distinction, i.e. whether suing in contract or in tort the 'reasonable foreseeability' test should apply where there is physical loss, whereas the 'reasonable contemplation' test should apply where there is economic loss. However, the distinction between physical and economic loss is difficult to apply.

(b) Scarman LJ's view places a heavy burden on the distinction between type and extent of loss. Was the lost profit on the ordinary laundry business really a different type of loss from the lost profit on the lucrative dyeing contracts in the *Victoria Laundry* case? If any illness to the pigs were contemplateable, why were the plaintiffs not at fault in continuing to feed the nuts to the pigs?

7.3.1.2   Measure of damages

How is the plaintiff's loss to be quantified?

Expectation, reliance and restitution interests

The terminology adopted here is taken from a well-known article by Fuller and Perdue ((1936) *Yale Law Journal* 52).

These three interests relate to the three main objectives behind an award of damages for breach of contract. Unfortunately, the interests often arise in different circumstances and may, on occasion, overlap.

Expectation interest (loss of bargain)   The basic object of damages for breach of contract is to put the plaintiff, as far as money can do it, in the same position he would have been in had the contract been performed, i.e. to compensate the plaintiff for loss of his bargain so as to protect his expectations arising out of the contract.

In order to quantify expectation loss the two situations envisaged in *Hadley* v *Baxendale* (see **7.3.1.1**) must be considered:

(a) Loss caused according to the usual course of things.

(b) Loss caused where special facts have been made known to the defendant.

These situations are best illustrated in the context of sale of goods cases:

(a) Loss caused according to the usual course of things: X agrees to buy Y's car for £2,000. Y breaks the contract and refuses to deliver the car, because he has sold it to Z for £2,500. X's loss is a car valued at £2,000.

X, in order to put himself in the position he would have been in had the contract been performed, would have to purchase a similar car in the open market at the market price. It follows that X's loss will be the difference between the market price at the time delivery was due, and the contract price. If the market price were £2,400, X's loss will be £400, and this will be the damages figure. (This rule is embodied in s. 51 of the Sale of Goods Act 1979, in sale of goods cases.)

However, in the above example, suppose X had contracted to sell the car to P for £2,500. This means that X is buying from Y for £2,000 and selling to P for £2,500. X cannot recover his loss of £500 because the loss is too remote under the rule in *Hadley* v *Baxendale*, unless Y is aware of the special circumstances, i.e that X is reselling to P.

You should be aware that there is some complicated case law in this area, involving car dealers selling new cars to buyers who then break the contract. The decisions centre on whether or not there has been the loss of a sale, which in turn depends upon whether or not there was an available market for the type of vehicle in question. The authorities are *W.L. Thompson Ltd* v *Robinson (Gunmakers) Ltd* [1955] 1 All ER 154; *Charter* v *Sullivan* [1957] 1 All ER 809. Apparently different considerations apply to sales by dealers of secondhand cars: *Lazenby Garages Ltd* v *Wright* [1976] 2 All ER 770. (You can investigate these cases in *Cases and Materials* (7.1.2.1).)

(b) Loss caused where special facts have been made known to the defendant: The extent of the loss recoverable will depend upon the degree of the defendant's knowledge. In *Victoria Laundry Ltd* v *Newman Industries Ltd* (7.3.1.1), the plaintiffs could not recover the full £262 per week because the defendants did not actually know of the lucrative dyeing contracts. But they were entitled to recover some of the loss from lost dyeing contracts because the defendants knew that dyeing was part of the plaintiffs' ordinary business.

As you will appreciate, in both situations (a) and (b), there can be difficulty in assessing the damages, but that alone is not a bar to a successful claim. This is illustrated by the case of *Chaplin* v *Hicks* [1911] 2 KB 786, where the defendant, a theatrical manager, proposed to hold a meeting of 50 actresses from whom he would select 12 to give them remunerative employment. He agreed to invite the plaintiff, but failed to do so, and she sued for breach of contract. The defendant argued that nominal damages only should be payable since the plaintiff had only a one in four chance of success. Nevertheless, it was held that the plaintiff should receive £100 compensation.

SAQ 84

Can you identify a remoteness of damage difficulty arising out of the decision in *Chaplin* v *Hicks*?

Chaplin v *Hicks* is traditionally discussed as a case raising issues concerning measure of damages, i.e. should the plaintiff have been awarded damages on the expectation basis for a speculative, loss or should she have been limited to a claim for the reliance interest? However, it can also be asked whether a one in four chance of success represents a loss which was 'not unlikely to occur'.

Sometimes a different approach is adopted when the goods delivered or the works carried out are defective. Here, the courts will calculate the measure of damages according to the cost of cure or the difference in value between what the goods/works are worth and what they would have been worth had the contract been performed properly. The cost of cure is recoverable only when it is reasonable to recover on that basis.

Ruxley Electronics & Constructions Ltd v *Forsyth* [1995] 3 All ER 268
The plaintiff contracted with the defendants for the construction of a swimming pool with a maximum depth of 7ft 6in. The plaintiff emphasised the importance of the depth as he wished to use the pool for diving, and he needed the depth in order to feel safe. The defendants constructed the pool with a maximum depth of 6ft 9in, which was only

6ft deep at the relevant diving point. There was evidence that the pool was safe for diving and its value undiminished. In order for the pool to be made to comply with the contract specification, it would have been necessary to rip out what had been installed and put in a new pool at the cost of about £21,000.

The House of Lords, reversing the decision of the Court of Appeal, held that the cost of cure was not recoverable and the plaintiff was awarded £2,500 for lost amenity.

Reliance interest   An alternative basis is to put the plaintiff into the position in which he would have been if the contract had never been made, by compensating him for expenses incurred in reliance on the contract, apparently even if that expenditure is incurred before the contract is entered into.

Anglia Television Ltd v Reed [1972] 1 QB 60
The plaintiff wished to make a TV film, and to that end incurred expenses of £2,750 in employing a director and designer. The plaintiff then contracted with Reed to play the part of the leading man. Reed repudiated the contract very late on, and the plaintiff, having failed to find another actor to fit the part, abandoned the film. The plaintiff claimed damages for wasted expenditure rather than loss of profits, because he had no idea of what his profit would have been, if any.

The £2,750 pre-contract expenditure was recoverable because it led to a loss which, after breach, could no longer be avoided.

On the other hand, the plaintiff will recover nothing if the defendant can show that he, the plaintiff, made a bad bargain, so that there was no expectation loss, and the wasted expenditure would have been incurred whether the contract had been broken or not. In *C & P Haulage v Middleton* [1983] 1 WLR 1461, it was held that the burden rests upon the defendant to show affirmatively that the plaintiff has made such a bad bargain.

SAQ 85

CCC Films (London) Ltd v Impact Quadrant Films Ltd [1985] QB 16
The defendants granted the plaintiffs a licence for $US 12,000 to exploit and distribute three films, the rights to which were owned by the defendants. The defendants breached the contract by sending uninsured video tapes of the films which were lost, and failed to replace them. The plaintiffs claimed the $US 12,000 as wasted expenditure.

The defendants claimed that the onus was on the plaintiffs to show they had not made a bad bargain, i.e. that they would have made sufficient profits from the exploitation of the films to cover the $US 12,000 expenditure; otherwise, the $US 12,000 expenditure would have been incurred whether the defendants were in breach of contract or not.

Explain, with reasons, whether the plaintiff will be successful or not.

The burden of proof rested upon the defendants to show that the plaintiffs would not have recouped the $US 12,000 expenditure. Since the defendants had submitted no such evidence, the plaintiffs' claim succeeded.

Restitution interest   In some circumstances, the plaintiff may have conferred a benefit upon the defendant in return for the defendant's promise, e.g., X pays Y in advance for goods which Y then fails to deliver. The court will compel Y to restore the value of the benefit he has received (the advance payment), the restitution interest, in order to prevent unjust enrichment.

Relationship between expectation, reliance and restitution interests   The expectation interest is the normal measure of damages. However, in a speculative transaction, where the expectation interest may be difficult or impossible to calculate, the plaintiff may prefer the reliance interest and he is free to choose between the two.

A further question is whether the plaintiff can combine his claims. In *Anglia Television Ltd v Reed* (above), Lord Denning said that the plaintiff had to choose between the expectation interest and the reliance interest, and could not claim both. However, this statement, while correct in the context of the case, should not be taken to be of general application.

ACTIVITY 35

Write down below a legal rule which would allow the plaintiff to combine the various interests in his damages claim?

You might have said that in *Millar's Machinery Co. Ltd* v *David Way & Son* (1935) Com Cas 204, the plaintiff recovered the price (restitution), the installation expenses of machinery (reliance loss), and his net profits resulting from the breach (expectation loss).

In conclusion, there is no objection to combining types of claim unless it enables the plaintiff to recover more than once for the same loss. In other words, there shall be no double recovery, e.g., X is paid £100 in advance by Y for goods which X ultimately fails to deliver. Y cannot recover both his £100 payment (restitution) and the full value of the goods at the due date of delivery (expectation loss).

Damages for disappointment or injured feelings

Since the general aim of damages in contract is to put the plaintiff in the same financial position he would have been in, compensation is usually restricted to economic/financial loss, though damages are recoverable for physical injury caused by breach of contract. Damages for disappointment or injured feelings are not usually recoverable.

Nevertheless, if the object of the contract is the provision of a service designed to lead the plaintiff to expect a happy or pleasurable experience, or greater peace of mind, then an award of damages may be granted to reflect the loss of that expectation.

Jarvis v *Swans Tours* [1973] QB 233

The plaintiff solicitor booked a skiing holiday with the defendants. The brochure described the holiday as a houseparty with parties, a yodeller, bar and skiing, and said the proprietor spoke English. The holiday proved to be something of a disappointment. In the first week there were 13 people present. In the second week the plaintiff was alone, there were no parties and the proprietor did not speak English. The bar was open one evening only in the second week, the yodeller was a local man in a boiler suit who quickly sang four or five songs on his way home from work and then left, and long skis were available only two days per week.

The Court of Appeal awarded the plaintiff £125 compensation for his disappointment.

Compensation for disappointment/injured feelings is not otherwise available, either for breach of a contract of employment (*Addis* v *Gramaphone Co. Ltd* [1909] AC 488), or for breach of commercial contracts in general (*Bliss* v *S E Thames Regional Health Authority* [1985] IRLR 308; *Hayes and Another* v *Dodd and Another* [1990] 2 All ER 815).

Damages for loss caused to third parties

In general the plaintiff can recover no more than nominal damages for a breach of contract which causes loss to a third party, who is a stranger to the contract: *Beswick* v *Beswick* [1986] AC 58. We covered this at **2.5.1** and if you cannot remember it, you should look at it now.

However, some interesting ideas emerge from the case of *Jackson* v *Horizon Holidays Ltd* [1975] 1 WLR 1468. The plaintiff booked a holiday with the defendants for himself, his wife and two three-year old children. The brochure described the hotel as 'of the highest standard', listing numerous facilities, none of which materialised, and the plaintiff's holiday was ruined. The Court of Appeal awarded the plaintiff damages, including £500 for 'mental distress'.

James LJ quantified this figure as consisting of the plaintiff's own distress and his additional distress caused by the disappointment of his wife and his children: Lord Denning MR said that the plaintiff had made a contract for the benefit of both himself and his wife and children, and could therefore recover in respect of their loss as well as his own. This is clearly contrary to *Beswick* v *Beswick*.

Explain why this view is clearly contrary to *Beswick* v *Beswick*.

Jackson v *Horizon Holidays Ltd* was considered by the House of Lords in *Woodar Investment Development Ltd* v *Wimpey Construction UK Ltd* [1980] 1 WLR 227, in which the House disapproved the approach of Lord Denning MR, but supported the actual decision, either on the basis of James LJ, or alternatively on the ground that cases such as booking family holidays or ordering meals in restaurants might 'call for special treatment'. Thus the doctrine of privity of contract is upheld and the refusal of courts in modern times to infer trusts of contractual rights maintained. We considered trusts of contractual rights in **Chapter 2** and if you cannot remember it, please look at it now to refresh your memory.

However, it may be that the trust of contractual rights is merely dormant rather than dead.

Linden Gardens Trust Ltd v *Lenesta Sludge Disposals Ltd* [1994] 1 AC 85 X engaged Y to carry out work on his property, in circumstances where both parties understood that X was highly likely to transfer the property to Z. X transferred the property to Z before Y's defective workmanship amounted to a breach of contract. Z could not sue because assignment of contractual rights was contractually excluded. On the face of it, since X no longer had any interest in the property, it looked as though its damages would be merely nominal. The House of Lords did not agree. Lord Browne-Wilkinson pointed to the need 'to provide a remedy where no other would be available to a person sustaining loss which under a rational legal system ought to be compensated by the person who has caused it'. Because both parties knew at the time of contracting that the property was going to be occupied and possibly purchased by third parties, it was foreseeable that damage caused by a breach would cause loss to a later owner and not merely to the original contracting party. Thus, said Lord Browne-Wilkinson:

> it seems to me proper, as in the case of the carriage of goods by land, to treat the parties as having entered into contract on the footing that (the original owner) would be entitled to enforce the contractual rights for the benefit of those who suffered from defective performance.

This would appear to resemble a trust of contractual rights in many respects, apart from not being so christened, but presumably it is restricted to situations where the contract is to be followed by an actual transfer of property to the third party.

7.3.2 MITIGATION OF LOSS

7.3.2.1 Duty of injured party to minimise his loss

A principle running through the law relating to damages is that the injured party cannot recover compensation for loss which could reasonably have been avoided. There is a duty to mitigate loss, i.e. to minimise loss where it is reasonable to do so. For example, if the buyer of goods wrongly rejects them, the seller must try to mitigate his loss by reselling the goods unless there is no available market.

Mitigation is illustrated by the case of *Brace* v *Calder* [1895] 2 QB 253, where the plaintiff was employed for a term of two years by a partnership. Five months later the partnership was dissolved by the retirement of two members, which (technically) in law meant that the plaintiff was automatically wrongfully dismissed. Two partners continued with the actual business and asked the plaintiff to work for them. He refused and sued for breach of contract, claiming his wages for the full two years. It was held that by refusing the offer of re-employment the plaintiff had failed to mitigate his loss, and was entitled to nominal damages only.

However, the plaintiff need take only **reasonable** steps to mitigate, e.g., he would not be expected to embark upon hazardous and uncertain litigation (*Pilkington* v *Wood* [1953] 2 All ER 810), and the burden of proof that the plaintiff has failed to take reasonable steps to mitigate rests upon the defendant.

7.3.2.2   Mitigation of loss and anticipatory breach

Where there has been an anticipatory breach, the plaintiff can either accept the breach as terminating the contract and sue immediately for damages, or he can refuse to accept the breach and await the due date for performance. If he accepts the breach he has a duty to mitigate his loss; if he does not accept the breach he has no duty to mitigate.

Cheshire, Fifoot and Furmston's Law of Contract suggests that the reasoning is logical, though the result may be grotesque. This is illustrated by the House of Lords decision in *White & Carter (Councils) Ltd* v *McGregor* [1962] AC 413, a decision defended by Treitel who points out that its application must be very limited indeed. The facts are that WC were suppliers of litter bins to local councils. They were not paid by the councils but by traders who hired advertising space on the bins. McGregor agreed to hire space for three years, but cancelled the contract on the same day that it had been entered into. WC refused to accept the cancellation, prepared the advertisements and placed them on bins for the three-year period. WC then sued for the contract price, having made no attempt to sell the advertising space to anyone else. The House of Lords held by a 3-2 majority that WC could recover the full sum and were under no duty to mitigate.

ACTIVITY 36

The view of Cheshire, Fifoot and Furmston (expressed above) is based upon the principle that the breach should be accepted whenever it becomes reasonable to do so. Can you construct a rule which reflects the decision in the case, thus indicating why it was not unreasonable of WC to refuse to accept the breach and to continue with the contract?

Despite the criticism and controversy which the decision has aroused, it is submitted, as Treitel suggests, that the decision is correct on its own rare and special facts.

Among the points you could have made are the following:

(a)   The burden of proof of failure to mitigate rests upon the defendant, but the defendant in *White & Carter* submitted no evidence on this point. If he had shown that *White & Carter* could have relet the advertising space without too much trouble, it would have been unreasonable of *White & Carter* to continue with the contract.

(b)   Lord Reid, deliverer of the leading (majority) speech in the House, pointed out that the rule in *White & Carter* applies only if 'the plaintiff has a legitimate interest, financial or otherwise, in performing the contract rather than claiming damages'. Thus, *White & Carter* were assumed to have such an interest (i.e. it was assumed no alternative advertising contracts were available) since McGregor had offered no evidence to the contrary.

You should read the following cases in *Cases and Materials* (**7.1.3.1**) where the 'legitimate interest' limitation has subsequently been approved, by the Court of Appeal in *Attica Sea Carriers Corporation* v *Ferrostaal Poseidon Etc., The Puerto Buitrago* [1976] 1 Lloyd's Rep 250, and applied by Kerr J in *The Odenfeld* [1978] 2 Lloyd's Rep 357, and by Lloyd J in *Clea Shipping Corporation* v *Bulk Oil International Ltd, The Alaskan Trader (No. 2)* [1984] 1 All ER 129.

(c) Lord Reid said that it is most unusual for one party to be able to perform the contract without the cooperation of the other party, as was the case here. It follows that this case does not apply if the other party's cooperation is required in order to perform the contract. Please refer to the judgment of Megarry J in *Hounslow LBC* v *Twickenham Garden Developments Ltd* [1971] Ch 233 in *Cases and Materials* (**7.1.3.1**).

7.3.3 LIQUIDATED DAMAGES AND PENALTY CLAUSES

7.3.3.1 Liquidated damages clauses

Normally the plaintiff will be awarded **unliquidated** damages, which means that the amount will be fixed by the court. However, particularly in commercial contracts, the parties will often provide in the contract for a particular sum to be payable upon the occurrence of one or more specified breaches of contract. This is known as a **liquidated damages** clause.

All the injured party needs to prove is the breach and the fixed sum will automatically be payable. An example of this would be a provision in a building contract that for each day late in completion of performance of the contract a payment of £100 shall be due. Even if the actual loss is greater/smaller than the fixed sum, nevertheless, it is the fixed sum which will be payable.

Cellulose Acetate Silk Ltd v *Widnes Foundry Ltd* [1933] AC 20
The defendant agreed to construct a special plant for the plaintiff within 18 weeks. The contract provided for £20 per week to be payable for each week taken beyond 18 weeks. The plant was completed some 30 weeks late, and the plaintiff claimed his actual loss of £5,850.

The clause was a liquidated damages clause, although described as a penalty clause, and that the plaintiff recovered £600 only, i.e. 30 × £20.

Why do you think that the House of Lords decided in *Cellulose Acetate* that this was a liquidated damages clause rather than a penalty clause?

You may have concluded that the clause was intended to provide for payment of a sum below the estimated loss. This is inconsistent with the nature of a penalty clause which is designed to terrorise the other party into performing the contract. Both parties must have known that the actual loss would exceed £20 per week, so that one object of the provision was to limit the contractors' liability. However, it was not a pure limitation clause (and, therefore, probably not subject in modern times to the Unfair Contract Terms Act 1977) because the contractors would still have had to pay £20 per week even if the owners had lost less.

This leads us to consideration of the nature and effect of a penalty clause.

7.3.3.2 Penalty clauses

A liquidated damages clause must be a genuine pre-estimate of loss and not a penalty. A penalty is a 'payment of money stipulated *in terrorem*', designed to force the offending party to perform the contract. Such clauses will not be enforced.

If the plaintiff's actual loss is less than the sum specified in the penalty clause, he can recover only his actual loss. But if the plaintiff's actual loss is more than the sum specified in the penalty clause, he can elect either to sue for the specified sum or to claim unliquidated damages in the normal way.

7.3.3.3 How does the court distinguish between a liquidated damages clause and a penalty clause?

The court will try to ascertain the intentions of the parties.

The fact that a clause is described as a penalty or liquidated damages clause is inconclusive; the real question is whether, from an objective viewpoint, the parties intended the clause to be a genuine pre-estimate of loss or an *in terrorem* clause. You should now look back at *Cellulose Acetate Silk Ltd* v *Widnes Foundry Ltd* (at **7.3.3.1**).

Some useful guidelines were laid down by Lord Dunedin in *Dunlop Pneumatic Tyre Co.* v *New Garage and Motor Co. Ltd* [1915] AC 79.

(a) The clause will be held to be a penalty if the sum stipulated is extravagant in amount in comparison with the greatest loss which could conceivably be proved to have followed from the breach.

(b) Where the promisor's obligation is to pay a certain sum of money and the contract provides for a larger sum to be paid in the event of breach, this is a penalty.

(c) If a single lump sum is payable on the occurrence of one, or more or all of several events, some of which may occasion serious and others more trifling damage, there is a presumption that it is a penalty clause.

(d) It is no obstacle to the sum stipulated being a genuine pre-estimate of damage that the consequences of the breach are such as to make precise pre-estimation an impossibility.

The difficulties of applying guidelines (c) and (d) in situations where it is virtually impossible to prove the precise financial loss which will follow from breach of the various contingencies is illustrated by two contrasting cases.

Dunlop Pneumatic Tyre Co. v *New Garage and Motor Co. Ltd* [1915] AC 79
The defendant bought tyres from the plaintiff and agreed that he would not tamper with the manufacturer's marks, sell below list price, sell to suspended persons, or exhibit or export tyres without the plaintiff's consent. The liquidated damages clause provided that £5 was to be paid for every tyre sold or offered in breach of the agreement.

Is this a liquidated damages or a penalty clause? Give reasons for your answer.

The clause was a liquidated damages clause, because the sum fixed was reasonable and not extravagant (a genuine attempt to pre-estimate loss).

Ford Motor Co. v *Armstrong* [1915] 31 TLR 267
The defendant bought cars from the plaintiff and agreed not to sell below list price, not to sell cars to other dealers and not to exhibit cars without permission. He also agreed that for every breach he would pay £250 as being 'the agreed damage which the manufacturer will sustain'.

Is this a liquidated damages or a penalty clause? Give reasons for your answer.

The clause was a penalty. It was substantial, arbitrary and fixed *in terrorem,* its very size preventing it from being a genuine pre-estimate of loss.

You should notice that the court's control of penalty clauses applies only to a **breach** of contract, and not, for example, to a hirer exercising termination rights under a hire purchase contract:

Bridge v *Campbell Discount Co.* [1962] 1 All ER 385, which you can read in *Cases and Materials* (**7.1.4**), provides an excellent illustration of this distinction.

Lastly, in *Robophone Facilities Ltd* v *Blank* [1966] 1 WLR 1428, Diplock LJ expressed his approval of liquidated damages clauses as reflecting good business practice in commercial contracts, since both parties know where they stand right from the outset. He felt that the courts should not be too quick to declare such provisions to be penalties.

7.4   Equitable Remedies

You will recall that we examined the remedies of rescission and rectification in the chapters on misrepresentation and mistake. Discussion here will centre upon specific performance and injunctions. You should remember at all times that equitable remedies are not available as of right, only at the discretion of the court.

7.4.1   SPECIFIC PERFORMANCE

A decree of specific performance is an order of the court compelling the party in breach to perform his contractual obligations. Its most frequent application is to property transactions, as where, for example, the vendor of a house refuses to complete the sale. The court will order the vendor to transfer the title to the house to the purchaser.

There are numerous restrictions on the availability of specific performance. Can you think of any reasons why this should be?

Your list of reasons why the availability of specific performance is restricted may have included:

(a) It will not be granted where an award of damages is an adequate remedy. So it is not normally available for breach of a contract of sale of goods, because the buyer can normally obtain similar goods elsewhere and claim damages if he has to pay more than the contract price. But it may be granted if the goods are unique, e.g., a veteran car, an antique, or in exceptional circumstances. A case on the latter issue arose in *Sky Petroleum Ltd* v *VIP Petroleum Ltd* [1974] 1 WLR 576. The defendants had agreed to supply the plaintiffs with petrol for their petrol stations. The defendants refused to maintain such supplies during the period of the oil crisis. The plaintiffs sought an interlocutory injunction to prevent the defendants from withholding supplies, which would effectively have amounted to temporary specific performance.

Do you think that the injunction was granted? Give reasons for your answer.

The court granted the order, since the plaintiffs had no alternative sources of supply due to petrol shortages caused by the oil crisis.

Similarly, since land is classed as unique, the purchaser of land can obtain specific performance, even though you might have thought that damages would have been an adequate remedy.

(b) The requirement of mutuality. One party will be entitled to specific performance only if specific performance would be available to the other party. It follows that since specific performance is never awarded against a minor, it will never be granted in favour of a minor. (A minor is a person under the age of 18 years.)

(c) Specific performance will not normally be granted if constant supervision by the court would be required. Basically this depends upon how strong the plaintiff's claim is and the degree of supervision required, so it is not a hard and fast rule. In *Ryan* v *Mutual Tontine Westminster Chambers Association* [1893] 1 Ch 116, the plaintiff leased a flat from the defendant. The lease imposed an obligation upon the defendant to provide a resident porter to be constantly in attendance. The porter provided was frequently absent as he had a part-time job as a chef in a restaurant. The court refused specific performance on the constant supervision ground.

You might like to contrast this case with *Beswick* v *Beswick*, which we considered at **2.5.1**, where specific performance was granted because the degree of supervision required was considerably less. If you cannot remember the case please go back and look at it now.

Specific performance has been awarded of certain building contracts in exceptional circumstances. In *Wolverhampton Corporation* v *Emmons* [1901] 1 QB 515, the plaintiff corporation acquired land for an improvement scheme and sold part of it to the defendant, who contracted to demolish the existing houses on the site and to build new ones. The demolition was carried out and plans for the new houses were approved. The court ordered specific performance of the obligation to build for three reasons: (i) the defendant's obligations were precisely defined by the plans; (ii) damages would not be an adequate remedy if a site belonging to the corporation in the middle of a town were left vacant instead of being occupied by houses which would yield rates; (iii) the corporation could not get the work done by another builder since the defendant had possession of the site.

The concept of constant supervision was explained by the House of Lords in:

Co-operative Insurance Society Ltd v *Argyll Stores (Holdings) Ltd, The Independent*, 5 June 1997

Argyll decided to close their Safeway supermarket in the Hillsborough Shopping Centre because it was losing money. This was a breach of a covenant in the lease, which obliged them to keep the premises open for retail trade during normal business hours. Argyll were prepared to pay damages but the Court of Appeal ordered specific performance. This order was reversed by the House of Lords on the constant supervision ground. Supervision would have involved the court in having to give rulings as to whether Argyll were carrying on business in compliance with the order. The possibility of having to give an indefinite series of such rulings in order to ensure the execution of the order was regarded as undesirable.

(d) Specific performance will not be granted of a contract for personal services.

A typical example is a contract of employment, and, indeed, s. 16 of the Trade Union and Labour Relations Act 1974 prohibits an order for specific performance against an employee compelling him to work.

(e) Specific performance will be granted only where it is equitable to do so: 'He who comes to equity must come with clean hands.' If the plaintiff has acted unfairly in the performance of the contract, specific performance will not be awarded.

(f) Undue delay in commencing proceedings will defeat a claim for an equitable remedy.

7.4.2 INJUNCTIONS

An injunction is an order from the court telling a person to stop committing a wrong. Such injunction may be either **mandatory** or **prohibitory**.

7.4.2.1 Mandatory injunctions

A mandatory injunction orders the defendant to take positive steps to put right what he has done wrong in breach of contract. Such an order is a drastic measure and will be awarded only where vitally necessary. Whether it should be granted or not is subject to a 'balance of convenience', test and it may be refused if the prejudice suffered by the defendant in having to restore the original position heavily outweighs the advantage to be derived by the plaintiff from such restoration.

A mandatory injunction was granted in *Wakeham* v *Wood* (1982) 43 P & CR 40, where the defendant, in breach of a restrictive covenant, erected a building so as to block the plaintiff's sea view. The court granted a mandatory injunction because the defendant had committed the breach deliberately, with full knowledge of the plaintiff's rights, and damages would not have been an adequate remedy.

7.4.2.2 Prohibitory injunctions

Such an injunction will be granted to enforce a negative stipulation in the contract, i.e. the defendant will be ordered not to break the stipulation. Prohibitory injunctions may be particularly important where a breach of a contract of employment is involved. But the effect of granting the injunction must not be to compel a party to perform the contract, as this would be tantamount to granting a decree of specific performance of a contract for personal services.

Lumley v *Wagner* (1852) 1 DM & G 604
W agreed to sing for two nights per week for three months at L's theatre in Drury Lane, and not to use her talents at any other theatre without L's consent. W abandoned the agreement, and for a larger payment agreed to sing for G at Covent Garden. L sought an injunction to prevent W from performing for G.

Give reasons as to why you think the injunction should or should not have been granted.

The injunction should be granted because it did not actually compel W to sing for L – she could have chosen not to sing at all. However, the decision has received much criticism because the effect of the injunction was to put W under such economic pressure that she was indirectly compelled to perform the obligation to L.

An interesting contrast can be seen in two further cases:

Warner Bros. Pictures v *Nelson* [1937] 1 KB 209
The defendant agreed to work as a film actress exclusively for the plaintiff for 12 months under a contract made in the USA. The defendant came to England and entered into a contract with another company to make a film. She also appeared in the theatre and made personal appearances. The plaintiff claimed an injunction.

Give reasons as to why you think the injunction should or should not have been granted.

The injunction was granted. It was not tantamount to a decree of specific performance because it extended only to the film actress activities, and the defendant, who was a talented lady, was capable of making a living in other ways.

Page One Records Ltd v *Britton* [1968] 1 WLR 157
The defendants, The Troggs pop group, appointed the plaintiff as their manager and agent for a five-year period. The contract provided that the plaintiff was to receive 20 per cent of all moneys earned, and that the defendants would not engage any other person as manager or agent or do the job themselves. The Troggs became famous overnight, earned really good money and repudiated the contract.

The plaintiff sued for damages and an interlocutory injunction restraining the defendants from appointing any other manager until the trial.

No injunction should be granted as it would be tantamount to specific performance of a contract for personal services.

How would you distinguish this decision from the decision in *Warner Bros.* v *Nelson*?

Warner Bros. v *Nelson* was distinguished on the grounds that Nelson (alias Bette Davies) was intelligent and talented and could earn good money in many ways. The Troggs, however, were not capable of earning good money any other way, and could not possibly continue without a manager or agent.

7.5   Restitution

7.5.1   INTRODUCTION

The law of restitution itself is a topic having much wider scope than merely the law of contract. We are concerned here with that small part of the law of restitution which skirts the fringes of the law of contract, and is sometimes referred to as 'quasi-contract'.

7.5.2   WHAT DOES RESTITUTION MEAN?

Restitutionary remedies seek to restore money paid or the value of a benefit conferred in circumstances where no contract exists e.g. because the parties have made an agreement which turns out to be void or because the parties' negotiations never reached the stage of forming a contract.

Can you draft a general principle which the court might adopt in deciding whether the law should intervene in the above circumstances?

The justification for the intervention of the law is to prevent 'unjust enrichment'. The broad parameters of 'unjust enrichment' have been set out by Goff and Jones in the *Law of Restitution*, 3rd ed., 1988. They are (a) that the defendant has been enriched by some benefit given to him; (b) that the enrichment has been acquired at the expense of the plaintiff; and (c) that the retention of the benefit by the defendant would be unfair or unjust.

7.5.3 IN WHAT CIRCUMSTANCES CAN AN ACTION IN RESTITUTION BE IMPLEMENTED TO RECOVER MONIES PAID

Such an action can be implemented in three situations.

7.5.3.1 Total failure ofconsideration

An excellent example is that any monies paid in advance in a contract which is subsequently frustrated may be recovered in circumstances where there has been total failure of consideration. We looked at this in operation earlier on in **Chapter 5** in *The Fibrosa* [1942] 2 All ER 122 (see **5.6.4.1**, p. 128).

Return to p. 128 to refresh your memory of *The Fibrosa*. You should recall that consideration in this context has a different meaning to the normal meaning of consideration. Can you write down what this difference is?

You will recall that in the context of contract formation, consideration can be constituted either by performance or by promise of performance. However, in the context of restitution, consideration relates to performance alone. Thus the plaintiff can recover in restitution when he has received no part of the performance to which he is entitled.

Clearly if a promise could amount to consideration in this area then there would rarely, if ever, be a total failure of consideration.

You should note that a restitutionary claim will not be available where the failure of consideration is partial only.

Whincup v *Hughes* (1871) LR 6 CP 78
The plaintiff paid a watchmaker a premium of £24 to apprentice his son to him for six years. After one year the watchmaker died, but it was held that the plaintiff could not recover his premium because the failure of consideration was only partial. (The circumstances of this case would now be covered by the Law Reform (Frustrated Contracts) Act 1943.)

However, in some cases it may be possible for the plaintiff to convert a partial failure into a total failure of consideration by returning any benefit he has received from such performance as has taken place. Such a situation may arise where the plaintiff has the right to repudiate the contract because of the other party's defective performance. The result of the act of repudiation is to produce a total failure of consideration. For example, if a purchaser pays in advance for goods which, when delivered, are not of satisfactory quality, he may repudiate the contract for breach of the term implied by s. 14(2) of the Sale of Goods Act 1979 (see **Chapter 4**) and claim back the purchase price on the basis of total failure of consideration.

ACTIVITY 39

Return to Chapter 5 and look at the cases on performance. Write down the names of two cases where the plaintiff would be unable to return the benefit received.

It is likely that you will have discovered *Sumpter* v *Hedges* and *Bolton* v *Mahadeva*, both cases where work has been done on the plaintiff's land or property and cannot be returned. Thus the plaintiff here would be unable to establish total failure of consideration.

Similarly, the use of the benefit under the contract by the plaintiff may prevent total failure of consideration.

Hunt v *Silk* (1804) 5 East 449
The plaintiff paid £10 to the defendant in return for the defendant's promise to give him immediate possession of certain premises, to repair them and to execute a lease of them in his favour within ten days. The plaintiff obtained possession, but left soon afterwards when the defendant failed to carry out the rest of his promise. He also sued to recover the £10 as money had and received.

State with reasons whether you think the plaintiff will succeed or not.

It was held that he had occupied the premises, albeit for a short period of time, and thus could not recover his £10, though, of course, he might have been able to claim damages for breach of contract.

The above decision may appear to produce difficulties in cases involving the sale of goods.

Rowland v *Divall* [1923] 2 KB 500
The plaintiff, a car dealer, bought a car from the defendant for £334, repainted it and sold it on to a third party. It transpired that the car had been stolen, although the defendant had dealt with it in good faith. The police repossessed the vehicle on behalf of the true owner. The plaintiff sued to recover from the defendant the £334 which he had paid.

Return to the account of *Rowland* v *Divall* at 3.5.2.1 and identify the term of the contract breached by the defendant.

Yes, the defendant was in breach of the term now implied by s. 12 of the Sale of Goods Act 1979 that he has the right to sell the goods (or expressed differently that he will pass on good title to the goods)

SAQ 96

Will the plaintiff succeed in recovering his £334 from the defendant on the basis of total failure of consideration, bearing in mind that he had four months usage of the vehicle prior to selling it?

You might have thought that the plaintiff would fail but you would be wrong. The plaintiff had paid the price to acquire ownership, which he had not got and it was from this defect that his right to repudiate arose. The use of the car in this context was totally irrelevant to the contract for the sale of the vehicle. He recovered his £334.

This rule would seem to make good sense in the case of a dealer, who purchases to resell and who therefore must have title, but is it justifiable in the case of a consumer, who purchases in order to use the goods in question?

7.5.3.2 Mistake of fact

This situation arises, for example, where there has been a common mistake which avoids the contract, which must, of course, be a mistake of fact and not one of law. If your memory is hazy on this distinction refer back to *Couturier* v *Hastie* and *Solle* v *Butcher* at **6.5.1.1** and **6.5.1.4**.

Money paid under a mistaken belief in the truth of a fact which, if true, would have entitled the payee to payment is recoverable by the payer.

Kelly v *Solari* (1841) 9 M & W 54
The plaintiff was a director of an insurance company which had paid out insurance money to the defendant on a life assurance policy taken out on her husband's life. In fact, the policy had lapsed due to non-payment of the premiums by the assured. The company had known of this, but at the time the money was paid the lapse had been overlooked. The plaintiff sought to recover the money from the defendant. It was held that the plaintiff succeeded.

An interesting question is whether, as in *Kelley* v *Solari*, the mistake must have led the plaintiff to believe a fact which, if true, would have meant that he was **legally** obliged to pay. Despite the reiteration of this requirement in a number of cases, the Court of Appeal has held that money paid under a mistake of fact which, if true, would have **morally** (but not legally) obliged its payment was recoverable.

In *Larner* v *London County Council* [1949] 2 KB 683, LCC, the defendants, passed a resolution to make up the pay of their employees who were on war service to the amount of their civil salaries. The plaintiff was an employee of the defendants who went off to war, and so received this increment. He was instructed by the defendants to inform them of any increase in service pay, but failed to do so. Consequently, LCC overpaid him. If the facts had been as supposed LCC would only have been morally, not legally, obliged to make the payments, but the mistake was held to be sufficient to justify recovery of the payments.

7.5.3.3 Discharge, under compulsion, of the defendant's liability to a third party

If X is compelled, either by threats of legal action or by some other pressure recognised by the law, to discharge Y's liability to Z, X will be able to recover his payment from Y.

Exall v *Partridge* (1799) 8 Term R 308
The plaintiff, with the defendant's permission, left his carriage on the defendant's premises. The defendant's landlord lawfully seized it by way of distress for rent due from the defendant. In order to redeem it the plaintiff had to pay off the defendant's rent arrears.

Can the plaintiff recover his payment from the defendant? If so, why?

Yes he can, because, otherwise, the defendant would be unjustly enriched at the plaintiffs expense.

7.5.4 RESTITUTIONARY CLAIMS ON A *QUANTUM MERUIT* BASIS FOR BENFIT CONFERRED

A *quantum meruit* is a claim for reasonable remuneration for services performed or things supplied.

We need to consider three situations here.

7.5.4.1 Breach of Contract

Let us suppose that under the terms of a contract X is to do a certain piece of work for Y for a sum of £2,000, payable upon completion. Y repudiates the contract when X has done part of the work, and X accepts this repudiation and regards himself as discharged from any further contractual performance.

SAQ 98

Explain whether X can recover the £2,000 contract price or, indeed, any remuneration at all.

You should have identified that X cannot recover the contract price, because the work has not been completed. However, he can claim the reasonable value of the work completed on a *quantum meruit* basis. In order to refresh your memory on this have another look at *Planché v Colburn* (**5.3.3**).

7.5.4.2   Void Contracts

It may be possible to recover remuneration on a *quantum meruit* basis where performance is rendered under a contract which, unknown to both parties, is void.

Craven-Ellis v *Canons Ltd* [1936] 2 KB 403
The plaintiff was employed as the managing director of the defendant company. Under the articles of association of the company the plaintiff was required to obtain his qualification shares within two months, failure to do so rendering him incompetent to act. The plaintiff failed to obtain his shares, but subsequently the company executed an agreement under seal agreeing to pay the plaintiff a certain remuneration. However, the directors' resolution to affix the seal to the agreement was invalid, which rendered the agreement void. The plaintiff sought to recover the promised remuneration. It was held that he had no contractual claim to the money, because the agreement was void, but that he could recover in respect of the services which he had rendered on a *quantum meruit* basis.

7.5.4.3   Services rendered in contemplation of a contract which does not materialise

Sometimes, particularly in the construction industry, a party commences work expecting a formal contract to be drawn up at a later stage. If the contemplated contract fails to materialise then the party who has undertaken the work may claim for the work done on a *quantum meruit* basis.

British Steel Corporation v *Cleveland Bridge & Engineering Co. Ltd* [1984] 1 All ER 504 (see also **1.7.1**).

Work was commenced on a major construction before all the elements of the contract had been agreed. Both parties confidently expected that final agreement would be reached, but such turned out not to be the case. The major stumbling block to agreement was a requirement by the defendants that the plaintiffs should accept unlimited liability for consequential loss in the event of delay, which the plaintiffs, not surprisingly, were not prepared to accept. The plaintiffs delivered on time all the steel nodes required of them apart from the last delivery, which was late due to a national steel strike. The plaintiffs sued for the value of the nodes; the defendants counterclaimed for damages for late delivery.

It was held that there was no contract due to failure to agree on price, delivery and applicable terms and conditions, but that the plaintiffs were entitled to payment on a *quantum meruit* basis.

Can you draft a legal principle indicating what the plaintiff must prove in these circumstances in order to be entitled to payment? There are two crucial factors.

The principle which you have drafted should have been similar to what follows. The plaintiff will have to prove: (a) that the work was done at the request of the defendant; or (b) that the work was freely accepted by the defendant.

Read the judgment of Steyn LJ in the Court of Appeal in *G. Percy Trentham Ltd* v *Archital Luxfer* [1993] 1 Lloyd's Rep 25 in *Cases and Materials* (7.3.2). On the basis of this judgment, suggest how a different approach might have been adopted in *British Steel* v *Cleveland Bridge* (above).

Yes, it might have been possible to construe the existence of a contract, even in the absence of an identifiable offer and acceptance, especially in circumstances where the agreement had been substantially acted upon.

However, can you identify why, other than because of the lack of identifiable offer and acceptance, Robert Goff J might have been reluctant to discover the existence of a contract in the *British Steel* case?

It would seem that by finding no contract to exist the plaintiff's claim for services rendered succeeded on a *quantum meruit* basis, whereas the defendant's counterclaim for damages for breach of contract for late delivery failed. This would seem to reflect substantial justice in the circumstances, in that it was the defendant's unreasonable insistence that the plaintiff's should accept unlimited liability for consequential loss in the event of delay, which was the major factor in preventing final agreement from being reached.

Nevertheless, the decision can be criticised in that it follows that either party could have abandoned the venture at any time, without giving notice to the other party, because there was no contact. This can hardly be said to reflect the reasonable expectation of the commercial world.

7.6 Conclusion

Common law remedies are available as of right, whereas equitable remedies are subject to the discretion of the court. In particular, they will not be granted where it would cause undue hardship. See, e.g., *Patel* v *Ali* [1984] 1 All ER 978, where Goulding J said the hardship must amount to 'an injustice'.

In the context of the law relating to damages, the remoteness of damage rules probably require intervention and rationalisation by the House of Lords.

Restitutionary remedies seek to restore money paid or the value of a benefit conferred in circumstances where no contract exists, usually because the agreement turns out to be void or because the parties have acted upon an agreement which never becomes a contract.

Sometimes restitution and damages provide alternative remedies. Where the total failure of consideration is caused by the other party's breach, the plaintiff will normally claim damages for expectation loss (loss of profits). If the contract was potentially advantageous, the expectation measure of damages will inevitably be a more attractive proposition than merely recovering money paid. If, however, the plaintiff has made a bad bargain (a contract, which, if performed would have produced a loss) he will be happy to exercise his restitutionary remedy in order to recover any money which he may have invested in the project.

7.7 End of Chapter Assessment Question

Cruisers Ltd, a business which hired out ocean yachts, ordered a new yacht for its fleet from Ted. The yacht was to be delivered on 1 May, ready for the beginning of the summer charter season. The contract provided for the payment of agreed damages of £5,000 per week for each week by which delivery was delayed.

The yacht was not ready for delivery until 1 July. As a result Cruisers Ltd lost charter fees of £3,000 per week for seven weeks, and a fee of £6,000 agreed with a television company, for the use of the yacht in the making of a television programme during the eighth week.

During the first four weeks of the delay Cruisers Ltd could have hired a similar yacht from another firm for a fee of £2,000 per week. Cruisers Ltd now claim damages.

Advise Ted.

See *Cases and Materials* (7.5) for the complete answer.

INDEX